American World Literature

American World Literature

An Introduction

Paul Giles

Registered Offices
John Wiley & Sons, Inc., 111 River Street, Hoboken, NJ 07030, USA
John Wiley & Sons Ltd, The Atrium, Southern Gate, Chichester, West Sussex,
PO19 8SQ, UK

Editorial Office
The Atrium, Southern Gate, Chichester, West Sussex, PO19 8SQ, UK

For details of our global editorial offices, customer services, and more information about
Wiley products visit us at www.wiley.com.

Wiley also publishes its books in a variety of electronic formats and by print-on-demand.
Some content that appears in standard print versions of this book may not be available in
other formats.

Library of Congress Cataloging-in-Publication data applied for

Hardback ISBN: 9781119431640
Paperback ISBN:9781119431787

Cover image: Cover photo of *A vanitas still life with an open book, a lute, recorders, scores,
a globe and an hourglass on a draped table* by Edward Collier (1702): © cea+
Cover design by Wiley

Set in 10/12pt Warnock by SPi Global, Pondicherry, India
Printed in Singapore by C.O.S. Printers Pte Ltd

10 9 8 7 6 5 4 3 2 1

Contents

Acknowledgments

In writing this volume, I have adapted material from a variety of sources, including my own books on American literature in its transatlantic context: *Transatlantic Insurrections: British Culture and the Formation of American Literature, 1730–1860* (University of Pennsylvania Press); *Virtual Americas: Transnational Fictions and the Transatlantic Imaginary* (Duke University Press); *Atlantic Republic: The American Tradition in English Literature* (Oxford University Press), as well as the broader treatment of this transnational theme in *The Global Remapping of American Literature* (Princeton University Press) and *Antipodean America: Australasia and the Constitution of American Literature* (Oxford University Press). More specifically, I have drawn with permission on various essays of mine previously published in a range of journals and edited collections: "Dreiser's Style," in *The Cambridge Companion to Dreiser*, ed. Lenny Cassuto and Claire Eby (Cambridge University Press, 2004); "Douglass's Black Atlantic: Britain, Europe, Egypt," in *The Cambridge Companion to Frederick Douglass*, ed. Maurice Lee (Cambridge University Press, 2009); "Transatlantic Currents and the Invention of the American Novel," in *The Cambridge History of the American Novel*, ed. Leonard Cassuto, Benjamin Reiss, and Clare Eby (Cambridge University Press, 2011); "Globalization," in *A Companion to American Literary Studies*, ed. Robert S. Levine and Caroline F. Levander (Blackwell, 2011); "Edmund Wilson, *Axel's Castle*," in *Essays in Criticism*, 61.3 (July 2011); "America and Britain during the Civil War," in *The Cambridge Companion to Abraham Lincoln*, ed. Shirley Samuels (Cambridge University Press, 2012); "The Novel after the Great War," in *Oxford History of the Novel in English, VI: The American Novel 1870–1940*, ed. Priscilla Wald and Michael E. Elliott (Oxford University Press, 2014); "Transatlantic Currents and Postcolonial Anxieties," in *Oxford History of the Novel in English, V: American Novels to 1870*, ed. J. Gerald

Kennedy and Leland Person (Oxford University Press, 2014); "Globalization," in *American Literature of the 1990s*, ed. Stephen Burn (Cambridge University Press, 2017). Some of the material on pedagogy was first addressed in "Transposing Pedagogic Boundaries: Global America in an Australian Context," *New Global Studies* 9.3 (2015). I should also like to acknowledge the many stimulating discussions with colleagues on topics related to this subject at the Institute for World Literature convened by David Damrosch at Harvard in July 2017.

1

The Theory of American World Literature

This book is designed to offer an overview of ways in which the subject areas of American literature and world literature have converged (and diverged) over the past 20 or 30 years. American literature is now widely regarded as engaging with global rather than merely local or national phenomena, and *American World Literature: An Introduction* attempts to set these changing conceptions of the subject in both critical and historical context. It also suggests how this perception of American literature as a global or "world" phenomenon has varied significantly across time, so that the intellectual investments of Cotton Mather in ideas of universal forms during the seventeenth century can be productively compared and contrasted to the resurgence of nationalist and transnational templates in the poetry of Walt Whitman 200 years later. In his preface to *Literary Theory: An Introduction*, published in 1983, Terry Eagleton wrote of how he had "tried to popularize rather than vulgarize the subject," and my intention here similarly is to address these complex historical and methodological issues in a way that might enlighten readers with little experience in the academic study of American literature, while still providing a sufficiently rounded view of these multifaceted matters to provoke interest in readers for whom the broad outlines of these debates will be more familiar.[1]

The term "American literature" was first used in the 1780s, in the aftermath of the political separation of the new United States from Great Britain, and it has always carried a nationalistic resonance. In his 1837 lecture "The American Scholar," given as a commencement address at Harvard, Ralph Waldo Emerson pointedly proclaimed how "[w]e have listened too long to the courtly muses of Europe," but the fact that he did not say "we have listened too long to the philosophical sages of Asia," still less "we have listened too long to the voices of indigenous peoples," exemplifies the way in which American intellectual culture initially conceived of itself in terms of a principled resistance to the ossified structures of a class-bound, aristocratic Europe.[2] The first university course in

American World Literature: An Introduction, First Edition. Paul Giles.
© 2019 John Wiley & Sons Ltd. Published 2019 by John Wiley & Sons Ltd.

American literature was not taught until 1875, by Moses Coit Tyler at the University of Michigan, and the subject initially flourished in less prestigious Midwestern universities, where its demotic qualities were thought to carry a broad, popular appeal for a less sophisticated clientele. Towards the end of the nineteenth century, American literature became a popular subject in student classrooms, but it was not then thought of as an appropriate field for intense scholarly research. Just as the study of English literature was generally conceived in British universities of the Victorian era as a soft option compared with more rigorous study of the classics (Latin and Greek), so American literature was long regarded among Ivy League academics as an easy option. The story goes that when F.O. Matthiessen, perhaps the most influential American literary scholar of the twentieth century, first proposed at Harvard in 1926 a PhD on Walt Whitman, he was advised by senior professors there that Whitman was an "exhausted" topic, and that his time would be better spent on the arts of Elizabethan translation. Matthiessen consequently produced a thesis that examined five important Elizabethan prose translations: Sir Thomas Hoby's rendering into English of Castiglione's *The Courtier* (1561), Sir Thomas North's translation of *Plutarch's Lives* (1579), John Florio's translation of Montaigne's *Essays* (1603), Philemon Holland's translations of Livy's *Roman History* (1600), and of Suetonius (1606).[3] A revised version of this dissertation was published in 1931 as *Translation: An Elizabethan Art,* and it is not difficult to see how a similar kind of quintuple method underpinned by a critical idiom of transposition also underpins the structure of Matthiessen's most celebrated work, *American Renaissance* (1941). Just as *Translation* focuses on the way in which English scholars converted five European classics into their native tongue, so *American Renaissance* seeks deliberately to prove to Harvard skeptics that Matthiessen's five chosen American writers – Emerson, Whitman, Henry David Thoreau, Nathaniel Hawthorne and Herman Melville – are as good as anything produced in the English Renaissance. The critical method again works through analogy, with American writers being set metaphorically within a comparative framework.

Matthiessen's work helped significantly to consolidate a field that had been given institutional momentum by the founding of an American literature group at the Modern Language Association of America (MLA) in 1921, and then by the establishment of the academic journal *American Literature* in 1929. Many of these "Founding Fathers" of American literary studies – there were, of course, no "Founding Mothers" – conceived of the subject in explicitly comparative terms. Norman Foerster, for example, wrote in *The Reinterpretation of American Literature* (1929) of how "[m]ore fully than any other, American culture is derivative, and consequently the study of American literature is essentially a study of comparative literature, a study in the international history of ideas and their literary expression."[4] In this same volume, Howard Mumford Jones emphasized what he called the "provincialism" of merely stressing "the Americanism of American literature," and he declared that Americanists must put aside their "morbid fear" that "comparisons" with writers such as "Shakespeare, Goethe or Dante" would prove "odious." Instead, wrote Mumford Jones, "we must group Europe and the United States into the homogeneous unity of Western culture; and seek to determine by comparison the differences and likenesses between them."[5] Again, "Western culture" is assumed to be the fulcrum of world civilization, and America is considered to be an interesting and significant variant in relation to this broader picture.

There were, of course, other influential voices at this time that sought to move beyond a narrowly formalist approach to this emerging subject. A.M. Schlesinger specifically criticized the first *Cambridge History of American Literature*, published in 1919, for not taking sufficiently into account the material culture and social context from which American literature had emerged. Citing the importance in US culture of such factors as "the popularization of the telephone, motor car, movie, and radio, and legislative attitudes toward such questions as censorship, international copyright, and a tariff on foreign bonds," Schlesinger argued in 1929 that "the development of literature is constantly affected by the forces which condition the whole course of social growth."[6] He thus anticipated a significant strand in Americanist criticism that sought not to treat letters as a privileged world apart but to relate literature to the social and political conditions that had produced it. This approach was also epitomized by V.L. Parrington's critical trilogy *Main Currents in American Thought* (1927–1930), which sought to align the development of American literature with a socially progressive agenda, driven by a democratic idealism that identified with the rural qualities of Jeffersonian populism and abhorred what Parrington considered the destructive influences of capitalist business and elitist social hierarchies. Parrington's introduction declared explicitly his intention to consider the transmission to America of certain old-world "ideals and institutions, and the subjection of those ideals and institutions to the pressure of a new environment, from which resulted the overthrows of the principles of monarchy and aristocracy, and the setting up of the principle of republicanism."[7] Such a critical pattern linking literature to society became more widespread during the Great Depression years of the 1930s, as scholars sought increasingly to explicate American literature in terms of its radical cultural politics and its differences from, rather than similarities to, European models. It was this nationalist slant, stressing the differential nature of the American domain, which crucially informed the development of the

American studies movement. This was given institutional shape by the foundation of the American Studies Association (ASA) in 1951 and by the first appearance of what was subsequently to become the ASA's official journal, *American Quarterly*, in 1949.

What is important to note, however, is that a dialectical double strand, involving the question of whether American literature should be seen as belonging specifically to the nation or to the wider world, has been inherent within the formation of this subject since its earliest days. The initial identification of American literature as a field of inquiry was driven as much by public affairs as by academic arguments. William E. Cain has written of how the first half of the twentieth century "was the period when American literature took shape as a subject and scholarly field," and he regards the fact that the case for American literature "was made inside and outside the academy" as representing "one of the most formidable achievements of modernism," bringing American literary culture into dialogue with a wider world.[8]

The visibility of American literature was significantly enhanced by the entry of the United States into World War I in April 1917 – poet Amy Lowell wrote of how the new "native school" in verse represented the "welding together of the whole country which the war has brought about" – and then by the pivotal role played by the USA in World War II. Both of these global conflicts had the effect not only of exposing American servicemen to a wider world, but also alerting this wider world to increasing American power and influence on the international stage.[9] When Conrad Aiken wrote in 1942 of how "for better or worse, American literature is henceforth a part of world literature," he was responding in part to a sense that, given the exigencies of modern military and communications technologies, the United States could no longer remain safely separated from European degradation and corruption by the reliance on what Thomas Jefferson in 1797 referred to as "an ocean of fire between us and the old world."[10] Hence, Donald Trump's notorious proposal of a wall between the United States and Mexico during his presidential campaign of 2016 can be seen as just the latest instantiation of a fantasy of partition that has long exercised the American cultural and political imagination. But the question of whether US cultural narratives should be understood as autochthonous products or as comparatively inflected designs has long been an issue susceptible to debate and disagreement.

Yet it was Jefferson's pastoral republicanism rather than Brown's interest in world geography that became most influential in the way American literature institutionalized itself during the 1950s and 1960s. Many of the subject's most influential critical formulations at this time – in R.W.B. Lewis's *The American Adam* (1955), Richard Chase's *The American Novel and its Tradition* (1957), or Leslie Fiedler's *Love and Death in the*

American Novel (1960) – promulgated, either explicitly or implicitly, a myth of American exceptionalism through which US conditions were represented as inherently different from those appertaining in the rest of the world. Thus, just to take one example of this, Chase argued for a categorical distinction between an American style of fictional "romance" and the English "novel," the former organized around a style of metaphysical quest, the latter merely around nuances of social class and manners.[11] In evoking such a dichotomy, Chase was effectively endorsing the antipathy of the American Transcendentalists towards British prototypes – Emerson in 1843 referred dismissively to English "novels of costume," saying they were "like the one orthodox sermon, which with slight variation is repeated every Sunday from so many pulpits" – and this also indicates the ways in which, in the wake of Matthiessen's influential work, nineteenth-century New England writers had become canonized as a template for American literature as a whole.[12] Many critics have subsequently pointed out the social hierarchies implicitly informing the fictions of Hawthorne and Melville, but in the way Chase envisaged the subject, the charm of American literature lay in the way it evaded such relative trivialities of social classification and aspired instead towards a more sublime artistic vision.

In any discussion of American world literature, then, it is important to remember how each of these three terms – "American," "world," and "literature" – is a contested rather than a naturalized entity. Apologists for American literary studies have sometimes tried to claim that the subject emerged organically from within the body of the nation, and this doggedly antitheoretical approach has remained an important influence on how the subject has been framed, from the work of Alfred Kazin in the 1940s to that of Greil Marcus at the turn of the twenty-first century. Kazin's emphasis on an unmediated social realism, like Marcus's focus on journalistic authenticity, took as its premise the assumption that a pragmatic American temper would simply put to one side the obfuscations of abstract preconception or rhetorical intertextuality, impediments that would threaten simply to get in the way of an appreciation by the writer or reader of their proximate American world. It is, of course, not difficult to understand the impatience felt by many towards more distant theoretical configurations, with the academic Hispanic Americanist Kirsten Silva Gruesz remarking in 2011 that she would prefer to hear about America from a Californian agricultural worker rather than a German graduate student.[13]

But such nostalgia for transparency always risks overlooking the fact that no subject can ever be approached neutrally, and any student of American world literature needs to recognize the fluctuating condition of all these key terms of classification. Although "America" is often used as

shorthand for the United States, America itself is not a nation but a continent, even though the term "American studies" has traditionally been
used to refer specifically to US culture. Attempts around the turn of the
twenty-first century to expand the definition of American studies to
encompass South America were met with resistance from US government
funding agencies, who had played an important role in helping to disseminate "American" values through underwriting overseas educational programs during the second half of the twentieth century. Such hard-nosed
political organizations were clearly unwilling to relinquish the impact of
this "soft power," in Joseph S. Nye's phrase, simply because of theoretical
anxieties about whether America should properly signify an entire continent stretching across both hemispheres rather than merely the territory
of the United States.[14] Some scholars today insist scrupulously on referring to "US literature" rather than American literature, but the latter term
has long been established in academic libraries and publishing, and there
is no indication at this point that the journal *American Literature*, for
example, is contemplating a change of title.

The meaning of the term "literature" has also varied considerably
across the ages. As Terry Eagleton pointed out, "[i]n eighteenth-century
England, the concept of literature was not confined as it sometimes is
today to 'creative' or 'imaginative' writing," but instead "meant the whole
body of valued writing in society: philosophy, history, essays and letters
as well as poems." According to Eagleton, indeed, what we now conceive
of as the "creative imagination" arose specifically from a nineteenth-century conception of the literary work embodying "a mysterious organic
unity, in contrast to the fragmented individualism of the capitalist marketplace."[15] Even if we do not entirely subscribe to the notion of "literature" being an invention of Romantic ideology that sought to position it
as a bulwark against the dehumanizing strain of industrialization, it is not
difficult to see that what we now think of as American literature has
encompassed many genres other than what we now consider the most
standard literary modes: novels, plays, and poems. The definition of
American literature conventionally incorporates the theological treatises
of John Winthrop in the 1630s, the intellectual history written by Cotton
Mather at the turn of the eighteenth century, the sermons of Jonathan
Edwards in the 1720s, the polemical lectures of Native American leader
William Apess and indeed the essays of Emerson himself written around
the same time. All these figures are represented in the widely used *Norton
Anthology of American Literature* as well as the competing *Heath
Anthology*, and they testify to an understanding of American literature as
a broad rubric. If the qualifying adjective *American* in the term "American
literature" is conventionally used as a form of nationalistic compression,
signifying the geographical circumference of the nation rather than any

hemispheric orbit, then conversely the noun *literature* is employed as a sign of expansion, a way of embracing within its capacious domain many varied styles of writing. Though William C. Spengemann's theoretical work is an exception to this rule, most early Americanist scholars who write on Mather or Edwards do not produce theoretical justifications for treating their subject as "literature," they simply assume that the term "American literature" is large enough, as Whitman famously formulated it in *Song of Myself*, to "contain multitudes."[16]

The same thing holds true of the modifier *world* within the phrase "American world literature." American literature has always related in various ways to a wider world, not only because it is necessarily part of this worldly domain, but also because the very idea of national identity depends upon a bounding and demarcation of space, a separation of "American" as a descriptor from more expansive or inchoate worldly co-ordinates. As R.W.B. Lewis and others noted, American culture has often been associated with a myth of exceptionalism that can be traced back to the days of the early Puritan settlers, as we see in Winthrop's sermon of 1630, "A Model of Christian Charity," where he justified the creation of an exiled colony in Massachusetts Bay on the grounds that it would serve as a "beacon" to the rest of the world: "For we must consider that we shall be as a city upon a hill. The eyes of all people are upon us." Winthrop rallied his fellow emigrants by declaring that their new community would be "a story and a by-word through the world," and the way in which he posits here a relation of reciprocity, through which the exemplary "city upon a hill" is validated by an external gaze, demonstrates the way in which this exceptionalist thesis is itself dependent on interaction with a world audience.[17]

During the first flourishing of American studies in the 1950s and 1960s, when the US economy was booming while many other countries were recovering only slowly from the austerities of World War II, the American "Beat" writers and others were held up throughout the world as examples of a cutting-edge, radical modernity, with Harry Harootunian subse-quently commenting on how Japan and other parts of East Asia were made at this time to feel that their local cultures were always inferior to the shiny new American model of modernity, with US culture seeming to involve by definition a commitment to futurity that left the rest of the world trailing in its wake.[18] Such forms of worldly engagements have fluctuated over time, of course, and America in the pre-Revolutionary eighteenth century, when it was still a collection of British colonies, enjoyed a markedly different relation to global space. The point here is simply that the term *world* in American world literature needs itself to be understood as a shifting signifier, no less than *American* and *literature*, and that to track the variations and interactions of these discrete entities over time is to bear witness to many different historical constellations. American world literature is a subject that changes its shape over time, and indeed that is the source of much of its interest.

It is also important to remember that this relation between American literature and the world always involves a process of multidirectional exchange, rather than merely the unilateral imposition of American values as a *desideratum* for the entire globe. Although postcolonial theory has emphasized the importance of writing back, the agency of various forms of resistance and the manner in which dominant and subordinate cultures interact in complicated ways, it has not always been the case that the United States has been particularly attuned to what Fredric Jameson described as "the radical difference of other national situations," with Jameson regarding it as "one of our basic political tasks ... to remind the American public" of such disparities.[19] Many of the international programs now established at the heart of the American university system do not seem particularly interested in engaging substantively with any overseas culture; their aim, in a more mercenary way, is simply to familiarize US domestic students with international conditions, so as to make them a more attractive employment prospect for US corporations in the global marketplace.

There are, of course, exceptions to this general rule, and Brian T. Edwards's careful work on local languages and cultures of the Middle East, and particularly on ways in which films such as *Argo* are understood quite differently across non-US cultural domains, might be said to epitomize international American studies at its most scrupulous.[20] But many programs driven by university administrators seek simply to appropriate alien cultures so as to further American interests, and there was a particularly egregious example of such insularity in 2014, when the University of California at Berkeley decided that it would establish a "global campus" a mere 10 miles from the main Berkeley site, making it what the Chancellor of the University of California system called "an international campus in the United States, right here in the East Bay ... where an exclusive group of some of the world's leading universities and high-tech companies will work side-by-side with us in a campus setting." The Chancellor at this time, Nicholas Dirks, expressed fears about the "limits on academic freedom" in other parts of the world, and he offered such concerns as a rationale for instead establishing the "global" campus in Richmond Bay, which he described as "a safe harbor in a safe harbor."[21] This project eventually fell through for lack of funding, but its "vision" does usefully encapsulate one particular strand of the American academy's engagement with the world, one that involves unabashed cultural and economic hegemony and imperial assimilation, rather than any kind of openness to otherness. There are many instances of American universities and publishing houses seeking to exploit a global moniker in theory while in practice presenting themselves almost entirely to a US market, and the Berkeley example illuminates the kind of pattern that tends to recur, albeit in less overt ways, on a routine basis. Although many American academics expressed outrage at the ascent of President Trump, his bullish sense of US superiority might be seen simply to express, albeit in a more extreme and indeed caricatured fashion, the assumptions that significant numbers of leaders in the American university world have long held.

International initiatives to expand the geographical remit of American culture across an institutional front have become associated in the early years of the twenty-first century with the resurgence of world literature as a field of scholarly inquiry. World literature as an idea is usually traced back to Goethe's first mention of *Weltliteratur* in 1827, when he suggested that "national literature is now a rather unmeaning term; the epoch of world literature is at hand, and everyone must strive to hasten its approach."[22] As John Pizer has observed, Goethe's paradigm was impelled in part by "the desire for a productive and peaceful coexistence among the nations of Europe after the divisive and destructive Napoleonic wars," and in that sense it represents an aspiration to rise above the fractious and bellicose nationalism of Goethe's own times.[23] Marx and Engels in their Communist Manifesto of 1848 linked the "exploitation of the world market" by the "bourgeoisie" to a process of international "intercourse in every direction, universal dependence of nations," with Marx and Engels finding a parallel between material and intellectual production: "The intellectual creations of individual nations become common property. National one-sidedness and narrow-mindedness become more and more impossible, and from the numerous national and local literatures, there arises a world literature."[24] However, this emerging dynamic of "world literature" was countered during the second half of the nineteenth century by a general revival of nationalist sentiment, with for example Friedrich Meinecke's *Weltbürgetum und Nationalstaat* (Cosmopolitanism and the National State), first published in 1907, arguing that cosmopolitanism was an outdated principle, and that nationalism was the progressive end to which history itself was tending.[25]

It is not difficult to understand, then, how the emergence of world literature as an idea in the nineteenth century was symbiotically entwined with questions of national identity and the problematic status of internationalism more generally. Transnational connections were impelled both by economic trade and developments in technology (such as the telegraph) that, as Marx and Engels noted, facilitated cross-border communications. On the other hand, an investment in the idea of the nation as what Ernst Renan in 1882 called a "spiritual principle" helped to underwrite the institutionalization of national literature as a quasi-sacred sphere of study, with Oxford University establishing its Honours School of English Language and Literature in 1893 as an academic correlative of this idealization of nationalist design.[26] Just as the myth of the American frontier was invoked by Frederick Jackson Turner in 1893, only two years after the US Census had officially declared the frontier closed, so it might be argued that myths of national formation and cultural independence arose specifically in reaction to the pressures being newly exerted on this concept in a more empirical sense. All the anthologies of national literature that flowed from presses in the early years of the twentieth century corroborated an intimation of what Sir Arthur Quiller-Couch, in the preface to his *Oxford Book of English Prose* (1925), described as the "sense of wonderful history written silently in books and buildings, all persuading that we are heirs of more spiritual wealth than, may be, we have surmised or hitherto begun to divine."[27] In English universities during this period, the academic study of literature at undergraduate level thus became associated with the inculcation of a set of moral values designed to build personal character and reinforce accepted national values.

Within this kind of pedagogical context, world literature also took on populist dimensions, offering a way of teaching large undergraduate classes with relatively accessible material. Although Columbia University established its Department of Comparative Literature as early as 1898, the focus there on reading works in their original language did not cut much ice with Richard G. Moulton of the University of Chicago, whose *World Literature and its Place in the General Culture* (1911) had no qualms about using works in translation. Moulton extolled the virtues of developing a student's broader qualities of taste and spirit, and he particularly damned the scholarship of philology, which he saw as unduly obsessed with factual minutiae. Moulton's antipathy towards "pure" scholarship was shared by Thomas Wentworth Higginson, sometime friend of Emily Dickinson, with Higginson complaining in his 1890 article "A World-Literature" of how the vast majority of Harvard University's literature classes were "wholly philological, not in any sense literary."[28] A bifurcation was consequently established whereby comparative literature and philology came to be regarded as more specialized subjects, ripe for graduate studies and academic research, whereas world literature was designated as a broader pedagogical category, suitable mainly for the undergraduate curriculum. This division held good through the first half of the twentieth century, with famous Columbia professor Lionel Trilling in 1958 holding his nose at the thought of world literature being "now part of the argot of our collegiate education," and Weldon M. Williams two years later comparing the typical world literature course to an American tourist's trip through the sites of Europe: "It may be that its quick forays into cathedrals and castles and mosques are too often like the achievement of the American tourist who boasted that he made it through the Louvre in ten minutes flat."[29]

It is important to remember, as Pizer observes, how world literature at this time was "a uniquely American pedagogic domain," with universities in other parts of the world tending to stick with more traditional formulations of national literature.[30] Sarah Lawall similarly commented in 1988 on how "Only in the United States do we find a systematic attempt to encompass the 'world' (however defined) in literature courses," and though this is certainly not the case in the twenty-first century, it nevertheless did hold true for most of the twentieth.[31] Trilling's disdain for world literature as a scholarly category in the 1950s would have been reinforced by the new professional visibility at that time of a distinguished cadre of comparative literature specialists: Erich Auerbach, René Wellek, and others. Many of these scholars had fled to the United States to escape the depredations of World War II in Europe, and Auerbach's ambition to establish comparative literature as an intellectual discipline beyond the claims of any petty nationalism sounds remarkably like Goethe's advocacy of *Weltliteratur* in 1827 as a counterpoint to the Napoleonic Wars. These comparative literature specialists were, as a mark of their professional accreditation, fluent in multiple European languages, and such standards would have enhanced the condescension of Trilling and others to what they took to be the vulgar prospect of world literature in translation.

The International Comparative Literature Association was founded at Oxford in 1954, but in its early years this Association followed the Goethean principle of conflating Europe with the world of knowledge, and nearly all of the language expertise of comparative literature specialists at this time was European in its provenance. The ICLA held regular congresses every three years, though these rotated on an exclusively European and North American axis – Montreal, Budapest, New York, Paris and so on – until 1991, when the ICLA first went to Tokyo, since when it has convened in South Africa, Rio de Janeiro, Hong Kong, Seoul, and elsewhere. This opening out of the field to Asian literature and culture, in particular, has raised concerns in North America about the academic coherence and scholarly integrity of the field. As J. Hillis Miller remarked in 2000:

> The old Eurocentric Comparative Literature made sense as a discipline because graduate dissertation committees, for example, could be made up of professors all presumed to be competent in all the languages and literatures covered in the dissertation. The situation is different when as is often the case nowadays, the

committee is made up, for example, of several professors who know Chinese, plus one specialist in Chinese. The latter is more likely to know European languages and methodologies than the former are likely to know anything about Chinese culture or literature or language, but the old rule that all the committee members have at least minimum competence in all of the work covered in the dissertation is broken in such cases.[32]

It is not difficult, of course, to appreciate the traditionalist bias inherent in Miller's concern, the assumption here that European and North American languages are central and Asian cultures correspondingly peripheral. But his observation does draw attention to the problem of practicality and viability that besets any attempt to encompass the world within an epistemological framework. Henry James was also influenced by a pragmatist cast of mind, not all of it deriving from the philosophical work of his brother William, and in a 1913 letter Henry James criticized his friend Henrik Christian Andersen's plans for a "World Centre" and his pamphlet on a "World Conference," with James writing:

> I simply *loathe* such pretensious [sic] forms of words as 'World' anything – they are to me mere monstrous sound without sense. The World is a prodigious and portentous and immeasurable affair, and I can't for a moment pretend to sit in my little corner here and 'sympathize with' proposals for dealing with it. It is so far vaster in its appalling complexity than you or me, or than anything we can pretend without the imputation of absurdity and insanity to do to it, that I content myself, and inevitably *must* (so far as I can do anything at all now) with living in the realities of things, with 'cultivating my garden' (morally and intellectually speaking) and with referring my questions to a Conscience (my own poor little personal), less inconceivable than that of the globe.[33]

J.M. Coetzee made a similar point in a 2001 interview, when he said that while he "would prefer to think more globally ... one can't write a sort of globally set novel. It has to be somewhere."[34] The aspirations of universal spirit, in whatever guise they manifest themselves, find themselves structurally bound to the ironies of terrestrial incarnation, and this, rather than mere academic politics or institutional conflict, is the primary reason why the idea of world literature exists in an uncomfortable space alongside its local or national counterparts. American world literature may be not quite an oxymoron, but it implies an interplay of competing and often contradictory forces that can by definition never achieve a state of stable resolution.

Within an academic context, the most persistent challenges to orthodox formulations of American literature have emerged in recent times
from exponents of comparative literature, who have complained of various ways in which the American literary subject has tended to be framed
too narrowly. Questions of language are perhaps the most obvious terrain on which these theoretical battles have taken place, with the
Longfellow Institute at Harvard, directed by Werner Sollors and Marc
Shell, lamenting how American literature has become consolidated in
scholarly terms as a monolingual category. Taking their cue from Henry
Wadsworth Longfellow, the multilingual Professor of Modern Languages
at Harvard in the 1860s, Sollors and Shell have pointed to the prevalence
of publications in many different languages throughout the United
States up until the early years of the twentieth century.[35] It is certainly
worthy of note how many Scandinavian-language newspapers were published in the immigrant communities of the Pacific Northwest, for
example, and it is important for any student of American literature to be
aware that Theodore Dreiser's first language – the vernacular he heard
at his family home – was German rather than English, just as that of Jack
Kerouac was Breton French. But it is also important to acknowledge
how the increasing hegemony of the English language within the United
States was driven not merely by chance, nor just by academic prejudice
against non-Anglophone tongues, but by specific government policies
mandating the imposition of a standardized English for the purposes of
social and political cohesion. When the first *Cambridge History of
American Literature* was published in 1919, it had two chapters devoted
to "Non-English Writings," but by the time of Robert Spiller's new edition
of the *Cambridge History* in 1948, this explicitly multilingual component
had been eliminated.[36] During the First World War, former president
Theodore Roosevelt declared: "We must ... have but one language. That
must be the language of the Declaration of Independence."[37] Hence the
suppression around this time of German-language publications, like the
legal suppression in 1868 of the teaching of French in Louisiana second-
ary schools in the aftermath of the Civil War, was designed deliberately
to shore up an ideal of national unity around Anglophone co-ordinates,
and the identification by Foerster and his collaborators during the 1920s
of American literature as a national enterprise carried as its correlative a
corresponding diminution in the visibility of languages other than
English.

This is not, of course, to deny the value of scholarship that examines
American literature's historical relationship to multilingualism, and such
scholarship takes many compelling forms, from studies of Puritan
encounters with Native American languages in the seventeenth century
through to Robert A. Orsi's analysis of the ethnic styles associated with

Italian immigrant communities in New York.[38] This multilingual dimension has been given added impetus in the twenty-first century by the increasing visibility of Spanish within the US national domain, with some forecasts predicting that the Hispanic population will outnumber the Caucasian by 2050, while contemporary fiction writers such as Sandra Cisneros and Cormac McCarthy sometimes use bilingual strands in their narratives, as if to mirror the hybrid nature of the new American world they are invoking. All this needs to be situated, however, against the countercurrent of a framework that is explicitly competing against monolingual, nationalistic paradigms. Foerster in 1929 specifically took issue with regionalist variations, whose focus on "local color" he saw as leading towards an inevitably "provincial" emphasis in American literary study, and he looked instead to Frederick Jackson Turner's conception of the frontier as a paradigm for what Foerster understood to be the dominant mythic tropes informing US culture.[39]

It is of course easy enough from our perspective to see what Foerster's mythic template overlooks: issues of race and gender, for example, as well as questions of multilingualism. But it is important to understand how the contours of this nationalist design have expanded and contracted over the past 400 years, with the focus on multiple languages being very far from a new phenomenon in the broader context of American literary studies, just as the idea of America as a redemptive new nation is an exceptionalist *topos* that can more usefully be analyzed in historical rather than philosophical terms. As an abstract idea, American exceptionalism is altogether nugatory, but as an affective concept it has long been powerful, and it continued to be so even among political leaders such as Obama who were skeptical of its rational justification. Obama's quasi-religious incantation in political rallies, "yes we can," was a fitting example of how the American body politic is beholden to a revivalist spirit of affirmation rather than a more clinical model of sober analysis.

Yet this exceptionalist affect also creates significant blindspots in terms of America's understanding of its relation to a wider cultural world. One of the most stringent recent interrogations of the underlying premises of American literary studies came in 2003 from a professor of comparative literature, Djelal Kadir, whose professional expertise lies primarily in South America rather than US culture as such. In his introduction to a special issue of *PMLA* entitled "America: The Idea, the Literature," Kadir accused American literary scholars of being implicated within the parameters of their own field to such an extent that they were caught up in the "redundancy" that "inexorably renders the knowing subject part of what it seeks to know." Tracing American literary studies back through Trilling, Matthiessen, and Parrington, Kadir argued that the field remains beholden to a "cultural logic of belated liberalism," one that hypostatizes the idea of difference and diversity, fiercely resists any "exogenous discourse on America," and seeks to reconcile the articulation of progressive values with the identity of America itself. One problem with such a form of "self-contemplation," argued Kadir, was that Americanist scholars tended to engage in a form of "unilateralist solipsism" that would flatten out "the irreducible complexity of what America has been," a site not just for the expression of utopian fantasies but an altogether harsher and more complex sphere, so that academically there was a need for testing such theorems of "identity construction" through "a comparative and relational refocusing of America in the larger world context."[40]

It is certainly the case that the conflation of progressive politics with American literary studies has produced an oddly slanted view of this particular scholarly domain. For example, Matthiessen's *American Renaissance*, brilliant as the book is, neglects almost entirely the significance of the US South as a formative influence in American literature – Matthiessen barely mentions Edgar Allan Poe, let alone the pro-slavery novelist William Gilmore Simms – and this led him to identify the optative "promise of America life" with an organic vision extrapolated from his five chosen New England and New York writers.[41] Kadir's argument in relation to Matthiessen was not that such radical energies were misplaced, but that they could lead towards a misleading understanding of the subject's wider compass, particularly when it was underwritten by the desire of US state agencies to promote an ideal of universal liberal order for political purposes. In the straitened economic circumstances of Europe after World War II, just as in the former Communist countries after the fall of the Berlin Wall in 1989, there were many academic departments that were glad to receive assistance from the US government to help fund their programs, but such collusion always tended to put these universities in the delicate position of treading a fine line between analyzing an idea and becoming an apologist for it. Whereas institutes of medieval studies that sprang up in many universities throughout the twentieth century were populated by scholars who were necessarily detached (at least in chronological terms) from medieval culture, institutes of American studies were sometimes run by professors who not only admired US culture but also drew their salaries from its government's information agencies.

There were, of course, various institutional conflicts within the profession that were brought into sharp relief by the intellectual disagreements associated with the strategic recalibration of American world literature around the turn of the twenty-first century. The 1990s might be understood in retrospect as a decade of blithe US hegemony, when market forces of globalization led Masao Miyoshi in 1993 to suggest that "Cable TV and MTV dominate the world absolutely," with political scientist

Francis Fukuyama similarly promulgating in 1989 an "end" to history.[42] This putative end of history itself came to an end on 9/11, 11 September 2001, after which US global relations could no longer be envisaged in terms of a unilateral process whereby the dominant culture could simply impose its liberal market values in a friction-free manner on the rest of the world. Although, of course, the sense of scale here is very different, the ASA in the latter years of the twentieth century had similarly tended to acknowledge international affairs only as an afterthought, but by the first decade of the twenty-first century the place of the United States in the wider world was very much in the forefront of new theoretical agendas. Kadir's International American Studies Association was founded in 2003 as a specific attempt to align American studies more with the axis of comparative literature, and several presidents of the ASA around this time made explicit efforts to integrate Americanist scholarship within a broader internationalist matrix, with Shelley Fisher Fishkin announcing a "transnational turn" in her presidential address of 2004, and Emory Elliott, president of the ASA in 2006–2007, working hard to ensure that what he considered to be two distinctive pressure groups within the organization – one committed to local politics and activist agendas, the other to a more internationalist nexus – did not splinter off into competing fragments.[43]

There were, of course, many intellectual developments at the turn of the twenty-first century that profoundly influenced American literary studies and expanded its conceptual orbit beyond the narrower sphere of nationalism. Particularly significant in this regard was the work of "queer" theorists such as Judith Butler and Eve Kosofsky Sedgwick on the contingent nature of sexual identities, as well as the broader work of deconstruction undertaken by a generation of French post-structuralists – Michel Foucault, Jacques Derrida, Jean-François Lyotard – who sought to reconceptualize social and psychological states as discursive rather than naturalized formations. In terms of American world literature, however, the most significant intervention associated with this transnational turn involved issues connected with slavery. It was not until the 1970s that African American writers such as Frederick Douglass achieved any kind of visibility on the syllabi of American literature courses, and it is now strange to think of how key critical works of the 1960s that celebrated a mythical sense of American freedom, such as Tony Tanner's *The Reign of Wonder* (1965) and Richard Poirier's *A World Elsewhere* (1966), completely overlooked ways in which such legendary forms of mobility were symbiotically bound up with racial subjugation of various kinds. Toni Morrison's *Playing in the Dark: Whiteness and the Literary Imagination* (1992), based on her Massey lectures at Harvard, made the compelling case that the shadows of race impacted just as tellingly upon classic

American literature by white writers such as Poe, Mark Twain, and Ernest Hemingway, and this exemplified the radical critical idiom that became commonplace in the last two decades of the twentieth century, through which questions of liberty and slavery were shown to be tied together both politically and aesthetically. Whereas Tanner and Poirier considered American narratives of freedom to be blissfully independent of repressive conventions, the work of Morrison and others demonstrated how such putative innocence was grounded upon a form of amnesia, what she called a "willful critical blindness."[44]

The very fact that the slave trade operated across a transatlantic axis, with slave cargo being shipped from Africa to Europe and thence to America, reinforced this revisionist view of how the United States could no longer be understood in isolationist terms, as what Henry Nash Smith in 1950 fondly described as a "virgin land" framed by its own mythologies of emancipation.[45] Many of the more traditional US cultural historians in the period after World War II liked to emphasize what Daniel J. Boorstin – an "apogee of exceptionalist thinking," according to Michael Zuckerman – regarded as the special qualities of American democracy, the manner in which it had successfully escaped from the class-bound hierarchies of Europe and constructed a society based around pragmatic progressivism rather than ideological conflict.[46] However, the new focus on how such democratic spirit had been forged on the backs of exploited racial minorities ensured that this new American studies was much less attached to conditions of consensual liberalism than Boorstin's academic generation had been. Paul Gilroy's *The Black Atlantic: Modernity and Double Consciousness* (1993), which described the triangulation of the slave trade across three continents and traced how such patterns of mobility and displacement came to influence articulations of national identity at every level, was only the most well known of many works around the turn of the twenty-first century that used both the metaphorical figure and the historical practice of slavery to bring American literary culture into alignment with a wider world. In Gilroy's reconceptualization of American literary paradigms, Richard Wright's intellectual dealings with existentialists in Paris were just as important as his involvement with antiracist activists in Chicago, and this version of systematic reciprocity, whereby US ideals of emancipation were exposed to alternative perspectives in relation to both high theory and material culture, served importantly to position the American slave experience within a larger discursive framework, one that emphasized its transnational provenance.[47]

This shift in the study of slavery from the particular conditions of the US South to the more exogenous circumstances of the international slave trade also had the effect of aligning the study of American literature with a critical framework of postcolonialism more generally. The ways in which British imperial power had operated in the Caribbean, or Spanish imperial power in South America, could no longer be differentiated so sharply from the idea of US empire within a global context. The prevalence of empire is far from a new theme in American literature – Herman Melville's first novel *Typee* (1846) features conflict between British and American naval forces in the Pacific over jurisdiction of what were then known as the Sandwich Islands (now Hawaii) – but because of the critical emphasis on Melville's qualities of allegorical "romance" in the "myth and symbol" approach to American literature that held sway after World War II, these questions of colonial and political rivalry as they manifested themselves in his novels tended to be disregarded as merely transitory or contingent affairs. In his essay "World Literature and US American Literature," Lawrence Buell noted that while twenty-first-century Americanists such as Amy Kaplan and Wai Chee Dimock express "divergent" critical positions – Kaplan in *The Anarchy of Empire* (2002) assessing US literary culture as "arrogant, self-centered, possessive"; Dimock in *Through Other Continents* (2006) regarding it as "infinitely curious, permeable, open to influence" – what they nevertheless both "have in common is a commitment never again to think of US literary history without regard to those of the rest of the world's cultures."[48] In this sense, the reconstruction of American literature as American world literature turns less upon political than on generational identification. While Kaplan and Dimock may approach American literary texts with different political perspectives, they both share a sense that the American literary subject should necessarily have a worldly rather than just a narrowly nationalistic focus.

The larger question of how American literature as a subject of scholarly inquiry relates to the resurgence of world literature as an academic field in the early years of the twenty-first century is a complicated affair, one that demands some understanding of how and why world literature has achieved this new state of prominence. There are, to be sure, the political and sociological aspects of globalization driven by information technology that need to be taken into account, with Mads Rosendahl Thomsen commenting in 2008 on how "it is difficult at present to give convincing arguments as to why anybody should be interested in studying the literature of one nation." Given the almost ubiquitous transmission of cultural products and narratives across national borders, and the states of hybridity that now characterize everything from poetry to television programming, Thomsen argues that "the traditional trinity of history, language and literature that provides the basis for many [national] studies seems to be untenable."[49] Franco Moretti in 2000 claimed that "the literature around us now is unmistakably a planetary system," while Aamir R. Mufti in *Forget English!* (2016) suggested that the re-emergence of world literature should be seen as a post-1989 phenomenon, one linked implicitly to the fall of the Berlin Wall and the dissemination of neoliberal capitalism across a global axis.[50] In Mufti's eyes, "World literature … is fundamentally a concept of exchange or, in other words, a concept of bourgeois society," one rooted in the belief that commodities can circulate across borders in a relatively uncontested manner.[51]

David Damrosch famously defined world literature as "work that gains in translation," and in his aptly entitled essay "How American is World Literature?," Damrosch argued that "shadowing the debates over Eurocentrism" in world literature was "a largely unacknowledged Americentrism, a factor that is at once repressed and pervasive in American comparatism," since the "relative invisibility of our American standpoint is itself a characteristically American trait."[52] Damrosch's point here is that world literature is covertly dominated by US expectations and assumptions, just as globalization in its post-1989 incarnation involved an export of American capitalism across international borders. In both cases, what was categorized as a "world" phenomenon was one that involved primarily an extrapolation of US interests across a global sphere. The risk was that just as President George H.W. Bush proclaimed a "new world order" after the demise of the Soviet Union, so advocates of "world literature" as an academic category would similarly adduce the world as their domain, in a move that institutionalized US interests and perspectives while effectively masking their provenance under a universalist rhetoric.

There have of course been stringent critiques of such "Americentrism," particularly from critics such as Pheng Cheah who have approached the subject of world literature from an explicitly postcolonial perspective. Defining "transnational literary relations" as "relations of power and domination," Cheah focused in particular on how "literature of the postcolonial South" operated as a challenge to normative conceptions of world literature based around North American (and European) hegemony, even if the examples Cheah adduced from the Philippines and other parts of Asia spoke more often to cultural resistance emerging from within the northern rather than the southern hemisphere.[53]

One example of how this notion of American literature as a global enterprise manifested itself in the twenty-first century on a popular level can be seen in the wild success of Azar Nafisi's *Reading Lolita in Tehran* (2003), which was published 18 months after the 9/11 attacks, and a few months after the US invasion of Iraq. Nafisi's book quickly went to the number one paperback best seller position on the *New York Times Book Review* list, and by September 2004 it was the fifth most borrowed non-fiction book in US libraries. Nafisi's polemic, based upon her memoirs of higher education in Tehran, flatters the expectations of its American audience by counterpointing US "free-dom" to "the texture of life in a totalitarian society."[54] The author updates the time-honored American opposition to "totalitarian" states by redefining the enemy not as Cold War Russia but as post-Revolutionary Iran, where the denizens of Nafisi's reading group find that "like Lolita we tried to escape and to create our own little pockets of freedom."[55] Citing Lionel Trilling, Leon Edel, and other prominent American critics of the 1950s, Nafisi thus holds up the "imagination" she takes to be inherent in classic works of Western literature – by Vladimir Nabokov, Scott Fitzgerald, Henry James, and Jane Austen – while contrasting these qualities to the repressive "ideology" she associates with the mullahs of Tehran.[56] Although this book vali-dates "empathy" as a prime liberal virtue, such a capacity to see the world from the viewpoint of others is not readily apparent in her satiri-cal portrait of an Iranian student's "long and garbled tirade about the valley of the ashes and the decadence of Gatsby's parties," in her dia-tribe against "the clutches of ignoramuses in the faculty who had no knowledge of literature," nor in the final section where the author ham-mers home her "hatred ... of evil totalitarian systems which Nabokov denounced."[57]

In this sense, as Anne Donadey and Huma Ahmed-Ghosh observed, Nafisi's work evidently "reinforces conservative assumptions" about how the "American literary canon" has "universal value," and this would no doubt have helped Nafisi's admittedly well-written "memoir" to find a ready audience in American book clubs and undergraduate classrooms.[58] Bizarrely, by April 2004 *Reading Lolita in Tehran* ranked second on the list of the most widely read books on US college campuses, and this clearly indicates ways in which curricular designs on American world literature centered in US universities tend to risk simply conflating US values with those of the rest of the world, in rhetorical acts of cultural imperialism that might have made Theodore Roosevelt blush. There was no attempt in Nafisi's work to understand alien cultures; more straight-forwardly, Iran was rhetorically contrasted with the United States in an effort to prove the supremacy of American values.

One of the American authors celebrated by Nafisi is Saul Bellow, with the Iranian-American particularly commending Bellow's *The Dean's December* (1983) because it deals "with the ordeals of the East and those of the West." Bellow's novel, which confronts the harshness of Soviet-backed political regimes in Eastern Europe, thus provides a Cold War counterpart to the struggle against Iranian forms of subjugation evoked by Nafisi, and it suggests how a Manichaean imagination, one involving the celebration of a spiritual sense of "boundless freedom" as opposed to suffocating systems of darkness, is a rhetorical trope that has structured

American approaches to world culture across many different historical eras and political circumstances.[59] Bellow himself, as Saul Noam Zaritt has emphasized, was among the Jewish-American writers in the post-World War II period who "very much wanted to be 'worlded'" in the sense of desiring "their works to circulate globally," to be canonized as literary figures who had achieved universal status," and who "wanted to escape the anxiety of seeming provincial."[60] The eponymous hero of Bellow's *Herzog* (1964) certainly reads many non-American philosophers – Hegel, Spinoza, Nietzsche, and so on – but his central goal is to reconcile these abstract thinkers with the brutal realities of his own Chicago world, thereby correlating local scenes with universal values.

Like his contemporaries Philip Roth and Norman Mailer, Bellow believed in the justice of his claim to be "universalized within world literature," rather than speaking merely as the representative of an ethnic or religious ghetto.[61] This, though, goes to the heart of the philosophical conundrum about whether American values should be considered particularistic or universal. When in 1987 Bellow wrote a foreword to his friend Allan Bloom's polemic *The Closing of the American Mind*, Bellow's assumption, like that of Professor Bloom from the University of Chicago, was that Western humanistic and artistic values were inherently superior to those of other cultures; "Who is the Tolstoy of the Zulus? The Proust of the Papuans?" Bellow famously remarked in 1988, "I'd be glad to read them."[62]

The emphasis of Bloom and Bellow on the uplifting quality of Western culture was also commensurate with the fact that the subject of world literature grew rapidly in US undergraduate classrooms after World War II as an extension and development of the "Great Books" programs that had become established in higher education after World War I. The traditional classicism of the "Great Books" ideal – Homer, Virgil, Dante, and so on – gradually morphed into a greater willingness to encompass works from outside Europe. Philo M. Buck Jr, a professor of comparative literature who edited one of the first world literature anthologies in 1934, expanded his paltry selections from Asian literature in his third edition, published in 1951, so as to enhance the selection of works from China and Japan.[63] But this pedagogical model of world literature, like Bellow's idiom of worldliness, was firmly centered in assumptions of a global sphere dominated by Western interests, into which the rest of the world was admitted only on sufferance.

It is no coincidence that some of the most prominent contemporary theorists of world literature, such as Moretti and Pascale Casanova, came to this field from an intellectual position outside the United States, with their more sociological modes of analysis refusing the residual romanticism that would put US culture at the center of all that it surveys. Moretti's model of literary production almost entirely eviscerates affect in favor of economics, replacing any analysis of fiction's imaginative charms with more impersonal charts and graphs that quantify the profusion of fiction as it circulated within the commercial marketplace, while Casanova's claim for Paris as the guarantor of a certain intellectual imprimatur carries Pierre Bourdieu's conception of "taste" as a marker of social distinction and hierarchy into the world of publishing.[64] From an American perspective, the work of both Moretti and Casanova involves a certain analytical coldness, challenging the kind of exuberance through which Bellow seeks to integrate Chicago with an embrace of the wider world, while substituting instead depersonalized formulas through which world literature is understood as a network formed by a global literary marketplace involving both cultural and economic capital.

This is not dissimilar in kind from Immanuel Wallerstein's "world-systems analysis," with Wallerstein suggesting in 2003 that the world was witnessing a gradual "decline of US hegemony," in part because the American attempt after 1945 to maintain its strategic control over the world's nuclear arsenal had become impossible, due to the proliferation of nuclear weapons that inevitably went along with developments in scientific knowledge. Wallerstein argued that this erosion of American supremacy was not the result of mere errors in political policy, but indicated a more structural shift associated with changes in information technology that allow capital investment and other kinds of data to be moved across national borders much more easily.[65] Such transnational mobility of capital facilitates outsourcing, along with an increasing awareness across the planet of the ecological limits of toxification and the likely non-renewability of energy sources. Such a shift in political focus from domestic issues to more intractable planetary challenges indicates how attempts by various American presidents to provide the public with "certainty about their future" effectively bring into play an allure of blanket reassurance through chimeras of security that are, in fact, "totally beyond [their] power to offer."[66]

This is not the place for a detailed analysis of the challenges to US geopolitical power in the twenty-first century. However, when considering the subject of American world literature, it is important to bear in mind that US global power can no longer be taken for granted in the way it was during the Cold War era. Political scientist John Ikenberry argued in 2011 that just as the "liberal hegemonic order" based around US values after World War II has eroded, so "the authority with which the United States has wielded power in this system has also diminished."[67] The rise of China and the rapid growth of other industries in Asia have contributed to these structural challenges to US power, and it is not difficult to see that the election of Donald Trump as president in 2016 arose in part from a widespread populist feeling that there was a need to "make America great again," to restore the United States to its former position of unchallenged supremacy. Trump's promise to build a wall on the southern border between the United States and Mexico, a pledge that attracted vociferous support during his presidential campaign, can in this context readily be understood as an attempt to turn back the clock, a fantasy of restoring the condition of the United States as an impermeable territory, one properly guarded against infiltration by foreigners. In fact, as Sandro Mezzadra and Brett Neilson have observed, "the border has inscribed itself at the center of contemporary experience," with "borderscapes" now being apparent on computer and television screens, in financial markets, in linguistic matrices, and so on.[68] The issue of "borderlands," wrote Azade Seyhan in relation to the fiction of Sandra Cisneros, is no longer confined merely to a line on a map, but should be understood as the historical condition for new critical formations.[69] In this sense, Trump's promise of a wall separating the United States and Mexico involves an imaginary resolution to a more all-encompassing issue, an attempt to control the proliferation of internal borders through a visible emblem of national security that would, in truth, address the issue at little more than a symbolic level.

Given how clear-cut divisions between "inside" and "outside" have been rendered redundant and that borders "sit no longer at the margins but at the center of our political lives," as Mezzadra and Neilson put it, the question of American world literature should be understood as appertaining to something more capacious than merely the trials and tribulations of immigrants.[70] Novelists such as Gish Jen and Jhumpa Lahiri have become very popular in the United States because their narratives tell familiar stories of immigrant struggle and eventual triumph, with their protagonists moving from China and India respectively to a United States that is conceived, in the time-honored manner, as a land of the free. Both Jen and Lahiri have received multiple accolades in the United States, including in Lahiri's case the award of the 2014 National Humanities Medal from President Obama, precisely because their fictions endorse a vision of assimilation that has been a staple of the American body politic since Hector St Jean de Crèvecoeur was writing about the integration of immigrant farmers into American life in the 1790s. This is not, of course, to disparage in itself the work of Jen or Lahiri, which combines a planetary reach with an accessible and transparent domestic style, along with acute sensitivity to the subjective vacillations of immigrants' experience. It is, however, to suggest that the idea of American world literature in the twenty-first century involves a more complicated and multipolar conception, one in which neither the boundaries of national geography nor the parameters of ethnic demarcation can be so clearly identified.

In its etymology, the word "translation" carries resonances beyond the process of mere linguistic exchange, with the Latin term *translatio* referring not only to a transfer of meaning but also to a transfer of property. Mezzadra and Neilson cite Thomas Hobbes in *Leviathan* (1651): "All contract is mutual translation, or change of Right."[71] To consider *translation* in this wider discursive sense is to suggest how it is a key factor in the operations of the transfer of goods across a wider public sphere, with law and economics as well as language becoming incorporated within the broader remit of translation. In this sense, the pressures placed by translation on American literature's domestic sphere have the effect of interrogating the conventions of liberalism, along with what comparative anthropologist Elizabeth A. Povinelli has described as "the fantasies necessary to act in a liberal society and how these fantasies are protected and projected into social life through specific textual practices."[72] One version of American world literature is an export model that involves a principled extension of basic human rights to all global citizens, a position taken by Martha C. Nussbaum's essay "Patriotism and Cosmopolitanism," which, citing as its epigraph Diogenes the Cynic's claim to be "a citizen of the world," effectively advocates a universalization of Western liberal values.[73] But another version of American world literature involves a more unsettling model of parallelism and reciprocity, where narratives external to the United States are mirrored, sometimes disturbingly, within its borders.

The purpose of this introductory study is to consider how the field of American literature might usefully be approached in different ways if it were to be understood as American world literature rather than simply American literature with a nationalist bent. History of all kinds is necessarily written backwards, reconfiguring patterns of the past in accordance with preoccupations of the present, and to trace the global provenance of American literature back through time is not to distort it but to offer an alternative interpretive angle to the one typically promulgated by nationalist literary historians in the twentieth century. For example, as Philip F. Gura has argued, early American literature specialists were characteristically attracted to the poetry of Edward Taylor in the 1660s because they could see ways in which it might be seen to prefigure the metaphysical style of Emily Dickinson in the 1860s, and they thus tended to emphasize "continuities" in American literary history by appropriating the colonial period as a proleptic anticipation of the nationalist era.[74] Albert Gelpi, another critic committed to the idea of American literature as an organic unity, similarly found affinities between Taylor and the "knots and crotchets" of Ezra Pound's poetic style.[75]

In this light, to reconstitute a model of American world literature is necessarily to read against the grain, but the impetus of such re-reading is not intended to be merely heterodox and countersuggestible. By greatly expanding the nationalist contours within which American literature has conventionally been framed, and by tracing ways in which it has over every historical period interacted in complex ways with the wider world, it becomes possible to understand the subject not just as a pastoral alternative to the Western canon, but as something integral to its construction. The marketing of American literature, particularly by overseas booksellers, has too often involved simply a piling up of "Beat" novels or civil rights autobiographies, as if to reinforce a commercial stereotype of America as the land where "we shall overcome." Without at all denigrating the claims of freedom and protest, the aim of this book is to position American literature within a more rounded sphere, where worldly considerations – colonial conquest, religious disputes, interaction with Islam, questions around taxation and representation, controversies associated with global trade, and so on – can be seen to have informed the subject since its earliest days.

American literature as a nationalist enterprise has tended perhaps too often to reify tropes of self-reliance and to regard Emersonian typologies of individualism as typifying the trajectory of the subject at large. By contrast, the broader domain of American world literature encompasses a wider conceptual as well as geographical circumference and it lays out a terrain of global engagement through which other national spheres see their domestic preconceptions interrogated or reversed. American literature has thus always had a worldly purchase, interfacing with wider domains in a way that offers both threats and opportunities, and the purpose of this book is to suggest the variegated ways in which these worldly dimensions have expanded and contracted over time.

References

1 Eagleton, T. (1983). *Literary Theory: An Introduction*, vii. Oxford: Blackwell.
2 Emerson, R.W. (1971). The American scholar (1837). In: *The Collected Works of Ralph Waldo Emerson, I: Nature, Addresses and Lectures* (ed. R.E. Spiller), 69. Cambridge: Harvard UP.
3 Gunn, G. (1975). *F. O. Matthiessen: The Critical Achievement*, 32, 35. Seattle: U of Washington P.
4 Foerster, N. (1928). Introduction. In: *The Reinterpretation of American Literature: Some Contributions toward the Understanding of Its Historical Development* (ed. N. Foerster), xi. (New York: Harcourt, Brace and Co.).

5 Jones, H.M. The European background. In: *The Reinterpretation of American Literature* (ed. N. Foerster), 74–75, 65.
6 Schlesinger, A.M. American history and American literary history. In: *The Reinterpretation of American Literature* (ed. N. Foerster), 171, 178.
7 Parrington, V.L. (1927). *Main Currents in American Thought: Volume 2, 1800–1860. The Romantic Revolution in America*, vii. New York: Harcourt, Brace and World.
8 Cain, W.E. (2003). Literary Criticism. In: *The Cambridge History of American Literature, Volume 5. Poetry and Criticism, 1900–1950* (ed. Bercovitch, S.), 345. Cambridge: Cambridge UP.
9 Cain, "Literary Criticism," 375.
10 Cain, "Literary Criticism," 404; Jefferson, T. (1984). Letter to Elbridge Gerry, 13 May 1797. In: *Writings*, 1044. New York: Library of America.
11 Chase, R. (1957). *The American Novel and Its Tradition*, 12–13. Baltimore: Johns Hopkins UP.
12 Emerson, R.W. (1904). Europe and European books. In: *The Complete Works of Ralph Waldo Emerson: Natural History of Intellect, and Other Papers*, 375–376. Boston: Houghton Mifflin.
13 Gruesz, K.S. Transnational Americas and the Literatures of the United States. MLA Convention, Los Angeles, 8 January 2011.
14 Nye, J.S., Jr. (2004). *Soft Power: The Means to Success in World Politics*. New York: Perseus Books.
15 Eagleton, *Literary Theory*, 17, 19.
16 Spengemann, W.C. (1994). *A New World of Words: Redefining Early American Literature*. New Haven: Yale UP; Whitman, W. (1973). Song of Myself. In: *Leaves of Grass* (ed. S. Bradley and H.W. Blodgett), 88. New York: Norton.
17 Winthrop, J. (1985). A Model of Christian Charity. In: *The Puritans in America: A Narrative Anthology* (ed. A. Heimert and A. Delbanco), 91. Cambridge: Harvard UP.
18 Harootunian, H. (2000). *Overcome by Modernity: History, Culture, and Community in Interwar Japan*, 23–26. Princeton: Princeton UP.
19 Jameson, F. (1986). Third-world literature in the era of multinational capitalism. *Social Text* 15(Autumn): 77.
20 Edwards, B.T. (2015). *After the American Century: The Ends of U.S. Culture in the Middle East*, 84–138. New York: Columbia UP.
21 "Berkeley Global Campus: A New, Bolder Vision for Richmond Bay." Berkeley New Center, 30 October 2014. https://chancellor.berkeley.edu/sites/default/files/BGC-NewsArticles--Dec18.pdf (accessed 24 November 2017).
22 Damrosch, D. (2003). *What Is World Literature?*, 1. Princeton: Princeton UP.
23 Pizer, J. (2006). *The Idea of World Literature: History and Pedagogical Practice*, 21. Baton Rouge: Louisiana State UP.

24 Marx, K. and Engels, F. (1998). *The Communist Manifesto* (1848; rpt.), 39. London: Verso. See the discussion of this passage in Arac, J. (2017). Getting to world literature. *Novel* 50(3): 331–332.
25 Pizer, *The Idea of World Literature*, 67.
26 Renan, E. (1990). What is a nation? (trans. Martin Thom, 1882). In: *Nation and Narration* (ed. H.K. Bhabha), 18. London: Routledge; Kumar, K. (2003). *The Making of English National Identity*, 222. Cambridge: Cambridge UP.
27 Sir Arthur Quiller-Couch (1925). Preface. *The Oxford Book of English Prose* (ed. Quiller-Couch), xiii. London: Oxford UP.
28 Pizer, *The Idea of World Literature*, 89, 162.
29 Trilling, L. (1958). English literature and American education. *Sewanee Review* 66(3): 372–373; Williams, W.M. (1960). Intensive and extensive approaches in the teaching of world literature. In: *The Teaching of World Literature: Proceedings of the Conference at the University of Wisconsin, April 24-25, 1959* (ed. H.M. Block), 81. Chapel Hill: U of North Carolina P. See also Pizer, *The Idea of World Literature*, 103–104.
30 Pizer, *The Idea of World Literature*, 113.
31 Lawall, S. (1988). The alternate worlds of world literature. *ADE Bulletin* 90: 53.
32 Hillis Miller, J. (2000). 'World Literature' in the age of telecommunications. *World Literature Today* 74(3): 560–561.
33 James, H. (1984). *Letters, Volume IV: 1895–1916* (ed. L. Edel), 682. Cambridge: Harvard UP.
34 Coetzee, J.M. Interview with Peter Sacks. 8 November 2001. Lannan Foundation, https://podcast.lannan.org/2010/06/28/j-m-coetzee-with-peter-sacks-conversation-8-november-2001-video (accessed 24 November 2017).
35 Sollors, W. (1998). Introduction: after the culture wars; or, from 'English Only' to 'English Plus'. In: *Multilingual America: Transnationalism, Ethnicity, and the Languages of American Literature*, 5–6. New York: New York UP.
36 Pearce, T.M. (1942). American traditions and our histories of literature. *American Literature* 14(3): 280.
37 Shell, M. (2002). *American Babel: Literatures of the United States from Abnaki to Zuni*, 8. Cambridge: Harvard UP.
38 Orsi, R.A. (1985). *The Madonna of 115th Street: Faith and Community in Italian Harlem, 1880-1950*. New Haven: Yale UP.
39 Foerster, N. Factors in American literary history. In: *The Reinterpretation of American Literature* (ed. N. Foerster), 31, 28.
40 Kadir, D. (2003). America: the idea, the literature. *PMLA* 118(1): 10–11, 14–15, 21–22.
41 Matthiessen, *American Renaissance*, 12.

42 Miyoshi, M. (1993). A borderless world? From colonialism to transnationalism and the decline of the nation-state. *Critical Inquiry* 19(4): 747; Fukuyama, F. (1989). The end of history?. *The National Interest* 16: 3–18.

43 Fishkin, S.F. (2005). Crossroads of culture: the transnational turn in American Studies – Presidential Address to the American Studies Association, November 12, 2004. *American Quarterly* 57(1): 17–57.

44 Morrison, T. (1992). *Playing in the Dark: Whiteness and the Literary Imagination*, 18. Cambridge: Harvard UP.

45 Smith, H.N. (1950). *Virgin Land: The American West as Symbol and Myth*. Cambridge: Harvard UP.

46 Zuckerman, M. (1997). The Dodo and the Phoenix: a fable of American exceptionalism. In: *American Exceptionalism? U.S. Working-Class Formation in an International Context* (ed. R. Halpern and J. Morris), 20. Basingstoke: Palgrave Macmillan.

47 Gilroy, P. (1993). *The Black Atlantic: Modernity and Double Consciousness*, 146–186. Cambridge: Harvard UP.

48 Buell, L. (2001). World literature and U.S. American literature. In: *The Routledge Companion to World Literature* (ed. T. d'Haen, D. Damrosch, and D. Kadir), 452. Abingdon: Routledge.

49 Thomsen, M.R. (2008). *Mapping World Literature: International Canonization and Transnational Literatures*, 1. London: Continuum.

50 Moretti, F. (2000). Conjectures on world literature. *New Left Review* 1: 54.

51 Mufti, A.R. (2016). *Forget English! Orientalisms and World Literature*, 11. Cambridge: Harvard UP.

52 Damrosch, *What Is World Literature?*, 281, and (2009). How American is world literature?. *The Comparatist* 33: 13.

53 Cheah, P. (2016). *What Is a World? On Postcolonial Literature as World Literature*, 26, 194. Durham: Duke UP.

54 Nafisi, A. (2003). *Reading Lolita in Tehran: A Memoir in Books*, 28. Sydney: Hachette Australia.

55 Nafisi, *Reading Lolita in Tehran*, 30.

56 Nafisi, *Reading Lolita in Tehran*, 159, 30.

57 Nafisi, *Reading Lolita in Tehran*, 260, 155, 223, 415.

58 Donadey, A. and Ahmed-Ghosh, H. (2008). Why Americans love reading Azar Nafisi's *Reading Lolita in Tehran*. *Signs* 33(3): 637.

59 Nafisi, *Reading Lolita in Tehran*, 341, 28.

60 Zaritt, S.N. (2016). Maybe for millions, maybe for nobody: Jewish American writing and the undecidability of world literature. *American Literary History* 28(3): 544.

61 Zaritt, "Maybe for Millions," 558.

62 Atlas, J. Chicago's Grumpy Guru. *New York Times Magazine*, 3 January 1988. www.nytimes.com/1988/01/03/magazine/010388-atlas. html?pagewanted=all (accessed 24 November 2017).

63 Pizer, *The Idea of World Literature*, 95.

64 Moretti, F. (2007). *Graphs, Maps, Trees: Abstract Models for Literary History*. London: Verso; Casanova, P. (2004). *The World Republic of Letters* (trans. M.B. DeBevoise, 1999), 25–26. Cambridge: Harvard UP.

65 Wallerstein, I. (2003). *The Decline of American Power*, 185, 1, 306. New York: New Press.

66 Wallerstein, *The Decline of American Power*, 250, 212.

67 Ikenberry, J. (2011). *Liberal Leviathan: The Origins, Crisis, and Transformation of the American World Order*, 7. Princeton: Princeton UP.

68 Mezzadra, S. and Neilson, B. (2013). *Border as Method, or, the Multiplication of Labor*, vii, 9. Durham: Duke UP. Mezzadra and Neilson attribute the term *borderscape* to the work of Australian critic Suvendrini Perera (12).

69 Seyhan, A. (2001). *Writing Outside the Nation*, 103–104. Princeton: Princeton UP.

70 Mezzadra and Neilson, *Border as Method*, 311.

71 Mezzadra and Neilson, *Border as Method*, 271.

72 Povinelli, E.A. (2002). *The Cunning of Recognition: Indigenous Alterities and the Making of Australian Multiculturalism*, 155. Durham: Duke UP.

73 Nussbaum, M.C. (1994). Patriotism and cosmopolitanism. *Boston Review* 19(5): 3.

74 Gura, P.F. (1996). *The Crossroads of American History and Literature*, 50. University Park: Pennsylvania State UP.

75 Gelpi, A. (1991). *The Tenth Muse: The Psyche of the American Poet*, 2e, 31–32. Cambridge: Cambridge UP.

2

Early American Literature in the World

2.1 Contact Zones and Extended Scales

In Iris Murdoch's 1968 novel *The Nice and the Good*, the narrator describes the academic career of its central character John Ducane, whose field is Roman law, observing that the "immense literature about Roman law has been produced from a relatively small amount of evidence, of which a substantial part is suspect because of interpolations." Murdoch's narrator goes on to comment on how "[t]here are certain areas of scholarship, early Greek history is one and Roman law is another, where the scantiness of evidence sets a special challenge to the disciplined mind."[1] Early American literature, by which is generally meant American literature before 1800, is of course not as distant chronologically as ancient Greece or Rome, and the quantity of data available about American cultural practices at this time is correspondingly much greater. Yet for many years, early American literature almost prided itself on being a scholarly world apart, something like an American equivalent of ancient history, where the very remoteness and apparent intractability of its materials lent the field an apparent scholarly integrity and almost otherworldly prestige.

The academic journal *Early American Literature* was first published in 1968 – as a continuation of the "Early American Literature" newsletter, which had begun two years earlier – and this academic enterprise arose out of a concerted belief among early Americanists that their subjects were being unduly marginalized within the academy and they consequently needed the support provided by their own institutional space. However, the notion of this being a rarefied and somewhat restricted area of study was reinforced by the way certain authors kept reappearing on the syllabi of early American literature courses. David Shields, in his presidential address to the Society of Early Americanists in 2001, described this pedagogical situation as being as predictable as that of an

American World Literature: An Introduction, First Edition. Paul Giles.

American FM radio station playing "classic rock." Whereas "stuck-in-a-rut" disk jockeys kept returning to the Eagles and Tom Petty, early Americanists kept returning on their "playlist" to Anne Bradstreet, Edward Taylor, and Benjamin Franklin.[2] Early Americanists often preferred to perpetuate the legend of a cultural "scantiness of evidence," as Murdoch's narrator terms it, so that the parameters of their field would stay pristine and contained, as well as remaining readily subordinated to the conventions of a retrospective academic ordering.

Shields's point was not, of course, that such canonical authors were not worth studying, but that the fetishization of such writers as the epitome of an American "spirit" effectively foreclosed a wide range of other intriguing writers that would enhance the scope and interest of this early Americanist cultural sphere. He pointed, for example, to Dutch authors in the New York area as an underresearched source, and recent critical attempts to expand the scope of early American literature as a multilingual phenomenon have helped significantly to alter the shape of this field. In addition, work on neglected African American and Native American figures, along with a renewed focus on women writers such as Mary Rowlandson, has had the effect of interrogating the linear teleology whereby early American writers tended to be read proleptically, with Benjamin Franklin, for example, too often understood to be an avatar of the liberal individualism that characterized the "way to wealth" in the fictions of the nineteenth-century novelist Horatio Alger, or even understood as a direct precursor to Scott Fitzgerald's *The Great Gatsby* (1925).

Early American literature has always been read historically, of course, with Edward Cahill and Edward Larkin commenting on how the "profound commitment to historicism" in "early American literary studies" always enjoyed a "vexed relationship to aesthetics," to the question of what particular poems or fictional narratives might mean in relation to style and affect.[3] But some forms of historicism have achieved a more established place within the trajectory of American literary history than others, and in particular the rhetoric of utopia and apocalypse that marked the seventeenth-century Puritan imagination has found greater favor among scholars than the more worldly, cosmopolitan idiom that characterized much eighteenth-century American writing. As if to exemplify how the Puritan conception of exceptionalism has become a template for subsequent American culture, the image of "a city upon a hill," as promulgated in Winthrop's 1630 sermon "A Model of Christian Charity," was cited in President Ronald Reagan's 1989 "Farewell Address to the American People," with Reagan saluting Winthrop as "an early 'Freedom Man,'" while, as if to indicate how Winthrop's metaphorical status was not to be classified merely upon party political lines, it was also appropriated by John F. Kennedy in his 1961 address to the Massachusetts Legislature (now commonly known as his "City Upon a Hill" speech), as well as by Barack Obama in his 2006 commencement address at the University of Massachusetts.

It should hardly come as a surprise when phrases such as "city upon a hill" are taken out of their formative context and commodified for subsequent recycling. Although the world of political marketing involves a particularly extreme example of such reductive sloganeering, this kind of retrospective appropriation is also characteristic, in one form or another, of historical writing at every level. For these reasons, it is worth making a particular effort in studying "early" American literature and culture to remember that the outcomes of the nationalist project in this revolutionary era never appeared certain, and that to reimagine seventeenth-century figures within their own times and places is to reconstitute a much more variegated sense of the American scene. John Winthrop was actually born in East Anglia in 1588, where he was Lord of the Manor and served for many years as sheriff in Groton, Suffolk, a legislative precursor to his administrative career in Massachusetts Bay Colony and one that continued significantly to influence his understanding of relations among the various domains of law, state, and church. Most of the poets traditionally celebrated as "early American" writers – Taylor, Anne Bradstreet, Michael Wigglesworth – were also born in England, with their poetry involving implicit dialectics between Europe and America, a pattern made quite explicit in Bradstreet's "A Dialogue between Old England and New" (1650). In addition, the political pressures linked to Puritan emigration and the establishment of transatlantic colonies had a significant impact on the English Civil War of the 1640s, with American colonist Roger Williams publishing in 1644 during a visit to London *The Bloody Tenet of Persecution, for Cause of Conscience*, a defense of absolute liberty of conscience. This book produced such uproar that Parliament ordered all copies of it to be burnt, with Williams himself only avoiding the death penalty because he was already on his way back home to Providence Plantations. Sir Henry Vane the Younger was another emigrant who served one term as Governor of Massachusetts Bay Colony (1636–1637), before working closely with Oliver Cromwell during the Civil War, but Vane suffered retribution when he was charged with high treason by Parliament and subsequently executed in 1662, after the restoration of King Charles II.

To imagine "American" literature evolving in a straight line from puritanism to transcendentalism is thus as misleading as to imagine "English" literature as celebrating the unclouded triumph of monarchical values. The cultural traditions of both nations were criss-crossed by dissent and dispute across a broad political spectrum, and to trace the American influence upon English literature of the seventeenth century is as important as tracing the English impact upon its "American" counterpart.

Technically, of course, all these American settlements were in any case colonies of the British crown at this time, so theoretically it would make more sense to examine the poetry of Bradstreet, Taylor, and Wigglesworth within a postcolonial rather than a merely nationalist framework. Edward Watts and others have done important pioneering work in this regard, but their efforts have been hampered by a reluctance among early Americanist scholars to understand Winthrop and others within a postcolonial context. This has come about partly because such a framework would raise the specter of a depredation of Native American peoples by these Puritan exiles, thereby repositioning them as an exploitative rather than an oppositional or subaltern community, but it has arisen more fundamentally because early American cultural historians have frequently been of a somewhat curmudgeonly cast of mind and hostile to literary and cultural theory in all its guises. It is true, of course, that the power plays in seventeenth-century North America were complicated in nature, with American settlers being (in Watts's words) "both colonizer and colonized at once," and distant British authority in London being refracted in oblique ways through the legal jurisdictions of the colonies.[4] However, the decimation of indigenous communities did not in itself mean that early American institutions were immune from the various forms of coercion that typified monarchical power. The subsequent categorization of Winthrop and others in terms of their visionary impetus has perhaps tended to obscure the ironies and ambiguities that were always associated with the projection of authority in the "New World" of seventeenth-century America, and to retrace connections between the Old World and the New is thus to adduce a more nuanced picture of how these multifaceted tensions operated.

Merely to imagine seventeenth-century American literature as driven by a rhetoric of "redemptive exceptionalism," as does William V. Spanos for example, is thus seriously to compress the historical and geographical circumference within which such rhetoric worked itself out.[5] There is, of course, no doubt that a language of apocalypse driven by Puritan concepts of an imminent end to the world was instrumental in forming the temper of American writing at this time, but it is equally important to recognize the demurrals and skepticism with which such prophecies were sometimes greeted. Thomas Morton, the Anglican trader and explorer who founded the colony of Merrymount in Massachusetts, specifically made fun in his *New England Canaan* (1637) of the Puritan tendency to allegorize the natural world by transposing snakes into Biblical portents. Later in the seventeenth century there were violent Calvinist protests against the increasing secularization of urban culture under the burgeoning influence of commercial trade, while a more widespread reaction against the forces of modernization led to the religious "Great Awakening" in New England during the first half of the eighteenth century. The point here is simply that the religious cultures of pre-Revolutionary America were always fractious and contested, riven not only by doctrinal disputes among the competing churches but also by the political complexities incumbent upon the need to deal with the British crown and other trading centers of Europe.

One of the great strengths of the "New Historicist" criticism pioneered by Stephen Greenblatt and others during the 1980s was to deconstruct oversimplified descriptions of particular historical eras – "The Elizabethan World Picture," "The Medieval Synthesis" – and to highlight instead ways in which all cultures are necessarily partial and fragmentary. Rehistoricizing seventeenth-century America in this way allows us to exercise a similar line of caution when confronted by similarly monolithic frameworks: "The American Jeremiad," "The Puritan Ordeal," and so on.[6] It also allows us to understand how New England at this time operated in a transatlantic continuum with its colonial counterpart, both engaging with political directives from London and, not infrequently, taking issue with them. Michael Wigglesworth's poem *The Day of Doom* (1662) actually gains in resonance if set alongside John Milton's *Paradise Lost*, which was published just five years later in 1667, since both epic poems seek to recalibrate temporality in the light of the internecine civil strife that had dogged Anglo-American communities during the previous decades. Wigglesworth's poem anticipates the day of judgment dawning upon what he depicts as his lazy and complacent New England community, just as Milton's epic work reinterprets the Biblical story of Creation, but in both cases the power of these poems derives from the way their authors interweave questions of theology with the more secular dynamics of worldly politics. Wigglesworth's poem was set in what Roy Harvey Pearce called "rocking fourteeners, a version of the hymn line," and despite the poem's length of 224 stanzas, it is estimated that fully one-tenth of New England's population in the 1660s knew its grisly representation of an imminent apocalypse off by heart.[7]

It is also important to recognize how this powerful mythical notion of what Sacvan Bercovitch described as "The Puritan Origins of the American Self" tended to underestimate the extent to which America had long been permeated by non-Anglophone cultures.[8] Spanish influences, particularly in what is now the South and West of the United States, can be traced back to the fifteenth century, and the *Heath Anthology of American Literature*, whose first edition was published in 1989, incorporated as a canonical corrective to seventeenth-century

New England writing examples of work by Fray Marcos de Niza, Felipe Guama Powe de Ayala, and other writers associated in various ways with the imperial cultures of South America. The inclusion of a journal written in 1528 by Alvar Nuñez Cabeza de Vaca is particularly interesting, since it shows how this young Spanish nobleman coped with a commission from Emperor Carlos V to explore the Gulf Coast of America. Cabeza de Vaca chronicles his journeys around what is now Florida, Texas, and the mouth of the Mississippi, talking of his hostile encounters with Indian tribes "in a country too remote and malign," and, as Juan Bruce-Novoa has observed, he reconstitutes the inevitable failure of his mission of mapping and conquest through "the medieval genre of hagiography," whereby the saint's personal experiences turn worldly failure into a putative form of spiritual triumph.[9] In this way, Cabeza de Vaca exemplifies not a Puritan template of spiritual apotheosis but a Catholic style of transubstantiation and metamorphosis, one that combines Native American and Spanish customs into a hybrid model through which an encounter with the New World transforms more established traditions into something new. The geographical scope of Cabeza de Vaca's writing, focused around the borderlands with Mexico, also introduces a different perspective into the world of early American literature, broadening out its linguistic as well as its cultural circumference.

In addition, the language and culture of first peoples have recently received more extensive consideration from early Americanists, with Annette Kolodny writing of how it appears "certain" that the Norse were in North America around the year 1000 CE, and Paula Gunn Allen, herself from the Laguna Pueblo tribe of Native Americans, writing in 1974 of how "America needs a sense of history, a sense of America's place in eternal time."[10] Allen's argument is that American culture needs to be understood within a more expansive temporal framework, just as critics whose work is informed by the principle of transnationalism have attempted to set the country within a more expansive spatial framework. Such a multidirectional emphasis would work necessarily to complicate the older mode of millennial teleology through which America was bound metaphorically to a linear grid of apocalypse and redemption. Native American culture retains a certain enigmatic quality in relation to the wider trajectories of American literature, since historical records of indigenous civilizations remain vague, even though it seems quite possible that (for example) the city of Cahokia in present-day Missouri was actually more populous in the twelfth century than London. Recent archeological investigations have suggested that these mature and sophisticated civilizations might have been ravaged by natural disasters of one kind or another – earthquakes, plagues, and drought have all been put forward as possibilities. In any case, it is important to recognize how America was not invented by Christopher Columbus in 1492, nor by the Pilgrim Fathers 100 years later, but involved contact and conflict between settler colonialism in its various guises and a broad spectrum of indigenous peoples.

The extent to which early American literature was played out through a series of "contact zones," to use Mary Louise Pratt's term for interaction among diverse peoples, can be seen clearly enough in the reaction of Puritan writers to native peoples.[11] Roger Williams, who quarreled with the Church authorities in Massachusetts before being exiled to Rhode Island in 1638, published in 1643 *A Key into the Language of America*, an aid to communication with Native Americans, with Williams forming friendships among Indian tribes and helping to develop systems of cross-cultural mediation and negotiation. More generally, this idea of contact zones, involving conjunctions among disparate ethnic groups and heterogeneous spatiotemporal formations, might be said to characterize early American literature across a more expansive circumference. Rather than involving simply a nationalist teleology that would link Puritan America to its post-Revolutionary descendants, scholars more intent upon tracing ways in which American literature of the seventeenth and eighteenth centuries interacts with a wider world have focused on ways in which the terrain that was to become the United States was shaped by multiple vectors across space and time, ranging from the colonial centers of the Caribbean and Latin America to the more obscure prehistory of Native American traditions.

To reorganize early American literature in terms of an extended geographic and temporal scale is thus to place the culture of what is now the northeastern United States within a much wider discursive framework. Our understanding of Roger Williams's project, for example, is enhanced by a recognition of how deeply embedded Indian languages were within this native terrain, just as the *Narrative of the Captivity and Restoration of Mrs Mary Rowlandson* (1682) achieves part of its resonance from a shift in authorial perspective as this captivity narrative unfolds, whereby the English woman, held captive by a Wampanoag raiding party in Massachusetts, comes gradually to feel a sense of ambiguous kinship with Indian culture. Although she presents the "vast and desolate Wilderness" of the Massachusetts frontier as a "lively resemblance of hell," with the Indians appearing as "black creatures in the night," Rowlandson slowly comes to accommodate herself for survival, allowing a squaw to give her a meal and making clothes for Indian women in return. Indeed, various forms of dualism run all the way through Rowlandson's *Narrative*, with the narrator commenting on how spiritual identity found itself under threat from the corporeal presence of her Indian captors:

> And here I cannot but remember how many times, sitting in their wigwams, and musing on things past, I should suddenly leap up and run out, as if I had been at home, forgetting where I was, and what my condition was; but when I was without, and saw nothing but wilderness, and woods, and a company of barbarous heathens, my mind quickly returned to me ...[12]

Rowlandson presents herself here as torn between spiritual steadfastness on the one hand and the darkness of embodied life on the other. The latter becomes associated with survival, but also with trial and temptation, as the author self-consciously allegorizes her own captivity and "the wilderness condition," as she calls it, into an exemplum of regeneration and redemption. Within this context, human frailty and the weakness of the flesh come to appear reprehensible, with the author chronicling how she first thought she would rather die than be captured, but then thought again, thereby testifying to "our perverse and evil carriages in the sight of the Lord."[13] Memory in this light operates as a bulwark against the world she sees around her. Rowlandson keeps returning in the desert to the memory of her spiritual steadfastness, and Increase Mather in his preface to the book emphasizes the significance of memory by describing her *Narrative* as "a *Memorandum* of God's dealing with her, that she might never forget, but remember the same, and the several circumstances thereof, all the days of her life."[14] The power of the mind is here adduced as a defense against the threats of terrestrial metamorphoses, with the division of Rowlandson's narrative into "removes" – "The Twelfth Remove," and so on – seeming to "remove" her further from her Biblical home and to cast her further and further adrift into Indian territory. At the same time, such an opportunity for spiritual torment also allows Rowlandson the prospect of her final reward, and in the work's final paragraph she comments: "I hope I can say in some measure, as *David* did, '*It is good for me that I have been afflicted*." Like the Book of Exodus, which becomes here both a Biblical prototype and a narrative template, Rowlandson's journey accordingly culminates in salvation: "now we are fed with the finest of the wheat, and, as I may say, with honey out of the rock. In stead of the husk, we have the fatted calf."[15]

Sharon M. Harris has observed how Rowlandson's *Narrative* has tended to become a popular text in moments of national crisis, such as the American Revolution and the Vietnam war, and it is not difficult to see how its pattern of what Richard Slotkin described as "regeneration through violence" might be understood as "the structuring metaphor of the American experience."[16] The divisions and enduring torments of the narrator's experience – she mentions in the final paragraphs how "I can remember the time, when I used to sleep quietly without workings in my thoughts whole nights together; but now it is otherwise with me" – also speaks to a gothic strain that runs persistently through American culture, where the power of spirit is threatened and potentially compromised, sometimes fatally, by the torments of the flesh.[17]

Yet any understanding of Rowlandson's work as a quintessentially American text needs to be countered by a recognition of how it also circulated transnationally and transatlantically. Although information about her life is scarce, Rowlandson was probably born in England rather than America, where she was the daughter of a wealthy land-owner in the Massachusetts Bay Colony, and her *Narrative* was par-ticularly successful in England, with a fourth edition being published in London after the first three editions, which were published in America, had sold out within a year, with a fifth edition subsequently being published in England in 1720. Nancy Armstrong and Leonard Tennenhouse have underlined the way in which Rowlandson's *Narrative* helped to define and shore up the English community by its emphasis on how English people were threatened by the "wilderness" of the frontier, and they have also pointed to ways in which American captivity narratives helped to establish the eighteenth-century English novel. There are similarities between Rowlandson's *Narrative* and Samuel Richardson's *Pamela* (1740) and *Clarissa* (1748), novels in which the vulnerable heroines are taunted and captured, both literally and metaphorically, by a licentious master, and in this sense the aes-thetics of captivity carry a resonance that travels beyond their specific incarnation within the Puritan conversion narrative, with Armstrong and Tennenhouse drawing in their work on what they call a "logic of supplementarity, by which the colonial world revised the so-called cul-ture of origin."[18] Rather than conceiving the English and American literary traditions as separate phenomena, Armstrong and Tennenhouse emphasize instead the way they criss-cross and overlap, with Rowlandson influencing Richardson and her own text in turn being given a new level of prominence in London.

In this sense, Damrosch's definition of world literature as that which "gains in translation" might be understood in something more than just a linguistic sense.[19] While Rowlandson writes in English, it is precisely when her work is "translated" across the Atlantic that it comes to be most influential. Although conservative writers of the Augustan era such as Joseph Addison mocked "the saints' apparent propensity for reporting the exact order of events in their conversions," the fact that this colonial experience became an object of comedy demonstrates in itself ways in which it impacted upon the consciousness of the imperial center.[20] Samuel Butler's mock-epic poem *Hudibras* (1684) specifically lampoons what it takes to be the pompous self-righteousness of Puritan exiles, and the use of burlesque to keep alternative domains at bay implies how the distant horizon of America functioned at this time as a reactive mechanism for consolidating domestic British values. At the same time, through the "double coding" and "double-voiced" quality that is, as Linda Hutcheon noted, inherent in all parody, this conservative English satire of supposed American extremism was turned back on itself, so that by recasting the Puritan captivity narrative within a more socialized English form, Richardson was effectively bringing together domestic space with more alien gothic landscapes.[21]

The work of a later eighteenth-century American novelist, Charles Brockden Brown, whose inchoate fictions have similarly been read as a response to the chaotic political and cultural conditions of the new American nation, might also be understood in terms of a transatlantic romanticism, since Brown himself was a formative influence on the gothic productions of Mary Shelley and others in her circle. Indeed, according to Pamela Clemit, the radical group of writers in early nineteenth-century Britain centered around the Shelleys was "swift to claim [Brown] as one of their own," as a writer with a distinctive political imagination rather than merely the oddball figure he often appeared within the United States, and we know that Mary Shelley read *Wieland* just before starting work on *Frankenstein* in 1816.[22] In this sense, attempts by critics with a specifically nationalist agenda, such as Donald Ringe, to shoehorn Brown into a teleology of "American Gothic" have tended to overlook the transnational associations linking him to various forms of European romanticism, German as well as English.[23] Social and political context, in other words, needs to be countered by generic models of literary circulation that do not accord so directly with nationalist prototypes.

Brown himself had many interests in world geography, even drafting in 1809 a prospectus for a textbook to be entitled "A System of General Geography: Containing a Topographical, Statistical, and Descriptive Summary of the Earth." This was commensurate with the way he sided with Federalist Party activists at the turn of the nineteenth century who wanted to position the new United States at the fulcrum of world trade rather than retreating into the pastoralist isolationism that was then associated more with Jefferson's Republican Party, and Brown's novels, with their multiple movements across colonial frontiers, reflect this condition of global mobility. To reposition Brown horizontally, as it were, within a matrix of social and economic cross-currents that were circulating in this post-Revolutionary era is to present a very different picture of Brown from the "vertical" one that emerges if he is positioned simply as a gothic forerunner of Poe and Hawthorne. To rehistoricize Brown is to recognize him as the inhabitant of a wider cultural world rather than merely a stepping stone within a tradition of American Gothic.

English literature of the eighteenth century flourished in part through a dynamic of what Ronald Paulson has called "sacred parody," whereby the religious imperatives that had energized (and caused such violent dispute within) seventeenth-century culture were recast in aestheticized forms.[24] In his *Spectator* essays, for example, Addison re-read *Paradise Lost* not from a religious but from an explicitly aesthetic viewpoint, and this was in accord with what philosophers of the Enlightenment took to be the principles of an iconoclastic liberty. John Locke's *Essay Concerning Human Understanding* (1690) substitutes belief for faith, allowing human intelligence to proceed on the basis of empirical evidence without any certain knowledge of truth, and this fitted with a growing mood of skepticism within Western culture, whereby ideas of divine revelation and philosophical absolutes were coming to seem increasingly old-fashioned. The "Great Awakening" in America during the 1730s and 1740s, which involved Calvinist revivals in New England and provoked the powerful sermons of Jonathan Edwards, should not obscure the fact that this religious movement positioned itself in anxious opposition to what church leaders perceived to be a rising tide of cosmopolitanism, wherein secular values of cultural relativism were threatening to supplant the tenets of Biblical "truth."

In this sense, eighteenth-century American literature shared many of the characteristics of its English counterpart, with the travel narratives of Sarah Kemble Knight, Elizabeth Ashbridge, and other writers offering a more variegated view of American provincial life at this time than customarily emerges through New England sermons. Knight's account of her 1704–1705 round trip between Boston and New York was first published in 1825, and it includes the kind of details of wayfaring, the trials and tribulations of "victuals and Lodging," that one might expect to find in a novel by Henry Fielding. Ashbridge was born in England in 1713 but she embraced the Quaker religion after visiting relatives in Pennsylvania, and *Some Account of the Fore Part of the Life of Elizabeth Ashbridge ... Written by Her own Hand many years ago* (1755) describes her movements across the northeastern American colonies. Here she not only plays off different regions of the country against one another but also dramatizes her own internal conflicts between spiritual and secular affairs, what she describes as "the Tryal of my Faith."[25] Spengemann has identified this kind of instability as characteristic of early American prose narratives more generally, pointing out that Knight wrote her journal from notes set down while traveling rather than in a position of retrospective mastery when safely back at home, and he suggested that such differences between the world seen from an unchanging point and one seen from a world in motion serve to emphasize the ways in which American writers of this era respond deliberately to the sense of a "rapidly changing world."[26] Rather than surveying the world from a fixed vantage point, in other words, American writers became part of the world of mutability they were describing.

Perhaps such a style of metamorphosis is characteristic of Enlightenment writing in other countries as well, but this focus on the vestiges of materialism always seems to carry a more ironic charge within cultures organized around theocratic principles. In *Worlding America: A Transnational Anthology of Short Narratives before 1800*, German academics Oliver Scheiding and Martin Seidl include extracts from Edward Taylor's "Atlantic Voyage" of 1668, with Taylor's diary entries, chronicling "shark fishes" and "seafowls," offering a prosaic counterpart to the elaborate Biblical conceits wrapped up in his more tortured style of metaphysical poetry.[27] The kind of emphasis on worldly fortune that appears in Taylor's prose narrative allows us to get a clearer sense of how competing secular and religious pressures framed the culture of colonial New England, and in this sense the "worlding" of American literature involves not just its realignment in relation to different geographical co-ordinates, but also a displacement of the internal logic that has shaped the institutional formation of the subject. Scheiding and Seidl also include an "Early Description of Pennsylvania and the Sea Voyage from Europe" written in 1724 by Christopher Sauer, who was born in the German town of Ladenburg, and this again testifies to the way in which travel narratives across a transnational axis necessarily extend the compass of American literature through a wider world.

2.2   The Classical Counternarrative

Broadening out the world of early American literature beyond its traditional focus on New England thus allows for both regional and philosophical variations in the demarcation of this subject. The Virginia charted in William Byrd II's *History of the Dividing Line*, like the Maryland celebrated in Ebenezer Cook's mock-epic poem *The Sot-Weed Factor* (1708), evokes an America where divisions between abstract idealism and terrestrial incarnation bring about various forms of structural irony and literary comedy. *The Sot-Weed Factor* describes a heterogeneous world of Anglos and Indians, civic politics, and economic profit, whose idiom involves, as the poem says, "mixing things Prophane and Godly," thereby deliberately rejecting states of theocratic control or spiritual transcendence.[28] John C. Shields's *The American Aeneas: Classical Origins of the American Self* (2001) was offered as a deliberate riposte to Bercovitch's *Puritan Origins of the American Self* (1975), with Shields writing that he had "found the tenets of the Adamic myth (the Judaeo-Christian mythos) insufficient to explain the obvious secularity of the American people." Proposing this classical matrix as a counternarrative to the more established Puritan ethos, Shields described how eighteenth-century pastoral poets such as Joseph Green and Joseph Secombe looked back directly to Virgil rather than the Bible for their source material. He also argued that the Puritan suspicion of aestheticism had been replicated among subsequent American literary critics, who had tended to overlook the "powerful spirit of aestheticism" that "pervaded American colonial culture" because of their focus on "the hegemony of the Adamic myth."[29]

The idea of American literature deriving in part from classical rather than Puritan templates is particularly relevant in the context of eighteenth-century culture. Shields is right to say that Phillis Wheatley, the African American poet who in 1784 addressed her country as a "new-born Rome," was attempting self-consciously to bring together classical and Christian modes of discourse, and Carl J. Richard also took issue with Bernard Bailyn's more traditional view that eighteenth-century voices in America used classical allusions as mere window-dressing by stressing instead how various pagan philosophical values – stoicism, epicureanism, and so on – worked their way into the intellectual world view of the Founding Fathers.[30] Richard described Thomas Jefferson as a true "heretic" in the original Greek sense of "one who picks and chooses," integrating into his eclectic world view those aspects of classical philosophy he liked, while discarding those that he did not.[31] After the Constitution of the new United States had been promulgated, many remarked on the absence of any explicit Christian framework for this document, with Timothy Dwight, the staunchly Calvinist President of Yale College, complaining that the nation had "offended Providence" in the way it "formed our Constitution without any acknowledgment of God."[32] Isaac Kramnick and R. Laurence Moore have emphasized the radical nature of what they call this "godless constitution," whose sixth article stated explicitly that "no religious test shall ever be required as a qualification to any office or public trust under the United States."[33] The significance of such a radical change has perhaps been underestimated by traditional colonial historians who have tended rather to emphasize the personal devoutness of many of the Founding Fathers. But in fact, eighteenth-century America, in both its literature and its cultural politics, covered a broad spectrum of views between Calvinist orthodoxy and classical skepticism, and to reorient early American literature in relation to a wider world is to be made aware of some of the complexities involved in these variations.

The classical idiom of eighteenth-century American literature also introduces a playful dimension, one in which the earnestness of moral or religious teaching is balanced or supplanted by an emphasis on ludic rhetorical forms. One example of this can be found in the works of Mather Byles, whose *Poems on Several Occasions* (1744) are full of puns and paradoxes, with Byles's sophisticated wordplay speaking to the ironies of British monarchical power as he experienced it obliquely from the transatlantic distance of Boston. In his poem "On the Death of the Queen," for example, Byles contemplates how the "far-beaming" crown of Queen Caroline reproduced and "flash'd" its image over the seas separating Britain from America, while in his "Elegy Addressed to Governor Belcher on the Death of His Lady," Byles puns on the names of both himself and the Governor:

> Meantime *my* name to *thine* allied shall stand,
> Still our warm friendship, mutual flames extend;
> The muse shall so survive from age to age,
> And BELCHER'S name protect his *Byles's* page.[34]

The pun, here bringing together soul and body in incongruous juxtaposition through its burlesque wordplay on bile and belching, indicates how Byles uses rhetorical forms to link disparate categories ironically together. Byles was the grandson of Increase Mather and the nephew of Cotton Mather, and his poetry reflects a sense of this belated condition, turning religion and political authority into questions for ironic interrogation. Byles had a short correspondence with Alexander Pope – he sent three fawning letters to Pope, although to his disappointment he received but one in reply – and Byles's poetry furnishes an example of an American author attempting creatively to rewrite Pope within the context of Enlightenment America. Byles's career as well as his prestige came to an abrupt halt when he backed the wrong side in the War of Independence, leading him to be arrested and then exiled to Nova Scotia along with other loyalists before he returned to Boston to die there in 1788.

The fact that Byles has been more or less written out of American literary history exemplifies how what David S. Shields called the "belletristic" culture of eighteenth-century America, one that flourished through urban coffeehouses and salons as well as in the more polite clubs and taverns, has tended to be marginalized by a critical emphasis instead on the more ostentatiously serious productions of churches and colleges.[35] Eighteenth-century America offered a modernized version of courtly ritual, where the intellectual culture of urban societies manifested itself through the kind of parodic performances practiced by the likes of Dr Alexander Hamilton, who in his *History of the Ancient and Honorable Tuesday Club* produced a general burlesque on Thomas Hobbes's theory of state power. Whereas Hobbes recognized the danger posed by private societies to the hegemonic grip of state authority, Hamilton took delight in variegated human conditions that evaded the directives of centralized control, and his *Itinerarium* chronicles a journey through the northeastern regions of America in the 1740s. Shields describes the colonies of British America as "transmutable regions of exchange value," where the power of empire and the material values of commerce were transliterated into heterodox forms, and it was a sense of hybridity rather than purity that galvanized American literary culture through most of the eighteenth century.[36]

Part of the problem in correlating questions of aesthetics with early American literature is an ingrained assumption that aesthetic functions were necessarily interwoven with what Edward Cahill termed a "liberty of the imagination."[37] Jay Fliegleman complained how the idea that aesthetics should necessarily serve progressive political and social purposes might be seen as reductive, and one of the reasons Phillis Wheatley's poetry was undervalued for so long was because its deployment of neoclassical idioms and pastoral tropes ensures that a declarative voice becomes hard to identify.[38] Saunders Redding argued in 1939 that the "tame" and "chilly" aspects of Wheatley's poetry could be traced to "the unmistakable influence of Pope's neoclassicism upon her," and the use of such traditional genres was long held to inhibit the development of an authentic and independent American persona.[39]

More recently, critics have sought to identify subversive or emancipatory aspects within Wheatley's authorial voice, discussing ways in which her poetic skill negotiates intertextually with the conventions of the classical pastoral, so that Tom O. McCulley, for example, has talked of a "queer" Wheatley, one whose poetry involves "performative acts of linguistic self-identity re-created with subtlety from the very language of her oppressors." Drawing on the critical theories of Eve Kosofsky Sedgwick and Judith Butler, McCulley analyzed ways in which Wheatley's reconfiguration of neoclassical tropes effectively travestied "the normative expectations of identity-destroying words like 'black,' 'slave,' and 'female.'"[40] Given such complex intertextual calibrations, we can understand how Wheatley, like other American neoclassical poets of the eighteenth century, understood literary genre not as an imprisoning matrix but as a system to be parodied and upended.

In her poem "To the University of Cambridge," for instance, Wheatley apparently contrasts the "ethereal" purity of Harvard students with her own provenance in a world of African "gloom":

> While an intrinsic ardor prompts to write,
> The muses promise to assist my pen;
> 'Twas not long since I left my native shore

The land of errors, and *Egyptian* gloom:
Father of mercy, 'twas thy gracious hand
Brought me in safety from those dark abodes.
Students, to you 'tis giv'n to scan the heights
Above, to traverse the ethereal space,
And mark the systems of revolving worlds.

Yet this image of "revolving worlds" introduces a theme of transposition and metamorphosis that is carried through to the last stanza of the poem, where the concept of "sin" comes ironically to threaten the "privileges" enjoyed by these rich students. Wheatley as "Ethiop" thus casts herself in the role of *deus ex machina*, suggesting that the "baneful evil" of slavery threatens the "soul" of white America with "eternal perdition":

Improve your privileges while they stay,
Ye pupils, and each hour redeem, that bears
Or good or bad report of you to heav'n.
Let sin, that baneful evil to the soul,
By you be shun'd, nor once remit your guard;
Suppress the deadly serpent in its egg.
Ye blooming plants of human race divine,
An *Ethiop* tells you 'tis your greatest foe;
Its transient sweetness turns to endless pain,
And in immense perdition sinks the soul.[41]

In this way, Wheatley's "systems of revolving worlds" can be understood in a self-reflexive sense, since she uses her awareness of geographical alterity to interrogate Boston from an alternative point of view, through which the intellectual and spiritual "heights" of Cambridge life are demystified and the "endless pain" of slave traffic brought back into view.

We see a similar play with tradition in followers of Pope such as John Trumbull, whose modes of satire are not conducive to a style of "liberation," as such, but rather to a darker idiom of satire. One reason for the comparative neglect of such prolix works as *The Anarchiad* (1786–1787), written "in concert" by Trumbull and the Connecticut Wits (David Humphreys, Joel Barlow, and Lemuel Hopkins), is the fact that the poem's implicit conservatism and skepticism about human dignity and capacity for self-governance were anathema to the dogmatically progressive spirit of post-Revolutionary America. *The Anarchiad* is subtitled "A New England poem," and it explicitly reworks Pope's *Dunciad* within the context of Revolutionary America, mixing poetry and prose, past and present in an intertextual farrago that is more reminiscent of a work of postmodernist pastiche such as

Vladimir Nabokov's *Pale Fire* (1962). Through its use of parodic inversion, *The Anarchiad* signals the inevitable collapse of human "schemes" of overweening ambition:

> But give your tools not o'er—the human soul
> Sinks, by strong instinct, far beneath her goal.

Within this upside-down universe, the prize in the festivities goes to those who shut their eyes longest to the clear light of day, with the absurd hero Wronghead becoming "the sole conqueror in this game," someone who "is, thereupon, rewarded by the Anarch with a pair of spectacles, which showed every object inverted, and wrapped in a mist of darkness."[42]

Parrington called the Connecticut Wits "the first school of poetry in America," but their more macabre and sinister charms have proved too much for the less adventurous domain of American pedagogy, which has long tended to prefer works of sentimental uplift or fine feeling and has marginalized Augustan American aesthetics accordingly.[43] Trumbull and fellow Connecticut Wit Timothy Dwight were both tutors at Yale in the 1760s, where they tried to revive the ossified curriculum based around theology by introducing the study of contemporary English literature, focusing on poets such as Pope, Oliver Goldsmith, and James Thomson. However, Trumbull and Dwight are now themselves generally considered moribund figures, and this is in part because the specifically nationalist agenda framing the curriculum of American literature has tended to privilege a romanticized version of the independent subject. This bias can be related directly to the outcome of the War of Independence, which had the effect of silencing not only loyalists but also those educated writers who viewed the idea of human perfectibility askance.

Despite the popularity of Christian traditions in the American colonies, the works of materialist Enlightenment philosophers – Hume, Gibbon, Voltaire – also circulated widely in America, and it was this more self-consciously intellectual tradition that came to be marginalized after the events of the 1780s.[44] Trumbull's *M'Fingal* (1782) is a brilliant mock-epic poem that lampoons loyalist and patriot equally, but it has been badly neglected in the subsequent history of American literature because it fails altogether to accord with the rhetoric of what Philip Freneau in a poem read as a commencement address at Princeton in 1771 called "The Rising Glory of America." Indeed, John Shields has pointed out that in most anthologies of early American literature, far more space is devoted to prose than to poetry. In Carla Mulford's *Early American Writings*, for example, 972 pages are allotted to prose and only 152 to poetry, while in Kevin J. Hayes's *Oxford Handbook of Early American*

Literature, the ratio is 530 pages of prose to a mere 81 for poetry.[45] All of this has the cumulative effect of marginalizing early American poetry, although in fact its systematic reconfiguration of classical aesthetics in the service of an adventurous New World style, speaking to both the traditions and the paradoxes involved in serving at least two masters within an American colonial setting, represents some of the most interesting achievements of early American literature. *M'Fingal* itself went through 23 editions in the 40 years after its publication, so the poem's subsequent neglect speaks more to contemporary preoccupations, and particularly to the way in which Emerson has been canonized as the fountainhead of American literature, than to levels of interest in what Trumbull himself in a 1785 letter called the style of "high burlesque" within the literature of the early republic.[46]

Joel Barlow's *The Columbiad* (1807) is another poem written in a neoclassical vein that has been severely underappreciated within the pedagogical framework of American literature where patriotic uplift and sentimental affect have consorted in mutually reinforcing ways. *The Columbiad* deliberately situates America at the apex of a world system, one interconnected by the oceans as conduits of trade, with Barlow representing seas and canals as a symbolic means for connecting all nations in both a commercial and spiritual harmony.[47] This vision might be critiqued as fanciful or utopian, of course, but the force of its bravado can hardly be questioned, and the way Barlow's poem celebrates oceanic explorers – Cook and Magellan as well as Columbus – indicates his poem's central theme of global discovery. There is also an immersion here in the rhetoric of science, with Barlow representing the dynamic interplay of magnetic poles as a counterpart to a new ideology of commercial exchange in the way it adduces a new empire of liberty, one that defines itself in contradistinction to the old tyrannies of slavery and plague. Drawing also on imagery of astronomy and invoking scientists such as Copernicus who radically shook up the established world picture, Barlow's epic poem is impelled by an impulse to rotate the globe upon its axis, as in Book III of the poem where "Vast Amazonia, starr'd with twinkling streams/In azure drest, a heaven inverted seems."[48] This is commensurate with Barlow's political essay *Advice to the Privileged Orders* (1791), where he had aligned advances in astronomy with progressive political causes, suggesting that Ptolemy's assumption of Earth being at the center of the universe, now known not to be true, served historically to bolster the entrenched hierarchies of the feudal order. Conversely, so Barlow argued here, the more dispersed "Copernican system" of planets rotating around a distant sun could be seen to foreshadow the more democratic "rights of man" in the way it deliberately decentered fixed stars.[49]

The almost complete elimination of *The Columbiad* from the annals of early American literature is a clear indication of the historical preference among Americanists for work that celebrates their own domestic culture rather than addressing a world system. In a critical maneuver typical of Cold War scholarship, James Woodress in 1958 complained of how Barlow "placed an inflated value on his *Columbiad*, lavished great energy on it, and failed completely to realize that his humorous *Hasty Pudding* alone gave him a chance to be remembered as a poet."[50] "The Hasty Pudding," an agreeable enough but much less ambitious poem that appeared in 1796, deploys depictions of rural virtues and plain food to lambast the "gaudy prigs" who compare the man brought up on corn to "pigs," thereby validating a radical democratic perspective at the expense of courtly pretentiousness.[51] As J.A. Leo Lemay has argued, the intricate nature of the references to cosmopolitan society alluded to in this poem indicates how Barlow's attraction to folk culture was based on a sophisticated form of dialectic rather than any mere regionalist nostalgia, but nevertheless the accommodation of such domestic charms within a relatively circumscribed verse form has allowed "The Hasty Pudding" to become canonized in a way that the more prolix *Columbiad* never has been.[52]

The complexity of Barlow's intellectual systems, and in particular the way he moved between mock-epic poetry and political essays, has also made his work difficult for scholars trained in narrower literary fields to get a proper handle on. This multifaceted quality is also linked to the complex interrelation between poetry and politics in Barlow's work. In "A Letter to the National Convention of France, on the Defects in the Constitution of 1791, and the Extent of the Amendments which are to be Applied" (1792), Barlow observed that the "great leading principle, on which their constitution was meant to be founded, is the *equality of rights,*" and he expressed confidence that France, which he called "certainly at this moment the most enlightened nation in Europe," would bury "monarchy and hierarchy … in the same grave."[53] The ferocity of Barlow's support for post-Revolutionary France and his willingness to see the French monarchy violently eliminated set him at odds not only with Edmund Burke – whom Barlow called an "illustrious hypocrite" – but also with the political leaders in 1790s America, who were wary of becoming too closely associated with what they took to be the anarchic spirit of French radicalism.[54] As Richard Buel Jr noted in 2011, though Barlow today "is remembered as a minor literary figure," during his own times "he enjoyed international renown for his vision of a republican future," and the way his reputation has declined since his death in 1812 can be attributed directly, if partially, to the formulation of American literature as a nationalist rather than a worldly enterprise.[55] Of course, long poems of this era – Pope's *Dunciad*, no less than Trumbull's *M'Fingal* or Barlow's *Columbiad* – are now largely out of fashion with students, but William Wordsworth's *The Prelude* (which was published two years before *The Columbiad*) is still popular, and it is the more opaque intellectual quality of Barlow's writing that has helped to make his work apparently unapproachable.

The appropriation of cultural figures from the Revolutionary era for the purposes of patriotic nationalism has also had the effect of contributing to the neglect of Benjamin Franklin's significant contributions as a literary satirist. Franklin is now best known for his *Autobiography*, where he aligns his own rise to fame and fortune with the rise of the United States from a state of colonial subservience to political independence. However, Franklin produced many darker satirical essays in the pre-Revolutionary years that spoke to his sense of coercion by irrational forces that were philosophical as much as political in their motivation and provenance. Many of Franklin's satires of the 1770s – "An Edict by the King of Prussia," "Remarks Concerning the Savages of North America," "A Dialogue Between Britain, France, Spain, Holland, Saxony, and America" – are remarkable not only for their dark humor but also their recognition of power play and self-interest as guiding principles of human behavior. Franklin's style of satire draws copiously upon Jonathan Swift – he cites "an old Friend of mine, Mr Gulliver, a great Traveler," in a satirical letter to the *Public Advertiser* in 1766 – and this testifies to Franklin's status as an eighteenth-century man of letters who admired the music of Handel as well as the poetry of James Thomson and William Cowper, along with the writings of Pope, Addison, and Daniel Defoe.[56]

Just as the emphasis on Franklin the American patriot has obscured his links with wider generic traditions of satire, so the retrospective understanding of Franklin as an incorrigible optimist has underestimated the extent to which Franklin as a cosmopolitan philosopher of the Enlightenment envisioned human culture in ironic and skeptical terms. Franklin spent many years associating with radical philosophers while working as a diplomat in Paris, and he was also friendly with David Hume, with whom he stayed during a visit to Edinburgh in 1771. Franklin himself was 70 when the Declaration of Independence was signed in 1776, and although undoubtedly it was useful for the Founding Fathers to have such a well-known and reputable figure to support and uphold their cause, it should not be forgotten that the great majority of Franklin's cultural achievements preceded the advent of the new nation. Indeed, the first part of Franklin's *Autobiography* was written in England in 1771, before there was any move towards political independence, and the subsequent canonization of this text as an exemplification of

American literary nationalism itself involves a retrospective, dehistoricized reading. Franklin in a letter of 1768 described himself as suspected "in England, of being too much an American, and in America of being too much an Englishman," and many of his writings retain this kind of elusive, double-edged quality.[57]

The same issues of nationalist appropriation that have distorted appreciation of Franklin's literary contributions might be extended, *pari passu*, to Thomas Jefferson's status as an American philosopher. During a dinner to celebrate Nobel laureates, John F. Kennedy joked that there was a more distinguished gathering that evening at the White House than at any time since Thomas Jefferson had dined alone, and Jefferson has always been revered as a polymathic paragon of progressive thinking and doughty American independence. However, Jefferson, like Franklin, spent time working as a diplomat in Paris, where he became acquainted during the 1780s with Enlightenment thinkers such as the Marquis de Condorcet and with Pierre-George Cabanis, whose work on physiology Jefferson much admired. Cabanis described how sensibility lay at the heart of all things, including human intelligence, with the brain according to his understanding being directed by a nervous system through which all human organs and muscles were connected. Cabanis's major work, *Rapports du physique et du moral de l'homme* (Reports on Man's Physical and Moral Being), was not published in Paris until 1802, but Jefferson had the two volumes sent to him in Washington, and this indicates ways in which he was intellectually influenced by the general culture of sensibility that was a product of Enlightenment thought. Rather than the Christian theology that had dominated the early New England colonies, Jefferson took his intellectual lead from his favorite author Laurence Sterne, whose books Jefferson purchased during the 1760s, with the American statesman even going so far as to purchase extra pocket-size editions in the 1780s so that he could always carry volumes of Sterne around with him.[58]

Sterne's willingness to entertain irony and contradiction as an inherent part of the human condition carries particular resonance in the light of recent DNA testing proving that Jefferson fathered several illegitimate children with his female slaves, something that has of course put a dent in the conventional image of him as a patriotic exemplification of gentlemanly virtues. But Jefferson would in any case more accurately be understood as an epitome of Enlightenment values, someone who sought to dissolve theocratic dogma and to base his thought instead upon a more skeptical, materialist premise where mind and body are frequently at cross-purposes. Inconsistency, in other words, became for Jefferson both a philosophical and a political program. Jefferson's own exposure as a chameleonic figure thus speaks in significant ways to more cosmopolitan influences on his life and work, where the shadow of French libertinage consorted uncomfortably with the more standardized image of the "Sage of Monticello" that subsequently became ratified for domestic political consumption.

2.3   The Early American Novel's Transatlantic Axis

Cathy N. Davidson associated this culture of sentiment specifically with the early American novel, arguing that Susanna Rowson's best-selling *Charlotte Temple* (1791), a tale of an American girl despoiled by a dissolute English aristocrat, shows a deliberate attempt to invest early American literature with a sphere of sentiment coded feminine, something that could stand in opposition to the more abstract theories of state propounded within the legalistic writings of the Founding Fathers. In this way, Davidson identified in the early American novel a predominantly female discourse of sentimentalism, whose "distinctive voice" she understood as combating the "demoralizing derision of Anglo-European arbiters of value and good taste."[59] Although such a conception of the gendered nature of the early American novel is interesting and thought-provoking, it overlooks the fact that sentiment and sensibility were also constituent aspects of male writers at this time such as Charles Brockden Brown or indeed Jefferson himself, as we have seen. It also tends to downplay the transatlantic provenance of Rowson, who was born in Bristol, England, in 1762, and whose fiction often refracts the style of displacement that she experienced in her own life.

Rowson grew up in America between the ages of five and 16, then returned to live in England again between 1778 and 1793, before finally emigrating to the United States with her new husband. *Charlotte Temple* was actually written in England and first published there in 1791 as *Charlotte: A Tale of Truth*, before being repackaged with great success for the American market. With its popular theme of virtue in distress, however, *Charlotte Temple* is much less ambitious in scope than *Reuben and Rachel* (1798), Rowson's three-volume epic about the foundation of the United States, which starts off back in the days of Christopher Columbus and then traces the course of a family's history over some 300 years, through religious struggles in England, the Reformation, and emigration to Pennsylvania in the eighteenth century. By charting how this Dudley family criss-crosses the Atlantic over several generations in search of economic wealth and freedom of conscience, Rowson's novel invokes such displacement as both a precursor to and an emblem of the US national narrative: Reuben and Rachel willingly renounce their English titles at the end, saying they are "distinctions nothing worth" compared to the joy of having sons who are "true-born Americans," with the prospect of "blessings" for their "posterity."[60] In this sense, *Reuben and Rachel* sets out deliberately to rewrite the history of the new nation, projecting its roots back in time to lend the unstable new republic a distinguished historical antecedence, one based around a transatlantic axis rather than simply a culture of American exceptionalism.

The circulation of sentiment across a transatlantic axis was also facilitated by the regular movements of theatrical companies across national boundaries, as Joseph Roach has chronicled in an illuminating manner. Rowson herself was also a dramatist, and her play *Slaves in Algiers; or, A Struggle for Freedom* (1794), which pits Islamic bondage against the political freedom enjoyed by Americans, demonstrates ways in which modes of transnational comparison and contrast fitted comfortably with a theatrical emphasis on styles of performative appearance. Royall Tyler's play *The Contrast*, which achieved great success when it was performed in New York in 1787, deliberately plays off the virtuous qualities of American country bumpkin Jonathan against the desiccated hypocrisy of European aristocratic privilege: the play's prologue anticipates a piece "Where the proud titles of 'My Lord! Your Grace! / To humble *Mr.* and plain *Sir* give place."[61] But Tyler's play was just as popular when it was performed at the Ranelagh Gardens in London, and this suggests ways in which national stereotypes and political controversies in the post-Revolutionary era were turned quickly into artistic commodities, as authors sought to transpose philosophical disputes into the stuff of popular entertainment. Paul Gilroy's formative work on how slavery permeated different points across an Atlantic compass might in this sense be extended into discussion of how cultures of sentiment and sensibility similarly circulated across an expansive transatlantic domain, with early American literature being as much of a packaged and commodified phenomenon as the market world of commercial transaction and exchange that it both mirrored and replicated.[62]

The difficulty of defining early American literature is exemplified by Spengemann's claim that Aphra Behn's *Oroonoko* (1688) should be classified as the "earliest American novel" on the grounds that it is "a literary work written in English about America by someone who claims to have lived there."[63] In truth, Behn's reported trip to the Caribbean in 1663 and 1664 was of limited duration but *Oroonoko*, which sets its scene "in a Colony in America, called *Surinam*, in the West-Indies," does directly address issues of slavery and monarchical authority in the British overseas territories, issues towards which the author herself, as a Tory and a Catholic living in the reign of King Charles II, maintained an ambiguous stance. The plot of *Oroonoko* turns upon ways in which the eponymous hero, a "Royal Slave," rebels against the island's colonial rulers to highlight "the Miseries, and Ignominies of Slavery," but the narrative is more concerned with emphasizing the exemplary human characteristics of the slave leader than with interrogating the system of slavery as such.[64] As in *The Widow Ranter*, a play first performed a few months after Behn's death in 1689 that comically portrays the colony of Virginia as a haven for dozy officials addicted to punch and tobacco, the spoofing of local authority figures in *Oroonoko* does not extend to any stringent critique of the parameters of royal power.

What is apparent from Behn's example, however, is the extent to which America in the seventeenth and eighteenth centuries entered into British colonial consciousness. American literature of the eighteenth century was postcolonial in almost every aspect, with this subaltern status of this pre-Revolutionary culture being one reason that more recent Americanists have not taken kindly to what they conceive to be its apparently compromised condition, its supposed lack of cultural maturity and independence.

The extent of the cultural traffic across the Atlantic in both directions at this time is exemplified also by the case of Charlotte Lennox, who was nominated by Gustavus Howard Maynadier in 1940 as his candidate for the title of "first American novelist."[65] More recent research has shown that Lennox was born as Charlotte Ramsay in Gibraltar – rather than New York, as Maynadier thought – although she did live in the province of New York between 1739 and 1742, while her father was serving in the British army at Albany. Lennox's first novel, *The Life of Harriot Stuart, Written by Herself* (1750), is clearly based on her own experiences of what its heroine calls the "unsettled condition" of transatlantic displacement, recounting the heroine's adventures in London before her departure for America, and then her "wild and romantic" escapades with Indians and lovers in the New World before her eventual return to England.[66] Lennox's last novel, *Euphemia* (1790), returns to this transatlantic scene in a more sophisticated manner, incorporating familiar scenes of captivity melodrama – Euphemia's son Edward is carried off by Native Americans at the age of three, only to reappear as a "handsome Huron" at the end of the novel – but also contemplating in a more reflective way the quandaries of exile. Euphemia's father initially repairs to America to salvage his fortunes, but in the last volume Mrs Mountfort wonders to herself whether or not it would be wise to return home after the death of her husband: "I left England in the bloom of youth and beauty," she says, "how can I bear the thoughts of returning thither, thus altered, that none of my former friends would know me."[67] The kind of dilemma typically faced by characters in the novels of Henry James 100 years later about which side of the Atlantic to live is also played out in

Euphemia, embodying as it does a fully realized, complex world where questions of family, career, and even pension provision rotate in complicated ways upon a transatlantic axis. As Amanda Gilroy and W.M. Verhoeven have remarked, the form of the epistolary novel favored by Lennox and other eighteenth-century novelists, predicated upon the idea of correspondents distant in space, allowed authors to exploit a transnational framework to good effect.[68]

In the second half of the eighteenth century, then, the Atlantic becomes a contested discursive space where novelists and other writers take up opposing positions on many different aspects of Western culture. Just as political philosophers such as Edmund Burke and Tom Paine clashed over the meaning of democracy and revolution, so Hugh Henry Brackenridge's *Modern Chivalry* – published sequentially between 1792 and 1805, with additional materials appearing in 1815 and 1819 – mediates debates about contemporary manners and politics in America. The sprawling nature of Brackenridge's narrative reflects the continual revisions in the author's own views on the state of Pennsylvania, shifts in perspective that can be seen as analogous to the manifold forms of supplementarity running through his multivolume work, whose final episode appeared 27 years after its first installment. In this sense, as Jared Gardner notes, the structure of eighteenth-century American fiction was specifically designed to accommodate "contradictory positions," not on account of any "insufficiency of the nascent literary culture," nor any psychological "instability of the individual author," but because discursive cross-currents were what the early American novel was all about. Rather than simply expounding the virtues of nationalism, the early American novel deliberately positioned itself within a wider world, correlating and contrasting republican perspectives to those emanating from other sources. Again, the epistolary form was ideally suited to such a "complex weave of contradictory voices," and, as Gardner says, Hannah Foster in *The Coquette* (1797) positions herself as "editor/curator" of the letters she reproduces rather than as their mere fabricator, thereby allowing within her work a hypothetical space for voices beyond the author's own.[69]

The early American novel's formal situation, as a rhetorical site for the mediation of contrasting positions, might be seen as a correlative to its fixation at the end of the eighteenth century on the dynamics underpinning the War of Independence. Looking back at early American literature from the hegemonic status enjoyed by the United States during the second half of the twentieth century, as so many Americanists did, it was easy to forget how tentative and exploratory was the status of this new nation at the turn of the nineteenth century and how the uncertain fate of the new United States was thought inevitably to relate to how its cultural formations could accommodate or repel the wider world. The War of Independence was a motif to which American novelists kept returning long after the last shot had been fired, partly because of patriotic pride at the Revolutionary outcome, but also partly because the trauma of that era created a general sense of discomfort in the American body politic that took many years to work through.

One of the most popular novels of the 1790s in the new United States was *The History of Constantius and Pulchera, or Constancy Rewarded*, first published anonymously in 1794, a book which went through many editions. Patriotically subtitled "An American Novel," *Constantius and Pulchera* describes how the romance between its central protagonists was forestalled by the intervention of "Monsieur le Monte, only son and heir to a rich nobleman in France," who turns the head of Pulchera's father and forces her to flee from such a "cruel parent." Despite crossdressing in "a neat suit of red regimentals" in an effort to avoid detection, Pulchera, in her guise as Lieutenant Valorus, is "captured by a forcible British cruiser" and detained in Canada.[70] True love eventually works itself out, of course, but it is significant that the authenticity of this romantic sentiment is correlated with, and verified by, the ritual of transatlantic crossings – "we will cross the Atlantic, we will revisit the land of freedom" – and also by a fictional use of the Revolutionary war as an analogy to this quest for self-fulfillment. In a narrative sense, *Constantius and Pulchera* turns upon the erotics of suffering, on characters being placed perpetually in a "frightful and horrible situation" yet somehow managing to survive unscathed, so that, as the novel's preface cannily puts it, the "repeated misfortunes" of Pulchera not only "cause the tear of Sensibility to fall" but also offer to readers "a peculiar source of amusement."[71]

Cross-dressing is also integral to Herman Mann's novel *The Female Review* (1797), which is similarly set during the Revolutionary War and which follows the fortunes of Deborah Sampson, who absconds from the marriage arranged by her mother in their small New England village and runs away to serve as a man in the American army. *The Female Review* is narrated in the first person, and the novel's detailed attention to the history and geography of the war – it is replete with dates, and with closeup descriptions of military personnel such as Washington, Cornwallis, and Lafayette – gives it the air of being a hybrid blend of fact and fiction; indeed, it attempts to authenticate its narrative in the final pages by quoting from a 1784 New York newspaper about the case of a female soldier who passed by the name of "Robert Shurtlieef." What is most noticeable about the character of Deborah Sampson, however, is how she implicitly conflates gender reversal with national rebellion: "All nature seemed in one combustible convulsion," she remarks, adding that within the scenario of insurrectionary war it would appear "[a]s if nature had been convulsed."[72] It is not difficult here to infer parallels between America's violent disruption of Britain's naturalized social hierarchies and the heroine's determination to "swerve from my sex's sphere"; Sampson attempts to justify both her own rebellion against parental dictates and America's political uprising by describing British authority as "cruel and unjust." The overall effect of this historical novel, published nearly a generation after American independence had actually been won, is not only to mythologize these "events [as] the most singular and important we have ever known," but also to acknowledge the widespread feelings of disturbance and anxiety that went along with such heroic insubordination.[73]

One of the side effects of the war's outcome was to divide the eighteenth-century novel, and indeed Anglo-American culture generally, into two discrete national traditions. This, however, created intense difficulties for the large body of American loyalists; historians today estimate that while about two-thirds of those living in the American colonies supported the struggle for independence, fully one-third did not. After 1783, this loyalist minority tended to keep quiet, feeling that ritualistic invocations in the new United States of the heroic nature of this Revolutionary enterprise naturally tended to exclude them.

Nevertheless, as Sarah J. Purcell observed, the fact that a novel such as Samuel Jackson Pratt's *Emma Corbett* (1780) was consumed so avidly in America, even though it was published by a British author at the height of the conflict, reflects "the ubiquity of these rifts" in the American colonies around the struggle for secession.[74] Drawing upon the metaphor of the Anglo-American family as one organic nation, a trope that informed much conservative thinking at this time, *Emma Corbett* mournfully chronicles a family torn apart by the war. Pratt's novel suffuses the international theme with many subtle psychological ambiguities and reversals. The main English character, Charles Corbett, sympathizes with the American cause, even though the suitor to his daughter Emma, Henry Hammond, is a staunch British patriot who fights to put down what he calls his "refractory fellow-subjects." Corbett, by contrast, abhors what he calls "this assassination of America" and tells Hammond that his desire "to go forth *amongst* your countrymen *against* your countrymen" is "shocking to my nature"; but the story ends up badly for paterfamilias Corbett, who loses not only his property interests in America but also most of his family to death on the battlefield.[75] Lamenting "that civil fury which hath separated the same interests of the same people," Corbett foresees that the wounds of this conflict will lead to "deep-mouthed gashes in the heart of Britain."

On one level, *Emma Corbett* can be read as a British colonial novel – Sir Robert Raymond, one of the candidates for the hand of Emma, has recently returned from an administrative tour of duty in India – but its central character is strongly critical of British policy toward America. Just as many American post-Revolutionary novelists portrayed Britain as an unnaturally cruel parent, so Pratt's novel organizes its discourses of family sentiment around representations of civil war as a transgression against the laws of nature: "Nature herself lies bleeding on thy shore," laments Corbett, "and there the inhuman mother has plunged the dagger (with her own barbarous hand) into the bowels of her child!"[76]

In light of this focus upon war, Davidson's model of late eighteenth-century American fiction as impelled by a progressive, feminist sentiment needs to be qualified by a recognition of how, as Terence Martin observed back in 1957, the early American novel usually fell "into one of two categories, the historical and the sentimental." Although the "virtue in distress" formula of the "American sentimental novel" was very popular, historical fiction – often focused on the Revolutionary battlefield and, by extension, the fate of the nation – was equally recognizable.[77] One writer of this era who straddled both categories was Isaac Mitchell, who published a series of novels reconfiguring gothic forms of melodrama within a carefully delineated American social setting. *Albert and Eliza* (1802) takes place in colonial New York, in the early settlement of North America, and it represents the ocean as a stimulus to both romance and intrigue. The heroine comes from a family that had emigrated from England to New York with a splendid fortune, and when Albert is called away to Europe on a business trip she fears he might get distracted by "some trans-atlantic beauty" – although his failure to return home promptly is actually brought about by the misfortune of having been taken prisoner by an Algerian corsair on the Atlantic, carried to Algiers, and sold into slavery.[78] *Melville and Phalez* (1803), another novel first published in serial form, similarly spans wide geopolitical space – various scenes are set in Turkey, Russia, Switzerland, and other countries – while considering ways in which mercantile values pose an implicit threat to the stability of the American republic in this early national period. Set amidst a world of trade, gambling, and speculation, *Melville and Phalez* contemplates the viability of autonomous domestic virtue in a multipolar world.

Mitchell's most enduring work of fiction, however, was *Alonzo and Melissa*, another novel set during the Revolutionary war that was first published in serial form in 1804. The work was then revised by the author and published in book form as *The Asylum* in 1811, and it remained popular in the United States throughout the nineteenth century. Mitchell's novel shadows modern American landscapes, in which the natural world and its seasons are lovingly evoked, with the specter of gothic intrigue represented here as a perverse force from the Old World whose malign influence threatens the protagonists' happiness. Again, trade and travel are integral to the story, and when Alonzo sets sail from America to Europe, his native shore appears to him "like a semicircular border of dark green velvet on the edge of a convex mirror."[79] It would appear from this evocative image as though the Atlantic Ocean itself were the prime mover behind the fortunes of these characters, with its scene of traversal a correlative to their perennial fear of finding themselves, both spatially and metaphorically, at "cross-purposes"; at the end of the novel, the narrator reports with a sigh of relief how "No *cross purposes* stood ready to intervene their happiness." The real *deus ex machina* who engineers this happy ending is none other than Benjamin Franklin, described here as "the great dispenser of all mercies," who encounters Alonzo in Paris and, on the strength of his old acquaintance with Alonzo's merchant father, ensures safe passage back to America for the hero.[80]

In a note appended to the serialized version of *Alonzo and Melissa*, which was published in the Poughkeepsie weekly newspaper *Political Barometer* from June 5 through October 30, 1804, Mitchell acknowledges that the story has been told "with too much rapidity for the contour of a perfect Novel." He says he would have liked to place more emphasis on "the most important events of the American war," but that such narrative detail would have been too time-consuming for his newspaper readers.[81] Mitchell amply remedies these deficiencies in *The Asylum*, putting in many more elaborate descriptions of naval battles and other aspects of warfare while changing the name of one of the central characters from "Beauman" to "Bowman," as if to emphasize this revised version's more naturalized, realistic tone. He also includes in *The Asylum* what he calls a "Preface: Comprising a Short Dissertation on Novel," an extended essay that bears comparison with Nathaniel Hawthorne's famous preface to *The House of the Seven Gables* 40 years later in the way it seeks to map out parameters and possibilities for the American novel. Mitchell attempts here to boost the status of the novel and redeem it from the charge of immorality, a charge made frequently by American Christian ministers, by claiming that such fiction should aspire to represent an idealized world in which "the scenery should be natural, the sentiment pure." He thus distinguishes the novel from the old generic model of romance, whose features of "licentiousness and impurity," as well as its reliance on "enchantments" rather than verisimilitude, led to a disproportionate emphasis on the "power of darkness." In this way, Mitchell radically reinterprets Western literary history to position its most exalted models as generic prototypes for the American novel:

> The most sublime specimens of fine writing, the most splendid productions of *belles lettres* genius, of either ancient or modern date, have been presented to us in the form of Novel. The Iliad of Homer, the Aenead of Virgil, Ossian's Fingal, Milton's Paradise, Dwight's Conquest, Barlow's Columbiad, and several other similar performances, are, in fact, epic novels, possessing the polished and superior advantages of lofty and majestic numbers.[82]

Just as American patriots at the turn of the nineteenth century regarded the new United States as a culmination of older civilizations, as westward the course of empire took its way, so Mitchell here somewhat bizarrely appropriates the Bible and *Paradise Lost* as precursors to his novelistic idiom. While admitting that the American novel still retains "irregularities" that derive from "the copious mixture of alloy" in its generic inheritance, Mitchell nevertheless seeks to justify this form by comparing it to Biblical parables in its capacity to impart "the most solemn and important truths."[83]

In this sense, the language of *The Asylum* – which the author claims to be "of the middle class, neither soaring to that sublimity which dazzles the understanding by its perpetual glitter, nor sinking to dull and trite inelegance" – is of a piece with his desire to evoke a world of "connexion and regularity" rather than "disorder and interruption." Such a sense of order is, in turn, aligned with a specifically patriotic impulse: "The production is entirely American," says Mitchell of *The Asylum*, and he goes on to validate its lyrical excerpts by insisting how "[t]he poetry is all from the geniuses of our own country."[84] It is true, of course, that various contradictions between gothic irregularity and pastoral sublimity are played out within the novel's narrative, and it is also true, as Joseph Fichtelberg has observed, that as a novelist committed to serial publication Mitchell was necessarily implicated within the chaotic world of international trade and commerce against which, through its final inward gesture of romantic retreat, *The Asylum* ultimately turns its face.[85] His novel can thus be read as an allegory of the emergence of American exceptionalism, of attempts at the beginning of the nineteenth century to carve out a discrete cultural and political space for the new nation that might set it apart from the rest of the world. Just as the lovers withdraw into "the native charms of their retired village," so the United States in this Jeffersonian era began to contemplate the virtues of blocking itself off from ancestral corruptions by an "ocean of fire."[86] It is, however, interesting to note that "asylum" at this time already carried what are now its more familiar associations of a home for the insane, and, as Davidson observes, the potential madness of isolation within a "happy, secluded ASYLUM" is also hinted at in the conclusion to Mitchell's novel.[87]

For all of its avowed patriotic zeal, then, *The Asylum* is implicitly haunted by various Atlantic cross-currents. In general terms, this idiom of conscious reduplication, predicated upon a pattern of intertextual dialogue or other structural double binds, is common throughout early American fiction. William Hill Brown's *The Power of Sympathy* (1789), once conventionally credited as the first American novel, cites Swift, Sterne, and, most significantly, Goethe's *The Sorrows of Young Werther*, a copy of which is found on the bedside table of the repentant seducer, Harrington, after he has killed himself. Goethe's novel originally appeared in Germany in 1774, with a first American edition published in translation in Philadelphia in 1784 and five more American editions appearing over the next 18 years. Because of its theme of adulterous love, Goethe's novel was of course generally deemed immoral in Christian America – one 1803 review declared it was among the class of books "which no parent should suffer to enter the hands of her child; which no bookseller should sell" – but Brown's novel might be said to represent a domestication of Goethe, in the way its seducer turned sentimentalist advances, under *Young Werther*'s tutelage, to his ultimate demise.[88] There is also an elaborately reflexive aspect to Brown's novel, exemplified not only by how Mrs Bourn is reading Sterne's *Sentimental Journey*, but also by Mrs Holmes's frequent critical remarks on literature: she talks, for example, of how ridicule is "evidently a *transatlantick* idea, and must have been imbibed from the source of some *English* Novel or Magazine." Brown's novel uses this play of intertextuality to interrogate the status of sentimentalism, or what its title classifies oxymoronically as "the *power* of *sympathy*." The inner world of emotional affect is here redescribed in relation to worldly force, and such a discourse of paradoxical transposition is commensurate with the character of Harrington himself, who is described as "a strange medley of contradiction – the moralist and the amoroso." Such contradictions are also integral to the emotional impulse of this kind of sentimental novel which, as Mr Worthy observes, mixes "pain" and "pleasure" in equal measure.[89]

The early American novel thus developed within an intellectual framework of sensibility, the grounding of knowledge in experiential perception rather than *a priori* concepts. Yet, as Julie Ellison has observed, sensibility in the late eighteenth century was "a transaction, not a character type," a form of exchange intimately linked to the circulation of commodities and, by extension, to slavery.[90] Bernard Bailyn has observed that the Atlantic was the first ocean ever to be located at the heart of an economy, while Stephen Shapiro argued that the American novel in its early years was shaped more by the bartering of both tangible and intangible assets – not only slaves but also sensibility and sentiment – across international borders, rather than by any incipient form of nationalism.[91] As we have seen in relation to Jefferson, the popularity in America of the works of Sterne and Jean-Jacques Rousseau testifies to the popularity in the new United States of radical Enlightenment ideas around sentimentalism, the intertwining of moral belief with human emotion. Also part of this movement were William Godwin – whose work Charles Brockden Brown much admired, and who admired Brown's novels in return – along with Mary Wollstonecraft and Wollstonecraft's lover Gilbert Imlay, whose novel *The Emigrants*, concerning the prospects for dissenters intending to migrate from Britain to America, was published in 1793. From this perspective, the patterns of displacement, comparison, and exchange that are self-evident in Olaudah Equiano's *Interesting Narrative* of 1789 might be said to epitomize American fiction in the late eighteenth century more generally. Just as Equiano's persona charts his (factual or fictional) movements from Africa and Europe to America, from slavery to freedom, so early American novelists negotiate the transference of cerebral commodities such as emotional sensibility and political dissent across a wide geopolitical spectrum.[92]

The constitutional doubleness of the early American novel, involving a condition of alienation as well as domesticity, is exemplified again by Peter Markoe's *The Algerine Spy in Pennsylvania*, which first appeared in 1787. Although Markoe's novel was published in Philadelphia and preceded *The Power of Sympathy* by two years, it is normally disqualified from the perhaps invidious title of "first American novel" on the grounds that its author was born at St Croix, in the Caribbean, and educated at Oxford University, even though after a career as a lawyer in London he took his oath to the State of Pennsylvania in 1784 and remained there until his death in 1792. *The Algerine Spy in Pennsylvania*, which was directly influenced by Montesquieu's *Persian Letters*, filters observations on the new United States through the eyes of "a native of Algiers," Mehemet, who has moved to Pennsylvania to report back on the condition of "the political Aetna of the world." The novel's prefatory note claims that "the work is but a translation," a rendering in English of letters written in Arabic and other languages, and this reinforces our sense of Markoe's novel situating itself amidst a global network of power. Mehemet comments, for example, on how the loss of America has made Spain less intimidated by Britain but more prone to regard "the American confederacy with a jealous eye," since "this new people" might threaten Spanish "possessions" on the American continent.[93] Algiers itself declared war on the United States in July 1785, encouraged to do so by the British who, having lost the War of Independence, wanted at least to drive American commerce out of the Mediterranean, and, as Markoe's novel implies, images of the Muslim world as an inveterate enemy of the American people were ubiquitous in the early years of the republic.

The Algerine Spy in Pennsylvania is, on one level, a typically American patriotic narrative, since by the end of the novel Mehemet becomes so convinced of the virtues of his adopted country that he decides never to return to Algiers. Mehemet particularly contrasts state tyranny in his African homeland with the prospect of freedom of speech in America: "Were an Algerine supposed to have imagined only in a dream what a Pennsylvanian speaks, prints, publishes, maintains and glories in," he says, "he would suffer the severest tortures." Yet the doubleness that runs through Markoe's spy narrative ensures that American "pillars of freedom" are always refracted through an idiom of estrangement, whereby the new United States is creatively reimagined from a position of alterity; American Christians, for example, are always referred to by Mehemet as "the Nazarenes."[94] This kind of transatlantic defamiliarization also informs Royall Tyler's novel *The Algerine Captive* (1797), which similarly plays American and Algerine, Christian and Muslim, off against each other. Tyler's novel, which features a former New England schoolmaster taken captive by the Algerines and forced to spend seven years away from home, foregrounds questions of historical and geographical perspective as it draws explicit parallels between the state tyranny in Algiers and the system of slavery in the southern United States, thereby facilitating what Timothy Marr has aptly described as "a critical transnational consciousness from the comparative perspective of Algerine space."[95]

The eighteenth-century American novel, then, developed across a transatlantic axis and was shaped by European prototypes as much as by US political pressures. It was a radically unstable form, mixing fiction, philosophy, and epistolary conventions, and this kind of formal hybridity coalesced with a historical era in which geographic boundaries were being reconceptualized and the limits of empire and nation radically redrawn. Noah Webster asserted in 1783 that "America must be as independent in *literature* as she is in *politics*," but this was clearly a proleptic statement rather than a description of the state of national letters at the end of the Revolutionary War, and the attempts in the next generation to enunciate a specifically American cultural tradition, as in the work of Mitchell and Rowson, often involved a conscious appropriation and reconfiguration of the past.[96] From the start, the affiliation of the American novel with a notion of US cultural identity was a fractious and ambiguous enterprise, one expounded vigorously by patriotic proselytizers but circumscribed by the amorphous quality of literary genre and by the always permeable boundaries of the nation itself.

2.4   Thomas Paine and Universal Order

The nationalist template that has framed the development of American literature and American studies has also had the regrettable effect of marginalizing the visibility and significance of Thomas Paine, who in fact wrote the three best-selling books of the eighteenth century. *Common Sense*, which was published in early 1776 and went through 25 editions that year, is said to have converted George Washington to the cause of independence. The book sold about half a million copies during the course of the American War of Independence, an astronomical figure for those times. *The Rights of Man*, published in two parts in 1791 and 1792, also sold about half a million copies over the course of 10 years.

Paine was born in Norfolk, England, in 1737 to a Quaker family, but he always enjoyed a difficult relationship with his native country. He worked for a while as a tax collector in Sussex, but typically enough, he lost this position by agitating for an increase in pay for excisemen. He then moved in 1774 to America, where he came to fame through the publication of *Common Sense* and by fighting as a soldier for the cause of American independence. He returned homesick to England for a visit in 1787, but on this trip he found the atmosphere of his old country extremely oppressive, resenting what he took to be the political hypocrisy of the government in London and also becoming embroiled in public disputes with Edmund Burke, who was then serving as a Member of Parliament for the Whig Party. *The Rights of Man* was a direct reply to Burke's *Reflections on the Revolution in France* (1790), which denied as a matter of principle the possibility of any purely theoretical idea of freedom. For Burke, no conception of "abstract principles" such as "the rights of men" was possible, since "in the gross and complicated mass of human passion and concerns, the primitive rights of men undergo such a variety of refractions and reflections, that it becomes absurd to talk of them as if they continued in the simplicity of their original direction."[97] For Paine, on the other hand, any form of mediation tended to obscure the clear-cut nature of ethical and political choices. Speaking about the French Revolution in *The Rights of Man*, he declares boldly: "The event was to be freedom or slavery."[98]

Paine said later that while *Common Sense* was adapted to the local conditions of American politics, *The Rights of Man* developed out of the British political situation, and he preserved this sense of disaffiliation from any one specific nationalist cause all his life. After the second installment of *The Rights of Man* had been published in 1792 the British government prosecuted him for libel, but Paine had by that point already left the country and the main purpose of this intervention by the

government in London was to stop him ever coming back. Paine consequently spent time in Paris, helping to draft the new French constitution,
but his career there was impeded by the fact that he could not speak
French very well, and in any case his cosmopolitan sympathies were not
especially amenable to the more fervent revolutionary spirits in France.
In a speech to the National Convention of France on 15 January 1793,
Paine argued for preserving the life of the French king, Louis XVI, by
pointedly describing himself as "a citizen of both countries," both the
new United States and the French republic after its 1789 revolution:

> Let then those United States be the safeguard and asylum of Louis
> Capet. There, hereafter, far removed from the miseries and crimes
> of royalty, he may learn, from the constant aspect of public pros-
> perity, that the true system of government consists not in kings,
> but in fair, equal, and honourable representation.
>
> In relating this circumstance, and in submitting this proposition,
> I consider myself as a citizen of both countries. I submit it as a citi-
> zen of America, who feels the debt of gratitude which he owes to
> every Frenchman. I submit it also as a man who, although the
> enemy of kings, cannot forget that they are subject to human frail-
> ties. I support my proposition as a citizen of the French republic,
> because it appears to me the best, the most politic measure that
> can be adopted.[99]

Paine's only reward for this act of Enlightenment *noblesse* was to find
himself imprisoned as a traitor to the French cause, and after his release
from jail in Paris, he moved back to America in 1802.

There, however, political circumstances had changed, and the post-
Revolutionary United States was becoming more cautious about the dissemination of radical philosophical ideas. Jefferson's own suspect
religious beliefs had become an issue in the presidential campaign of
1800, so he was anxious for reasons of expediency to dissociate himself
from the reputation of atheism that had become attached to Paine on
account of his years in Paris, while Benjamin Rush, previously a keen
supporter of Paine, refused to talk to him. Gordon S. Wood has observed
how Paine found himself out of kilter with the increasing religiosity of
the public sphere at the beginning of the nineteenth century – "As the
Republic became democratized," said Wood, "it became evange-
lized" – but the always provocative Paine undoubtedly did not help his
own cause, which was also jeopardized by his open letter in 1795 to
George Washington, accusing him of being a mediocre general and a bad
politician who drank too much.[100] Paine ended up dying in relative poverty and obscurity at a farm in New Rochelle, New York, in 1809, and as

Bertrand Russell remarked in 1935, Paine's subsequent fame "is less than it would have been if his character had been less generous," since when "public issues were involved, he forgot personal prudence." What Russell commended as Paine's "lack of self-seeking" might be seen from another perspective as a perverse proclivity for self-destruction, with Paine's lack of "worldly wisdom" helping to assure his ultimate state of alienation even from those who under other circumstances might have protected him.[101]

Nevertheless, while Paine's universalist tendencies and reluctance to compromise always put him at odds with local factions and interests, his writing remains valuable for the way it advances the prospect of America not just as a new nation but as a new world. *Common Sense* explicitly advocates "universal" rather than "local" perspectives:

> The cause of America is in a great measure the cause of all man-kind. Many circumstances have, and will arise, which are not local, but universal, and through which the principles of all Lovers of Mankind are affected, and in the event of which, their affections are interested ... It is repugnant to reason, to the universal order of things to all examples from former ages, to suppose, that this con-tinent can longer remain subject to any external power ... O ye that love mankind – ye that dare oppose, not only the tyranny, but the Tyrant, stand forth; every spot of the old world is over-run with oppression. Freedom hath been hunted round the globe – Asia, and Africa, have long expelled her; Europe regards her like a stranger, and England hath given her warning to depart. O! receive the fugitive, and prepare in time an asylum for mankind ... We have it in our power to begin the world over again. A situa-tion, similar to the present, hath not happened since the days of Noah, till now. The birth-day of a new world is at hand ...[102]

Paine does not celebrate the "birth-day" of the United States *per se*, but of a "new *world*," and in this sense he reads US emergence as an allegory of a new universal condition.

The Rights of Man turns upon a similar structural paradox, in the way it describes the rights of man as a universal phenomenon and natural rights as the foundation of civil rights. The book's title page describes its author as "Secretary for Foreign Affairs to Congress in the American War," and, as Paine knew full well, to affiliate himself with such a global conception of human rights positioned him as an antagonist to the old European powers, with Paine projecting himself as a spokesperson not for Old World hierarchy but for a New World rational order. This is why Paine specifically presents himself here as a comparatist, arguing that

Burke seeks deliberately to suppress any analysis of similarities or differences between the constitution of different countries, whereas Paine wants to bring them into juxtaposition through his "orb of reason." Burke's sense of inherited privilege, argues Paine, depends upon a contraction of perspective so that social hierarchies come to appear naturalized, as if they were produced instinctively, whereas his own style of principled "comparison" opens up the world to alternative systems of government and global horizons:

> Titles are like circles drawn by the magician's wand, to contract the sphere of man's felicity ... As the estimation of all things is given by comparison, the Revolution of 1688, however from circumstances it may have been exalted beyond its value, will find its level. It is already on the wane, eclipsed by the enlarging orb of reason, and the luminous revolutions of America and France ... In contemplating a subject that embraces with equatorial magnitude the whole region of humanity it is impossible to confine the pursuit in one single direction. It takes ground on every character and condition that appertains to man, and blends the individual, the nation, and the world.[103]

Whereas for Burke the very notion of comparison is destabilizing, Paine's rhetoric is all about spatial expansion – "the enlarging of the orb of reason" – and this enables him to countenance "the whole region of humanity."

Paine also links this explicitly to the "pacific system" of international commerce, arguing that there is no such thing as a nation flourishing alone in commerce and that an international economy based around a free market "needs no other protection than the reciprocal interest which every nation feels in supporting it." Again, this is to move away from a restricted series of circumscribed interests, predicated upon protectionism, and instead to render local worlds permeable to external forces, embracing intellectual influences as well as market agents:

> In all my publications, where the matter would admit, I have been an advocate for commerce, because I am a friend to its effects. It is a pacific system, operating to cordialize mankind, by rendering nations, as well as individuals, useful to each other ... If commerce were permitted to act to the universal extent it is capable, it would extirpate the system of war, and produce a revolution in the uncivilized state of governments. The invention of commerce has arisen since those governments began, and is the greatest approach

towards universal civilisation, that has yet been made by any means not immediately flowing from moral principles ... Commerce needs no other protection than the reciprocal interest which every nation feels in supporting it – it is common stock."[104]

Paine dated his own intellectual development from purchasing two globes in his youth and from his conversations about astronomy with John Bevis, a fellow of the Royal Society, and in *The Age of Reason* there is an extended discussion of the solar system and the spherical rotation of the planets, an idea that was, as Paine points out, viewed as a form of heresy when it was first propounded by Virgilius before being developed into a heliocentric planetary system in the sixteenth century by Galileo. Paine's point here is that vested interests always seek to guard their own localized and restricted space by closing down what they perceive as the threatening impact of a wider world, and he reinforces this theme of the transmission of ideas across a transnational expanse by appropriating scientific images of the way light is transmitted, saying that the revolutions in America and France "have thrown a beam of light over the world."[105]

Paine also presents this comparative perspective on religious issues. He describes himself not as an atheist but as a deist, believing "in one God, and no more," and hoping "for happiness beyond this life." Nevertheless, the tone of his writing is distinctly iconoclastic, as he exposes how established religions become intertwined with the political protection of vested interests:

Every national church or religion has established itself by pretending some special mission from God, communicated to certain individuals. The Jews have their Moses; the Christians their Jesus Christ, their apostles and saints; and the Turks their Mahomet; as if the way to God was not open to every man alike.

Each of those churches shows certain books, which they call *revelation*, or the Word of God. The Jews say that their Word of God was given by God to Moses face to face; the Christians say, that their Word of God came by divine inspiration; and the Turks say, that their Word of God (the Koran) was brought by an angel from heaven. Each of those churches accuses the other of unbelief; and, for my own part, I disbelieve them all.[106]

Paine also takes a sardonic delight in exposing links between Christianity and heathen mythologies, likening Noah's ark to an Arabian tale, and commenting in the *Rights of Man* on how "the word *prophet* ... was the Bible-word for poet," a form of linguistic play that allows him to align prophecy and poetry and thus to dismiss Christian theology as an "empty subject":

> It is curious to observe how the theory of what is called the Christian Church, sprung out of the tail of the heathen mythology … The Christian mythologists, after having confined Satan in a pit, were obliged to let him out again to bring on the sequel of the fable. He is then introduced into the garden of Eden in the shape of a snake, or a serpent, and in that shape he enters into familiar conversation with Eve, who is no ways surprised to hear a snake talk; and the issue of this *tête-à-tête* is, that he persuades her to eat an apple, and the eating of that apple damns all mankind. After giving Satan this triumph over the whole creation, one would have supposed that the church mythologists would have been kind enough to send him back again to the pit … to prevent his getting again among the women, and doing more mischief.[107]

It is easy enough in the light of such inflammatory remarks to understand why Paine would have been disowned by politicians of his own time such as Jefferson and Rush, while Theodore Roosevelt in 1888 disparaged Paine more vituperatively as a "filthy little atheist."[108] The more general point to make, however, is that Paine was an Enlightenment thinker who found himself increasingly out of place in the culture of sentimentality and religiosity that increasingly informed the American public sphere at the beginning of the nineteenth century and indeed afterwards. Intellectually, Paine's dedicated form of anti-clerisy was more akin to that of a French *philosophe* such as Denis Diderot, although Paine entirely lacked Diderot's canny, political capacity for self-preservation.

Paine is worth special consideration in the context of American world literature because he so clearly offers a different kind of vision of America's place within the world. The more traditional style of American studies was based on nationalist premises that took their cue from Jefferson's republican notion of an "ocean of fire" between the Old World and the New, but this model of American exceptionalism was a concept in which Paine was never interested. Nor was he particularly concerned with the kind of patriotic legacy inaugurated by George Washington. Instead, Paine's commitment to how America might present itself as an epitome of Enlightenment universalism offers a different kind of genealogy for discursive considerations of America's literary and cultural legacy. The marginalization of Paine that was set in motion by Washington and Jefferson has been perpetuated by later generations of Americanists, who have found Paine's style of rationalistic demystification and his antipathy towards established religions too much to countenance. But in fact, this kind of materialist consciousness played an important part in eighteenth-century American culture, and many of the novels and travel narratives of this time introduced transnational perspectives so as to position America within a broader global circumference. Thus when Paine declared in *The Rights of Man* that "My country is the world, and my religion is to do good," he was also expressing the kind of universalizing and secularizing perspective that was crucial to the general cultural formation of early American literature in the world.

References

1 Murdoch, I. (1969). *The Nice and the Good* (1968; rpt.), 171. London: Penguin.
2 Shields, D. (2001). The Archival Turn. Presidential Address, Society for Early Americanists Conference, Norfolk, Virginia, 8 March 2001.
3 Cahill, E. and Larkin, E. (2016). Aesthetics, feeling, and form in Early American literary studies. *Early American Literature* 51(2): 235.
4 Watts, E. (1998). *Writing and Postcolonialism in the Early Republic*, 2. Charlottesville: UP of Virginia.
5 Spanos, W.V. (2016). *Redeemer Nation in the Interregnum: An Untimely Meditation on the American Vocation*, 2. New York: Fordham UP.
6 Bercovitch, S. (1978). *The American Jeremiad*. Madison: U of Wisconsin P; Delbanco, A. (1989*). The Puritan Ordeal*. Cambridge: Harvard UP.
7 Pearce, R.H. (1961). *The Continuity of American Poetry*, 20. Princeton: Princeton UP.
8 Bercovitch, S. (1975). *The Puritan Origins of the American Self*. New Haven: Yale UP.
9 Bruce-Novoa, J. (1998). Alvar Nuñez de Vaca. In: *The Heath Anthology of American Literature*, 3e (ed. P. Lauter), Vol. 1, 129. Boston: Houghton Mifflin.
10 Kolodny, A. (2012). *In Search of First Contact: The Vikings of Vinland, the People of the Dawnland, and the Anglo-American Anxiety of Discovery*, 5, 331. Durham: Duke UP.
11 Pratt, M.L. (2008). *Imperial Eyes: Travel Writing and Transculturation*, 2e, 7. New York: Routledge.
12 Rowlandson, M. (1994). A true history of the captivity and restoration of Mrs Mary Rowlandson. In: *Colonial American Travel Narratives* (ed. Martin, W.), 12–13, 27. New York: Penguin.
13 Rowlandson, "The History," 15, 42.
14 [Increase Mather], "Preface to the Reader," in Rowlandson, "A True History," 7.
15 Rowlandson, "A True History," 47.

16 Harris, S.M. Mary White Rowlandson. In: *Heath Anthology* (ed. P. Lauter), 340; Slotkin, R. (1973). *Regeneration through Violence: The Mythology of the American Frontier, 1600–1860*, 5. Norman: U of Oklahoma P.

17 Rowlandson, "The History," 47–47.

18 Armstrong, N. and Tennenhouse, L. (1992). *The Imaginary Puritan: Literature, Intellectual Labor, and the Origins of Personal Life*, 216. Berkeley: U of California P.

19 Damrosch, *What Is World Literature?*, 281.

20 Caldwell, P. (1983). *The Puritan Conversion Narrative: The Beginnings of American Expression*, 163. Cambridge: Cambridge UP.

21 Hutcheon, L. (1985). *A Theory of Parody: The Teachings of Twentieth-Century Art Forms*, 14, 72. New York: Methuen.

22 Clemit, P. (1993). *The Godwinian Novel: The Rational Fictions of Godwin, Brockden Brown, Mary Shelley*, 106. Oxford: Clarendon Press.

23 Ringe, D.A. (1982). *American Gothic: Imagination and Reason in Nineteenth-Century America*. Lexington: UP of Kentucky.

24 Paulson, R. (2003). *Hogarth's Harlot: Sacred Parody in Enlightenment England*. Baltimore: Johns Hopkins UP.

25 Ashbridge, E. Some Account of the Fore Part of the Life of Elizabeth Ashbridge. In: *Heath Anthology* (ed. P. Lauter), 607.

26 Spengemann, W.C. (1977). *The Adventurous Muse: The Poetics of American Fiction, 1789–1900*. New Haven: Yale UP.

27 Scheiding, O. and Seidl, M. (ed.) (2014). *Worlding America: A Transnational Anthology of Short Narratives before 1800*, 39. Stanford: Stanford UP.

28 Cook, E. (1900). The sot-weed factor. In: *The Works of Ebenezer Cook, Gent. Early Maryland Poetry* (ed. B.G. Steiner), 23. Baltimore: Maryland Historical Society.

29 Shields, J.C. (2001). *The American Aeneas: Classical Origins of the American Self*, ix, 10. Knoxville: U of Tennessee P.

30 Wheatley, P. (1988). Liberty and peace. In: *The Collected Works of Phillis Wheatley* (ed. J.C. Shields), 134. New York: Oxford UP.

31 Richard, C.J. (1995). *The Founders and the Classics: Greece, Rome, and the American Enlightenment*, 2, 193. Cambridge: Harvard UP.

32 Hutson, J.H. (2008). *Church and State in America: The First Two Centuries*, 105. Cambridge: Cambridge UP.

33 Kramnick, I. and Laurence Moore, R. (2005). *The Godless Constitution: A Moral Defense of the Secular State*, 2e, 29. New York: Norton.

34 Byles, M. (1940). *Poems on Several Occasions* (1744) (ed. C. Lennart Carlson), 79. New York: Columbia UP.

35 Shields, D.S. (1997). *Civil Tongues and Polite Letters in British America*, xxv. Williamsburg/Chapel Hill: Institute of Early American History and Culture and U of North Carolina P.

36 Shields, D.S. (1990). *Oracles of Empire: Poetry, Politics, and Commerce in British America, 1690–1750*, 17. Chicago: U of Chicago P.

37 Cahill, E. (2012). Liberty of the imagination in Revolutionary America. In: *American Literature's Aesthetic Dimensions* (ed. C. Weinstein and C. Looby), 39–55. New York: Columbia UP.

38 Fliegelman, J. (1982). *Prodigals and Pilgrims: The American Revolution against Patriarchal Authority, 1750–1800*, 247. Cambridge: Cambridge UP. See also Weinstein, C. and Looby, C. Introduction. In: *American Literature's Aesthetic Dimensions* (ed. C. Weinstein and C. Looby), 29.

39 Saunders Redding, J. (1939). *To Make a Poet Black*, 11. Durham: U of North Carolina P.

40 McCulley, T.O. (2011). Queering Phillis Wheatley. In: *New Essays on Phillis Wheatley* (ed. J.C. Shields and E.D. Lamore), 193. Knoxville: U of Tennessee P.

41 *Collected Works of Phillis Wheatley*, ed. Shields, 15–16.

42 Humphreys, D., Barlow, J., Trumbull, J., and Hopkins, L. (1967). In: *The Anarchiad: A New England Poem (1786–87)* (ed. L.G. Riggs), 32, 35. Gainesville: Scholars' Facsimiles and Reprints (1861; rpt).

43 Parrington, V.L. (ed.) (1963). In: *The Connecticut Wits*, x. Hamden: Archon Books, (1925; rpt.).

44 May, H.F. (1976). *The Enlightenment in America*, 38, 226. New York: Oxford UP.

45 Shields, J.C. (2011). Two new, significant volumes treating Early American literature. *Eighteenth-Century Studies* 44(3): 412.

46 Trumbull, J. (1820). Letter to the Marquis de Chastellux, 20 May 1785. In: *The Poetical Works of John Trumbull*. Hartford, II, 232.

47 Tichi, C. (1979). *New World, New Earth: Environmental Reform in American Literature*, 147. New Haven: Yale UP.

48 Barlow, J. (1809). *The Columbiad: A Poem*, 82. London: Richard Phillips (1807; rpt.).

49 Barlow, J. (1796). Advice to the Privileged Orders (1791). In: *The Political Writings of Joel Barlow*, 28. New York.

50 Woodress, J. (1958). *A Yankee's Odyssey: The Life of Joel Barlow*, 24. Philadelphia: Lippincott.

51 Barlow, J. (2003). The Hasty Pudding. In: *The New Anthology of American Poetry: Volume I, Traditions and Revolutions, Beginnings to 1900* (ed. S.G. Axelrod, C. Roman, and T. Travisano), 119. New Brunswick: Rutgers UP.

52 Leo Lemay, J.A. (1982). The contexts and themes of 'The Hasty Pudding'. *Early American Literature* 17(1): 3–23.

53 Barlow, J. "A Letter to the National Convention of France," in *Political Writings*, 161, 170, 173.

54 Barlow, J. "Note on Mr. Burke," in *Political Writings*, 256.

55 Buel, R., Jr. (2011). *Joel Barlow: American Citizen in a Revolutionary World*, 4–5. Baltimore: Johns Hopkins UP.

56 Franklin, B. (1987). Contempt for the Thames. In: *Writings*, 584. New York: Library of America.

57 Franklin, *Writings*, 840.

58 Burstein, A. and Mowbray, C. (1994). Jefferson and Sterne. *Early American Literature* 29(1): 19–34.

59 Rowson, S. (1798). *Reuben and Rachel; or, Tales of Old Times*, 363. Boston.

60 Davidson, C.N. (2004). *Revolution and the Word: The Rise of the Novel in America*, 2e, 3, 150. New York: Oxford UP.

61 Tyler, R. (1997). *The Contrast*. In: *Early American Drama* (ed. J.H. Richards), 7. New York: Penguin.

62 Gilroy, *The Black Atlantic*, 1–40.

63 Spengemann, W.C. (1989). *A Mirror for Americanists: Reflections on the Idea of American Literature*, 45. Hanover: UP of New England.

64 Behn, A. (2003). *Oroonoko* (ed. J. Todd), 9, 61. London: Penguin.

65 Maynadier, G.H. (1940). *The First American Novelist?* Cambridge: Harvard UP.

66 Lennox, C. (1995). *The Life of Harriet Stuart, Written by Herself* (1750) (ed. S.K. Howard), 173, 75. Madison: Fairleigh Dickinson UP.

67 Lennox, C. (2008). *Euphemia* (1790) (ed. S.K. Howard), 389, 305. Peterborough: Broadview Press.

68 Gilroy, A. and Verhoeven, W.M. (ed.) (2000). *Epistolary Histories: Letters, Fiction, Culture*, 9. Charlottesville: UP of Virginia.

69 Gardner, J. (2000). The literary museum and the unsettling of the Early American novel. *ELH* 67(3): 745, 755.

70 *The History of Constantius and Pulchera, or Constancy Rewarded* (Leominster, MA, 1797), 14, 10, 43, 68.

71 *History of Constantius and Pulchera*, 93, 36, vii.

72 Mann, H. (1797). *The Female Review*, 208, 72. Dedham.

73 Mann, *The Female Review*, 108, 57, 54–55.

74 Purcell, S.J. (2002). *Sealed with Blood: War, Sacrifice, and Memory in Revolutionary America*, 69. Philadelphia: U of Pennsylvania P.

75 Pratt, S.J. (1782). *Emma Corbett, or, The Miseries of Civil War*, 3e. Philadelphia, II, 172; I, 6–7.

76 Pratt, *Emma Corbett*, II, 85; I, 161–162.

77 Martin, T. (1957). Social institutions in the Early American novel. *American Quarterly* 9(1): 73–74.

78 [Isaac Mitchell], "Albert and Eliza," *Political Barometer* (Poughkeepsie, NY), 1, No. 1 (8 June 1802): 1–2.

79 [Isaac Mitchell], "Alonzo and Melissa," *Political Barometer* (Poughkeepsie, NY), No. 118 (4 September 1804): 4.

80 Mitchell, I. (1811). *The Asylum; or, Alonzo and Melissa*, II, 185; II, 245. Poughkeepsie: Joseph Nelson.

81 Isaac Mitchell, "Note to 'Alonzo and Melissa,'" *Political Barometer* (Poughkeepsie, NY), No. 126 (30 October 1804): 4.

82 Mitchell, *The Asylum*, xix, xii, xxi.

83 Mitchell, *The Asylum*, xxi–xxii.

84 Mitchell, *The Asylum*, xxvi, xxvii–xxviii.

85 Fichtelberg, J. (2003). *Critical Fictions: Sentiment and the American Market, 1780-1870*, 17. Athens: U of Georgia P.

86 Mitchell, *The Asylum*, II, 277; Thomas Jefferson, letter to Elbridge Gerry, 13 May 1797, in *Writings*, 1044.

87 Davidson, *Revolution and the Word*, 327.

88 Grefe, M. (1988). *"Apollo in the Wilderness": An Analysis of Critical Reception of Goethe in America, 1806–1840*, 165. New York: Garland.

89 Brown, W.H. (1996). *The Power of Sympathy*, 28, 56, 51, 9. New York: Penguin.

90 Ellison, J. (1999). *Cato's Tears and the Making of Anglo-American Emotion*, 98. Chicago: U of Chicago P.

91 Bailyn, B. (1996). The idea of Atlantic history. *Itinerario* 20(1): 30; Shapiro, S. (2008). *The Culture and Commerce of the Early American Novel: Reading the Atlantic World-System*, 13, 40. University Park: Pennsylvania State UP.

92 For the suggestion that "the accounts of Africa and the Middle Passage in *The Interesting Narrative* were constructed" and that Equiano "probably invented an African identity," see Carretta, V. (2005). *Equiano the African: Biography of a Self-Made Man*, xix–xv. Athens: U of Georgia P.

93 [Peter Markoe], *The Algerine Spy in Pennsylvania; or, Letters Written by a Native of Algiers on the Affairs of the United States of America from the Close of the Year 1783 to the Meeting of the Convention* (Philadelphia, 1787), 61, v, 18.

94 [Markoe], *The Algerine Spy*, 97, 129.

95 Marr, T. (2006). *The Cultural Roots of American Islamicism*, 55. New York: Cambridge UP.

96 Weisbuch, R. (1986). *Atlantic Double-Cross: American Literature and British Influence in the Age of Emerson*, 62. Chicago: U of Chicago P.

97 Burke, E. (1968). *Reflections on the Revolution in France* (ed. C.C. O'Brien), 118, 152. Harmondsworth: Penguin.

98 Paine, T. (1792). *The Rights of Man, Part II*, in *The Works of Thomas Paine*, 16. London.

99 Paine, T. (1908). Reasons for preserving the life of Louis Capet. In: *The Writings of Thomas Paine*, vol. III (ed. M.D. Conway), 122. New York: Putnam's.

100 Wood, G.S. (1991). *The Radicalism of the American Revolution*, 331. New York: Random House.
101 Russell, B. (1957) The fate of Thomas Paine. In: *Why I Am Not a Christian: And Other Essays on Religion and Related Subjects*, 147. New York: Touchstone-Simon and Schuster.
102 Paine, *Common Sense*, in *Works*, iv, 29, 39, 59.
103 Paine, *Rights of Man, Part II*, in *Works*, 54, 43–44, 68.
104 Paine, *Rights of Man, Part II*, in *Works*, 71.
105 Paine, *Rights of Man, Part II*, in *Works*, 81.
106 Paine, T. (1796). *The Age of Reason*. In: *The Works of Thomas Paine*, 300. London.
107 Paine, *Age of Reason*, 308, 302, 304.
108 Roosevelt, T. (1888). *Gouverneur Morris*, 289. Boston: Houghton Mifflin.

3

National/Global

The Framing of Nineteenth-Century American Literature

3.1   National Agendas and Transnational Dialogues

Nineteenth-century American literature has traditionally been under-stood by Americanists based in the United States to be the classic period of their subject, the era in which the field produced its most notable and enduring writers. This in itself marks a difference from the way American literature is characteristically understood in the wider academic world, where it is usually understood as primarily a modern subject, with a focus on contemporary writing and a historical reach that often does not go back earlier than *The Great Gatsby*. The novelist Caryl Phillips, who studied English as an undergraduate at Oxford in the late 1970s, subse-quently recalled how no black author was included at that time on the main syllabus of English literary history, running as it did from Beowulf to Ted Hughes, and he consequently chose to devote his special focus on the American literature optional paper to the twentieth-century African American novelists Richard Wright and Ralph Ellison.[1] This pattern was not unusual within the twentieth-century European academy, where American literary studies were popularly understood as a welcome anti-dote to antiquarian stuffiness and historical convention, but it had the unwelcome side effect of tending to marginalize the study of nineteenth-century American writing.

There are complex institutional reasons for the development of this academic pattern, with American literature gaining popularity in Europe and other parts of the world after World War II as an epitome of the modern spirit and a refuge from the traditionalist emphasis that had hitherto propped up European language and literature departments, which were usually weighted heavily towards pre-1900 literature. This meant that American literature was often romanticized in terms of its antiauthoritarian dynamics, with a consequent emphasis on topics such

American World Literature: An Introduction, First Edition. Paul Giles.
© 2019 John Wiley & Sons Ltd. Published 2019 by John Wiley & Sons Ltd.

as Beat writing or the Civil Rights movement, an attenuated focus that tended to oversimplify the social and political complexities that framed the broad arc of American literature. Leaders of the European Association of American Studies spoke of feeling "betrayed" when Ronald Reagan became president in 1981, but this sense of betrayal arose only because their foreshortened cultural perspective had idealized the Kennedy legacy to such an extent that it effectively repressed recognition of how religious and political conservatism has been an integral part of American culture since the days of John Winthrop.[2]

Within the United States itself, Matthiessen's *American Renaissance* sought not only to define the literary canon of nineteenth-century American literature – Emerson, Thoreau, Hawthorne, Melville, Whitman – but also to make this national culture synonymous with a progressive nation-building agenda. Poe, notoriously, was excluded from *American Renaissance* on the grounds that he was "bitterly hostile to democracy" and lacked "the moral depth" of Matthiessen's chosen authors, while popular novelists of the mid-nineteenth century such as the South Carolina novelist William Gilmore Simms, who backed the wrong side in the US Civil War, were unceremoniously disbarred.[3] *American Renaissance* was a great formative critical work, of course, but Matthiessen's ideological predilections – excluding women and African American writers, as well as Southerners – have become clearer in the years since the book's publication in 1941.

What this also suggests, in a more general sense, is that the framing and academic consolidation of American literature in the second half of the twentieth century was symbiotically intertwined with a nationalist agenda. Henry Wadsworth Longfellow, for example, was by far the most widely read poet in nineteenth-century America, and he was one who, as professor of modern languages at Harvard until 1854, enjoyed academic and critical as well as popular acclaim: Hawthorne characteristically placed him "at the head of our list of native poets."[4] Longfellow's *Song of Hiawatha* appeared in 1855, the same year as Whitman's *Leaves of Grass*, but the difference in the early reception of these two books could hardly have been greater, with *Hiawatha* selling 30 000 copies during its first six months in print, while praise for *Leaves of Grass* was much more understated and mixed. Matthiessen, finding Longfellow's work "swamped" by "European influences," dismissed his style as "gracefully decorous" and intent upon using "metrical dexterity as an ornamental exercise," and the fact that Longfellow's bust was placed in Poets' Corner at Westminster Abbey in March 1884, within two years of his death, has tended subsequently to reinforce this popular understanding of his work as overly deferential towards genteel conventions.[5] Longfellow and Whitman were both remarkable poets in their different ways, of course, but the fact that Whitman's "Song of Myself" has come to be seen as representative of an American cultural ideal while Longfellow's multilingual facility has been relatively neglected indicates clearly enough the nationalist agenda framing the academic dissemination of American literature over the past 100 years.

It is difficult in this context to underestimate the extent to which the Civil War, including both its prelude and its aftermath, shaped American writing in the nineteenth century. Many of Poe's stories, "The Masque of the Red Death" (1842) and others, are haunted by gothic anxieties about encroaching blackness that have been linked by Teresa Goddu to fears of slave uprisings among the white community in Virginia, where Poe worked as a journalist in the mid-1830s, and in other parts of the US South.[6] "The Masque of the Red Death" represents "Prince Prospero" retreating into "the deep seclusion of one of his castellated abbeys" in an effort to avoid the pestilence of "Red Death" that has struck the country, but the "ebony clock" in his chamber, along with "the blackness of the sable drapery," create a sinister world within which the nobleman's "fine eye for colors and effects" leads him imaginatively to evoke an apocalyptic landscape, where "Darkness and Decay and the Red Death held illimitable dominion over all."[7] Though Poe's story does not address racial subjugation directly, its ambience of threat and impending darkness speaks to a fear common in white communities of the antebellum period that they were liable at any moment to be overwhelmed by slave insurrections.

According to legend, Harriet Beecher Stowe, who published the bestselling *Uncle Tom's Cabin* in 1853, was subsequently greeted by Abraham Lincoln at the White House as "the little lady who started the big war," and of course Stowe's sentimental description of how African American family life was disrupted on Southern plantations was brilliantly effective in galvanizing public opinion during the years leading up to this internecine conflict. But many other writers of the 1850s dealt with sectional issues in one form or another, even if in less explicit forms. Sacvan Bercovitch, for instance, has argued that Hawthorne's *The Scarlet Letter* (1850) projects through its principled ambiguities and attention to diverging points of view a rhetoric of national consensus, through which the author attempts to accommodate widely variant viewpoints within the constitutional framework of an American national body.[8] There has also been illuminating work on how the "political symbolism" of Melville's *Moby-Dick* (1851) responds implicitly to the crisis arising from the passage in 1850 of the Fugitive Slave Act, with Melville's *Pequod* cast as a "Ship of State" and the novel attempting formally to hold together a multiplicity of conflicting strands.[9] It is true, of course, that the plot of Melville's novel follows the *Pequod*'s course into the southern hemisphere, way beyond the domestic terrain of the United States, but it is obvious enough that the author also encompasses within his capacious narrative an implicit consideration of how the contentious agenda of "Manifest Destiny" was shaping the American cultural and political scene at this time. (The shared initials between Manifest Destiny and *Moby-Dick* are probably not accidental.)

Simms's *The Cassique of Kiawah,* published in 1859 on the eve of the Civil War, similarly addresses nationalist politics in an oblique manner, through the way in which, although set in the Carolinas and Florida during the seventeenth century, it emphasizes words such as *region, locality* and *territory* so as to adumbrate a radically different version of the relationship between regionalism and federalism to the one being promoted at this time by politicians and intellectuals in the Northern states. Simms attempts here to use his representation of a constitutionally "irregular" natural world to authorize and mythologize his sense of racial difference and local specificity, as if to emphasize how slavery had thoroughly embedded itself within the imaginative life of the antebellum South.[10]

It is, of course, hardly surprising that political divisions and controversies of this kind have helped to shape American literature, but the subject as it evolved during the course of the twentieth century tended to take its direction from Abraham Lincoln's professed goal to consolidate the United States as "one national family," a nation predicated upon "territorial integrity," whose Constitution, so he argued in 1864, represented the country's "organic law."[11] Lincoln began his own career as a policer of national boundaries during the Black Hawk War, Indian skirmishes "in what was then the West," and his lifelong attempt to define and circumscribe the parameters of the nation always impelled him towards a deep suspicion of anything that might undermine the idea of such "organic" unity.[12] Lincoln's professed belief in a nation whose "perpetual" Constitution was guaranteed by "universal law," as expounded in his First Inaugural Address of 1861, was regarded with some incredulity among the political classes in London, where the political framework of the new US republic was regarded as a much more contingent and mutable phenomenon.[13] In this sense, Lincoln's frequent elevation of the Constitution and other aspects of US life to transcendent status – linked by the "mystic chords of memory" to purportedly metaphysical dimensions of the nation's past and future – was widely understood in Britain as part of the president's dim-witted folksiness and religiosity. British lawyer and historian George Wingrove Cooke wrote scathingly in the London *Times* of 7 October 1862 of how Lincoln by his Emancipation proclamation "constitutes himself a sort of moral American POPE," while even Richard Cobden, the English advocate for free trade who was generally well disposed towards the Union, described Lincoln as "intellectually inferior."[14]

Conversely, it is in large part for this metamorphosis of national identity into a transcendent idea that Lincoln has so often been celebrated in the United States itself. Whitman's famous elegy "When Lilacs Last in the Dooryard Bloomed" deliberately associates the "corpse" of the slain president, "the sweetest, wisest soul of all my days," with the "varied and ample land, the South and the North in the light" that Whitman regards Lincoln's brilliantly integrative spirit as having encompassed politically.[15] This, of course, is the same cherished land that Whitman represents Lincoln's martyred body as traversing on its final journey, and it exemplifies how American literature of the nineteenth century has often been valorized for ways in which it embodies a national spirit.

It is interesting to note how Lincoln inaugurated his political career by protecting the territory of the American West against Indian incursions, since the shadowing of white civilization by Native American cultures was one of the areas in which the US national imaginary in the nineteenth century was susceptible to radically alternative ways of mapping the world. The Indian tribes formed not simply separate communities but separate nations, and the violent clashes on the frontier at this time involved not only immediate concerns for the appropriation of land but also more abstract questions about jurisdiction and sovereignty. The US national model of extending "from sea to shining sea," which was advanced after the Civil War by the opening of a transcontinental railroad in 1869, was clearly contradicted at every turn by the presence of indigenous peoples claiming autonomy and ownership of particular localities. In addition, the template of abstract interchangeability and "democratic social space," the federal idiom of a spatial continuum across the continent that Philip Fisher took to be a constitutive feature of nineteenth-century American writers such as Whitman, would evidently be countermanded by a more particularistic idiom of national community where ownership could be attached instead to specific local landscapes.[16] Such a juxtaposition of competing versions of national identity also licenses the analytical mode of transnationalism, which characteristically situates itself at points of intersection, where competing national frameworks come into discursive conflict. Native American scholar Robert Warrior has specifically linked indigenous scholarship to "the transnational turn," arguing how the move intellectually to cross borders that was characteristic of American studies scholarship in the first decade of the twenty-first century should be seen as particularly relevant to a situation where "intellectual trade routes" criss-crossed the American continent.[17] Jodi A. Byrd has argued that it was the presence of native peoples that paradoxically enabled the "discourses of savagery, Indianness, discovery, and mapping" that underwrote the development of American Empire, with the figure of the Indian in his eyes operating as "a ghost in the system," one that reveals settler societies "to be where they are and will have been all along: colonialist."[18]

Representations of Native American culture in American literature of the nineteenth century are, of course, varied and multifarious. Writing of Longfellow's *Hiawatha* in 1855, the Boston *Daily Traveler* regretted "that our pet national poet should not have selected as a theme of his muse something higher and better than the silly legends of savage aborigines."[19] Conversely, Lydia Maria Child's first tale, "Adventure in the Woods" (1826), subverts the pattern of standard Indian captivity narratives by recognizing the standards of family love that resonate in Indian communities, while particularly applauding the fact that they "never strike children."[20] Catherine Maria Sedgwick's *Hope Leslie; or, Early Times in the Massachusetts* (1827) is another novel that seeks to bring together white settler and Native American perspectives, in her case by evoking a historical scenario – the novel is set two centuries earlier, during the early Puritan settlement – that seeks to rewrite American history as a narrative of convergence and reconciliation rather than simply conquest and dispossession.

Whatever the ideological perspective involved, it is clear that Native American culture offers a challenge to American writers of the nineteenth century in terms of the enigmas it raises, the problems of temporal and spatial layering that remain unanswered. For example, in "The Bean-Field" section of Thoreau's *Walden* (1854), the narrator mentions the arrowheads that he has turned up while hoeing, objects that show how "an extinct nation had anciently dwelt here."[21] Colin G. Calloway, in his 2008 presidential address to the American Society for Ethnohistory, aptly observed that "America for too long has suffered from a national historical narrative that is narrow and nationalistic," and he asked whether a new understanding of Native American history might do more than simply contribute to an academic subfield, but instead have the potential to "push beyond understanding Indian motivations, perspectives, and agency to try to change the big picture."[22] Just as American history itself could gain from being reframed within the more extensive temporal contours adduced by Native American time, so American literature gains in chronological scope and thematic resonance by being set alongside the alternative national boundaries of Indian culture.

The major American writer in the nineteenth century who deals most explicitly with Indian affairs is James Fenimore Cooper. Cooper's five "Leatherstocking" novels, published between 1823 (*The Pioneers*) and 1841 (*The Deerslayer*), take as their central concern the cultural conflict between an indigenous society and a colonizing power that seeks to marginalize or displace them. As Susan Mizruchi has observed, Cooper's novels should be seen as having a "metahistorical dimension," particularly "in a cultural dialogue on how history should be viewed and written," and in this sense his narratives engage implicitly with the question of how US national identity might be mapped.[23] *The Pioneers*, published in 1823, is set in 1793, just after the War of Independence, and it identifies the idea of westward pioneering with the spirit of America, at the same time as respecting Natty Bumpo's hereditary rights as a Native American. All of Cooper's Leatherstocking novels involve the prospect of reconciliation between the nation as an abstract entity and the American landscape as a natural inheritance: "we understand rifts, and rapids, and cataracts," declares the eponymous hero in *The Pathfinder* (1840), who is said to be "untempted by unruly or ambitious desires, and left to follow the bias of his feelings amid the solitary grandeur and ennobling influences of a sublime nature."[24] Pathfinder himself is identified as being somewhere in between a white man and an Indian – "There is a soul and a heart under that redskin, rely on it" – and his relationship with the daughter of Sergeant Dunham, "the only marriageable white female on this frontier," exemplifies a symbolic accommodation between urban and rural America: "For the first time, Mabel felt the hold that the towns and civilization had gained on her habits seriously weakened."[25] Pathfinder's "frank and ingenuous nature" makes him particularly impatient with the "smooth-tongued courtesy" of the treacherous Muir, and one of the themes that runs throughout Cooper's novels is the way in which a "natural frankness of manner" associated with the American national character, as *The Spy* (1821) puts it, is contrasted with European wiles and deception.[26]

This dichotomy is expressed most clearly in *The Spy*, set during the War of Independence, where the landscape of American sublimity – "What a magnificent scene ... Such moments belong only to the climate of America" – is contrasted with a genteel British manner said to be "too apt to judge from externals."[27] Cooper here satirizes how an English column manifests itself "with an accuracy that would have done them honour on a field-day in their own Hyde Park." However, the American spy Harvey Birch, whose frequent changes of military costume become revealed towards the end of the novel – "British and American uniforms hung peaceably by the side of each other" – is subsequently commended by George Washington for having acted "with a strong attachment to the liberties of America," and this suggests how Cooper's divisions between American transparency and European concealment come to be problematized as the narrative unfolds. Cooper's style of picturesque, evoking as he does "the daily rising of this great curtain of nature," suggests in itself ways in which his American natural world is framed by artifice.[28] As a student of comparative cultures, concerned not only to compare European to American but also white American to

Indian, Cooper in his novels probes the places where such binary oppositions recoil upon one another, and where identity becomes a more complex, hybrid construction.

Cooper's sense of US culture being intertwined with European models was given journalistic expression in various volumes of travel writing that derived from his experiences in Europe. *Gleanings in Europe: England* was published in 1837, after the author had undertaken no less than six visits to that country: twice in 1806–1807 as a merchant seaman, then again in 1826, 1828, and 1833 (twice). Cooper's work fed into the intense debates about national identity that were taking place in the United States during the 1830s, with the author in his preface saying that 4 July 1776 represented "a declaration of political independence, only," and that there was a need also for "mental emancipation." He acknowledges here that his "view of England" is presented "with very conflicting sensations," since on the one hand it "was the land of our fathers, and it contained, with a thousand things to induce us to love it, a thousand to chill the affections."[29] The one word Cooper selects to epitomize the "national peculiarities" of England is that it "is a country of proprieties." It is a land dominated by social rules and etiquette, where the obsession with the class "ladder" – "every one is tugging at the skirts of the person above, while he puts his foot on the neck of him beneath" – leads to an absence of any "free and generous communion," of the kind that he recognizes within the more democratic society of America.[30] Describing this "hereditary principle" that permeates British society as "offensive to human pride, not to say natural justice," Cooper also complains that Walter Scott's "prejudice" in favor of "deference to hereditary rank" is an idea that "pervades his writing."[31] Other volumes of *Gleanings in Europe* deal with France, Italy, Switzerland, and the Rhine, and in all cases Cooper compares the state of European politics to what he takes to be the challenges of the new American republic. He extols General Lafayette, for example, as a prospective president of France after the Paris revolt of 1832 and implies that social progress would involve a relation of reciprocity, whereby the political order in Europe would become more liberal and humane under American influence at the same time as a greater cultivation was disseminated within the United States through the influence of Europe.

One of the oddities of American literature as an academic field, as it has been constructed since the middle of the twentieth century, is that so much more attention has been given to fiction of the 1840s and 1850s than to that of the previous two decades. In many ways, of course, this is quite understandable, since the fiction of Hawthorne, Melville, and others has been thought to exemplify an initial flowering of the American literary idiom, but one of the attendant effects of this particular temporal focus is seriously to underestimate the significance of writing from the 1820s and 1830s, when the idea of a national identity in American literature had not yet fully crystallized. Cooper's work from this period involves a comparative analysis of American culture that derives its power from a series of deliberate discursive juxtapositions with other domains.

For example, in his novel *The Headsman; or, the Abbaye de Vignerons* (1833), set in eighteenth-century Switzerland, the author outlines the various cultural conflicts between different cantons in old Europe. He describes how romance and probity are undermined by the archaic Berne custom whereby the role of headsman, or public executioner, would descend automatically in a hereditary line. Christine, the daughter of headsman Balthazar, feels this ancient custom is a "curse" upon her family, one that impedes her marriage prospects, and Cooper's novel contemplates various issues around fate and free will, social conservatism and progressive democracy.[32] It is easy enough to see how this emphasis on local divisions within Europe comprises a cautionary tale for the new federal republic across the Atlantic. The author talks of how "the authority of Berne weighed ... imperiously and heavily on its subsidiary countries, as is usual in such cases," with "these contracted districts possessing nearly as many dialects as there are territorial divisions"; and in this sense *The Headsman* might readily be construed as an allegory of confederation, an examination of the pitfalls involved in regional friction and dissension. Symptomatically, Cooper also talks at one point about the need for a nation to possess "unity commensurate to its means" so as to enable it to have "confidence in itself," since "small and divided states waste their strength in acts too insignificant for general interest."[33] Using a comparative poetics in this way, Cooper deploys Switzerland as a foil and counterexample so as to address by implication the political destiny of modern America.

It is, consequently, not difficult to see a continuum between fictional work such as *The Headsman* and the non-fictional commentaries on social and political affairs that Cooper published in his *Gleanings in Europe* series. The concern in this non-fictional work to identify national characteristics is mirrored in the unabashed national stereotypes of *The Headsman*, where Maso, for example, is said to have "the swarthy hue, bold lineaments, and glittering eye, of an Italian."[34] To put this another way, the 1830s was a decade when many travel writers were impelled to extrapolate an idea of national essence from their peregrinations, and much writing of this era seeks deliberately to compare and contrast different cultural formations in the interests of identifying and consolidating certain emergent forms of national identity.

The other way in which Cooper's fiction engages explicitly with a wider world is through his sea novels, works such as *The Crater* (1847) and *The Sea-Lions* (1849). According to Thomas Philbrick, Cooper's sea fiction was in his own lifetime "often considered his major literary achievement," even though it is the Leatherstocking novels that have appealed most to the nationalist assumptions of traditional Americanist criticism because of how they encompass the epic foundation of a society grounded upon the integration of Native Americans into the civic realm.[35] By contrast, the plot of *The Crater* revolves around the discovery of a new island in the Pacific and its sudden disappearance after a volcanic eruption on the ocean floor, an event that puts paid to the attempts of American governor Mark Woolston to establish on this Pacific island a new utopian colony. Written during the American war with Mexico, *The Crater* refers darkly to "outrages" against US national dignity, with the novel itself exemplifying Cooper's conservative fears about the potentially destructive tendencies of an overextended American public realm: "Were the people of the United States confined to one-half the territory they now occupy," observes the narrator of *The Crater*, "there can be little question that they would be happier, more powerful, more civilized, and less rude in manners and feelings."[36] *The Sea-Lions*, which focuses on a hunting expedition to Antarctica, similarly plays off home comforts against the disorienting seascape of the southern hemisphere, within whose orbit everything is reversed. Mary Pratt promises to marry mariner Roswell Gardiner if he comes to subscribe to the "law of faith" through exposure to the scenery of the "planet" that gives him "a just sense of his real position in the scale of created beings," and in this sense the frozen Antarctic landscape becomes a site of pastoral transformation, one that fundamentally consolidates Gardiner's understanding of the meaning of "home."[37] Margaret Cohen has suggested that the inherently "terrestrial bias of novel studies" has traditionally privileged questions of social interaction within particular local or national communities rather than movement across the "horizons of the globe," but Cooper's sea novels introduce an extraterritorial, planetary dimension that complements the social nuances portrayed in his other writing.[38]

The standardized alignment of the nineteenth-century American literary canon with an implicitly nationalist agenda is never shown to less advantage than in the critical marginalization of Washington Irving's skillfully double-edged narratives, which were published around the same time as Cooper's novels. Emerson characteristically upbraided Irving for lacking "nerve and dagger," but Irving's style of romantic irony and sophisticated self-deprecation was shaped by intellectual paradigms drawn from a complex pattern of transatlantic influences, ranging from the German romantics (Schlegel, Schiller) through to Byron, and Irving's self-effacing style should not simply be associated with any kind of personal pusillanimity.[39] Most of the scholarly attention that was paid to Irving in the twentieth century tended to focus on his few stories that are set in rural American landscapes, particularly "Rip Van Winkle" and "The Legend of Sleepy Hollow," in both of which the author juxtaposes an environment of nostalgic tranquility against a reluctant need to confront social and political change. However, the majority of Irving's narratives unfold either overseas – most of the scenes in the very popular *Sketch Book* (1819–1820) are set in England, while *Tales of the Alhambra* (1832) is located in Moorish Spain – or in situations where the territory remains inchoate and unmapped. It is the latter milieu that frames Irving's *Astoria, or Anecdotes of an Enterprize beyond the Rocky Mountains*, published in 1836, where the focus is on military conflicts and commercial struggles among fur traders around the town of Astoria in the Pacific Northwest during the War of 1812 between Britain and America.

Irving's imagination thus responded in a luminous fashion to situations of radical instability and uncertainty, where grand theoretical designs were liable to be punctured by the contingent march of events. His *History of New York* (1809) was described by Robert A. Ferguson as "the first American book to question directly the civic vision of the Founding Fathers," since it uses a dynamic of burlesque humor to interrogate the abstract principles upon which the revolutionary theory of independent governance was grounded.[40] Ferguson argued that Irving's deflationary humor in *A History of New York* seeks deliberately to cast aspersions on the idealist visions of "William the Testy," a fictionalized version of Thomas Jefferson, with Irving consequently doubting that the etiolated designs of an abstract republican democracy of the kind envisioned by Jefferson could ever be based sufficiently in empirical common sense or social custom. Using the double bind of German romantic irony as his *modus operandi*, Irving effectively subjects the utopian rhetoric of the New World to an aesthetic of defacement and despoilment, one predicated not merely upon a carnivalesque predilection for degradation, but on a more detached skepticism about the inherent wisdom of revolutionary ideals.

Another important work by Irving that has been badly neglected in recent times is his *Life and Voyages of Christopher Columbus* (1828), on which the author worked for 14 hours a day during 1826 and 1827, a schedule that quite belies the popular image of him as a gentlemanly idler, what Lewis Leary patronizingly called a "man of limpid style."[41] The brilliance of *Christopher Columbus* lies in its internalization of the burlesque principle that permeated Irving's earlier writing and its representation of global discovery as being based on a series of accidents, where the mariner thought he was sailing to "the extremity of Asia" and ended up finding America.[42] By highlighting the absurdity of Columbus's belief that present-day Florida was Japan, Irving does not demean Columbus but rather represents him as the epitome of a world where progress emerges through hazard rather than destiny. Whereas other nineteenth-century American historians such as Francis Parkman and George Bancroft were interested in how a sense of Manifest Destiny shaped the American spirit, Irving understands national narratives through a prism not of patriotic uplift but of ontological irony. In this sense, Irving deploys burlesque to empty out what he takes to be the puffed-up assumptions of American cultural institutions in the first half of the nineteenth century.

The integration of American transcendentalism into the mainstream of US cultural life reached such a high point during the second half of the twentieth century that many of Emerson's more quotable aphorisms – a man's wisdom is to "hitch his wagon to a star," and so on – were readily incorporated into high school commencement addresses and the like.[43] Emerson's prose essays, of course, have their pragmatically optimistic side, one that goes along with their philosophical skepticism, and it is not wrong to understand Emerson – in celebrated lectures such as "The American Scholar" (1837), "The Divinity School Address" (1838), and so on – as a proselytizer for patriotic values. "We have listened too long to the courtly muses of Europe," he famously declares in the former essay, adding that the scholar in America risks becoming "decent, indolent, complaisant," with "tragic consequence." Emerson recommends that American intellectuals, instead of being "cowed" by tradition, remake the world according to their own designs. "It is," he says, "a mischievous notion that we are come late into nature; that the world was finished a long time ago. As the world was plastic and fluid in the hands of God, so it is ever to so much of his attributes as we bring to it."[44] This justifies not only political and cultural independence but also an ethic of self-reliance, another of Emerson's famous themes, along with a reluctance to accept on authority any wisdom not corroborated by an individual's own experience.

Yet there is another side to Emerson's chameleonic intellectual style, one that in his 1835 lecture on Chaucer specifically repudiates the idea of originality: "There never was an original writer. Each is a link in an endless chain ... The greatest genius will never be worth much if he pretends to draw exclusively from his own resources."[45] In another 1835 lecture on medieval romance, "The Age of Fable," Emerson refers proprietorially to "our native English tongue," thereby positioning himself in a line of continuity with an historical tradition of English language and literature.[46] This is not to indict Emerson, since self-contradiction was an integral part of his own universalist aspirations, as it was for other transcendentalists. "Do I contradict myself?," asks Whitman in "Song of Myself": "Very well then, I contradict myself. / (I am large, I contain multitudes.)"[47]

Emerson's later writings, and particularly his 1860 essay "Fate," also postulate a markedly darker version of cognitive processes than a reader would infer from his essays of the 1830s and 1840s.

My point is simply that by foregrounding a highly selective version of Emerson's writings, American critics in the wake of Matthiessen have tended to institutionalize a partial version of Emerson as patriot and an advocate for independence, one not justified by a wider reading of his works. Although of course the consolidation of Emerson as a canonical figure after World War II did much to align the spirit of American literature with the public domain, it also had the detrimental effect of commodifying Emerson, packaging him within a few easily accessible nuggets rather than attending to the wider complexity of his oeuvre.

The same civic service was performed for Hawthorne's *The Scarlet Letter* (1850), which became a standard text in high schools because of its combination of literary prestige with what was for American teenagers an attractive portrait of Hester Prynne as a rebel against conventional religious authorities. As Lauren Berlant has shown in her work on how *The Scarlet Letter* was appropriated as a "utopian" vehicle, the multiple contradictions framing Hester's appearance within the theocratic community of seventeenth-century Salem, Massachusetts, tended to romanticize Hester's agency and consequently to downplay the incommensurability of interpretation that runs all the way through Hawthorne's novel.[48] One of the curiosities in teaching this novel is that undergraduate students sometimes assume, at least initially, that the events portrayed in it are contemporaneous with Hawthorne's own time rather than taking place 200 years earlier, and students often also overlook the way in which Hawthorne specifies the transatlantic provenance of his characters and their status in Boston as newly arrived "English emigrants." Governor Bellingham's "heirlooms," for example, have been "transferred hither from the Governor's paternal home" in England, while Arthur Dimmesdale's "scholar-like renown still lived in Oxford."[49] Hawthorne's structurally ambivalent text negotiates these multiple positions, of course, just as his last completed novel *The Marble Faun* (1864) plays off the cultural values and belief systems of New England characters (Kenyon, Hilda) against the states of aesthetic hybridity and ethical corruption associated here with the Old World figures of Rome. As Henry James observed in his pioneering critical work *Hawthorne* (1879), the "Puritan conscience" represented Hawthorne's "natural heritage," but the author's "relation to it was only, as one may say, intellectual; it was not moral and theological."[50] In its portrayal of idealistic New England protagonists trying to come to terms with the "labyrinth of darkness" embedded in Italian culture, *The Marble Faun* refuses closure in the way it establishes a sustained dialogue between cross-cultural perspectives. Indeed, Hawthorne's style of radical openness and ambiguity in this novel infuriated so many readers that the author was moved to add a "postscript" to the book's second edition, in response to what he called the general "demand for further elucidations respecting the mysteries of the story."[51]

The peculiar quality of *The Marble Faun* thus lies in the way it takes the more abstract aspects of New England transcendentalism – Emerson's idealism, Thoreau's asceticism, Whitman's solipsism – and investigates how such qualities might intersect with a fully incarnated social and historical context. In this sense, it is not dissimilar thematically to Hawthorne's earlier novel *The Blithedale Romance* (1851), which also considers how the idea of a utopian community might operate within a more mundane, embodied world of ordinary human jealousy and passion. *The Blithedale Romance* confines itself specifically to conflicts within the New England community whereas *The Marble Faun* extends its geographic range much more widely, but by foregrounding questions of artistic form in the latter novel – Miriam is a painter, Kenyon a sculptor – Hawthorne's novel implicitly interrogates the extent to which aesthetic substance can incorporate the full range of human experience across time and space. Hawthorne's characters here find themselves becoming enmeshed in statuesque legends, customs, and prototypes from all periods of Roman culture whose fate they cannot evade, so that *The Marble Faun* might almost be said to turn upon a discourse of archeology, constantly uncovering the sediments of time so as to bring, as the novel puts it, "the remoteness of a thousand years ago into the sphere of yesterday." There is a detailed account of archeological activities in Chapter 45 of the novel, a description of grappling with "earth-mounds" and "heaped-up marble and granite," together with an acknowledgment of the opacities and obscurities endemic to this attempt to recover fragments of the past.[52] In this sense, the valiant attempts on the part of Hawthorne's American characters to infuse history with a distinct teleological spirit, to read it transcendentally, are traversed textually by a penumbra of archeological indecipherability. Whereas in his journals Hawthorne often plays the role of an American diplomatic politician intent upon boosting national self-esteem, in this final novel he more ambitiously examines ways in which the inherited cultural assumptions of America and Europe intersect with each other in an unresolved dialectical tension.

All of Hawthorne's work, then, involves transatlantic dialogues of one kind or another. Writing of *Our Old Home*, Hawthorne's 1863 account of his travels in England, James noted Hawthorne's propensity to take delight in chronicling various aspects of English life, while "insisting, with a perversity that both smiled and frowned, that they rubbed him mainly all the wrong way."[53] *Our Old Home* contrasts what Hawthorne takes to be an American "modern instinct ... towards 'fresh woods and pastures new'" with the "heavy air" of typical English attachment to "a spot where the forefathers and fore-mothers have grown up together, intermarried, and died ... till family features and character are all run in the same inevitable mould," and he also asks pointed questions in *Our Old Home* about what he perceives as the gross inequities of the British class system, contrasting an "aristocratic" wedding with a similar event among the "ragged people": "Is, or is not, the system wrong that gives one married pair so immense a superfluity of luxurious home, and shuts out a million others from any home whatever? One day or another, safe as they deem themselves, and safe as the hereditary temper of the people really tends to make them, the gentlemen of England will be compelled to face this question."[54] Just as Mark Twain's *The Innocents Abroad* (1869), his account of a trip through Europe, takes pleasure in defining notions of American integrity through comically contrasting them with Italian corruption – noting how more than one Italian church claims to possess relics from John the Baptist, he remarks dryly: "we could not bring ourselves to think St John had two sets of ashes" – so Hawthorne, like other nineteenth-century American writers, articulates an idea of national probity through an engagement with, and a dialectical resistance to, transnational models.[55] Hawthorne comments in *Our Old Home* on how he "grew better acquainted with many of our national characteristics" during his time in England, and this is because his recognition of American identity emerged reflexively, or, in his own words, was "brought more strikingly out by the contrast with English manners."[56]

Given their commitment to a model of Platonic inclusiveness, then, the transcendentalists willingly embraced ironies and contradictions of all kinds. Whitman, who in "Song of Myself" attempted to expand his own personality into a synecdoche for the United States at large, proposed in "Salut au Monde" (1856) to extend this gargantuan spirit across the entire globe. However, as Dana Phillips has observed, "Whitman's racial politics are more complicated, more conflicted ... than his reputation for a broad and easy tolerance of others suggests," and "Salut au Monde" postulates an implicit hierarchy of races, counterpointing his own incarnation of global geography – "Within me latitude widens, longitude lengthens" – against other races that he represents here as altogether inferior: "the swarms of Pekin, Canton, Benares, Delhi, Calcutta, Tokio," the "Austral negro," the "dwarf'd Kamtschatkan," all of whom are for Whitman the "menials of the earth."[57] Other Whitman poems of the 1860s, such as "A Broadway Pageant" and "A Passage to India," implicitly celebrate the growth and development of US commerce and its capacity to gain a hegemonic position in world trade markets. Whitman in this sense anticipates what was to become a familiar stance in American political rhetoric over the next 150 years, where the aggrandizement of US cultural values was elided into a progressive vision for the whole world. Just as Whitman welcomed the opening of Pacific trade routes as a global rather than a specifically national event, so successive American presidents have promoted the circulation of open markets and the values associated with them as a guarantor of liberal enlightenment and testimony to the power of individual choice, in social as well as economic affairs.

All of the mid-nineteenth-century writers canonized by Matthiessen enjoy a similarly paradoxical relation to global and national concerns, since they address themselves overtly to planetary issues but refract them overtly through nationalistic agendas. To think of Melville in relation to American world literature is not at all anomalous, since all of his works chart complex correlations between local scenes and the wider sphere. *Moby-Dick*, though it starts out in a provincial whaling community in Nantucket, traverses the oceans in a way that parallels intellectually Melville's aspiration to rival the discursive range of the classical philosophers and writers he cites as prefatory "extracts" to his novel. Yet Melville's troubled interaction with the world of American criticism exemplifies the difficulties he encountered in attempting to negotiate a path between national and transnational engagement. Although his first novel *Typee* (1845) was eulogized by Evert Duyckinck and the patriotic "Young America" movement that was strongly influenced by Duyckinck for the way it opened up the Pacific Ocean to an American voice, these Young America critics were considerably less enthusiastic about the way in which Melville's later fictional narratives, such as *Mardi* (1849) and *Moby-Dick* itself, seemed increasingly to deviate from scenes of the familiar into more obscure metaphysical realms. Melville experienced a great deal of difficulty with American publishers in the 1850s, even going so far as to allow *Pierre* (1852) to be edited in the interests of making the book (supposedly) more accessible to a domestic audience. At the time of Melville's death in 1891, he was more or less forgotten as a writer in the United States, and his rediscovery early in the twentieth century arose partly because of the enthusiasm of a group of acolytes based in England, centered around Leicester lawyer James Billson, who fervently championed the virtues of his writing. This revival in Melville's critical fortunes also owed much to the way in which his idiomatic complexities and ambiguities were given a new lease of life by the interest in modernist aesthetics that developed after World War I, and indeed D.H. Lawrence's *Studies in Classic American Literature* (1923) was one of the first critical works to take Melville's fractured style as symptomatic of an American cultural condition more generally.[58]

It is all the more ironic, then, that New Historicist readings of Melville that developed during the 1980s tried to circumscribe him again within a domestic circumference, this time typically through the critical matrix of slavery. It is true, of course, that Melville's texts engage in various ways with race and slavery, as indeed they engage with many different aspects of American domestic politics. But his aim was always to interrogate received beliefs, to take conventional wisdom as a starting point for further scrutiny rather than as a discursive *fait accompli*, a quizzical position epitomized by the enigmatic remark of the narrator Ishmael in *Moby-Dick*: "Who ain't a slave? Tell me that."[59] Ranging across various types of slavery, from racial to economic to ontological, *Moby-Dick* resists any fixed position, just as Melville's neglected epic poem *Clarel* (1876) sends its fictional protagonists across the seas to explore the ossified institutions of Europe and the sanctified sites of the Holy Land. Even Melville's novella *Billy Budd*, which was found among the author's papers and published after his death, encapsulates a deliberately comparative perspective, since the action here is set aboard a British Royal Navy ship at the time of the Napoleonic Wars and contemplates ways in which sexuality has become sublimated into discourses of established authority and power.

By using transnational vantage points to gain distance upon particular scenarios, Melville specifically avoided reducing psychological and social questions to issues deriving merely from local politics. The representation of Captain Vere in *Billy Budd* in terms of his repressed attraction to the midshipman gains all the more intensity for the way in which it becomes aligned with British imperial power, as though the empire itself were based upon a complex intercalation of patriotic and erotic fantasies. Melville hence exploited his background as an American novelist not simply to write about America, but to appropriate America in order to approach world events from an alternative angle of vision. Unlike Hawthorne, who worked for a while as American consul in Liverpool and who was always able to accommodate himself to normative expectations, Melville's narrative genius was linked to a style of radical skepticism, one that led him compulsively to turn any given social equation on its head. If Hawthorne was a social conservative whose fictional narratives expose themselves to liberal ambiguities, Melville was a psychological anarchist whose humdrum everyday life as a customs inspector for the city of New York – a routine he started in 1866 and followed for 19 years, unable to make a living from his writings – ran alongside a radical desire to subvert the tenets of all domestic orthodoxies.

It is easy to forget that Melville began his career as a writer in a United States that looked cartographically very different from how it appeared in the postbellum period, with his career spanning the age in which the

United States became geographically and politically consolidated into the transcontinental model that we recognize today. When, for example, Richard Henry Dana published his account of California in *Two Years Before the Mast: A Personal Narrative of Life at Sea* (1840), he was writing about a place that was still legally part of Mexico. Dana's characteristic comments on the shiftless Spaniards – "The Californians are an idle, thriftless people, and can make nothing for themselves" – derive in part from the author's deliberate counterpointing of Yankee industry with Catholic sloth, an opposition that emerges from Dana's distinct sense of Boston as "home" and the West Coast as a region where Americans are regarded as "foreigners."[60]

Again, the outcome of the US war with Mexico that took place in the late 1840s, together with the consequences of the Civil War that reconstructed the nation after 1865 in its current geographic formation, have tended historically to obscure the extent to which America in the mid-nineteenth century was a collection of disparate political territories rather than a unified national domain. When the English military explorer and spy George Ruxton published his novel *Life in the Far West* in 1848, many American readers imagined that it had been written by an indigenous Rocky Mountain trapper, rather than an agent who was intent upon reconnoitering the landscape and sending back reports to London about US designs on the Oregon Territory. Although the Young America movement tried to promote the idea that US national destiny was always designed to manifest itself in particular ways, this pressure group came into being at a time when many in America believed that the "natural" western boundary of the United States was in fact the Rocky Mountains rather than the Pacific Ocean. During the 1840s, the British consul to California, intent upon preserving British imperial trade with China and the Far East, was sending back urgent messages to the Peel government in London about the strategic importance of making sure the United States did not obtain control of the port of San Francisco.

3.2   Slavery's Global Compass

Although nineteenth-century American literature emerged from a context where nationalist agendas were paramount, it also unfolded within a framework within which alternative transnational spaces provided crucial zones of alterity within which US domestic values were held up to reflexive scrutiny. In this sense, transnationalism is carried over from specific historical contexts into the more amorphous realms of literary form and genre. Transatlanticism does not just affect the particular scenes that fiction describes but also the ways in which they are artistically organized. When Frederick Douglass's first autobiographical narrative appeared in 1845, his account of what he calls his "escape from slavery" – with facts about the Underground Railroad ostentatiously suppressed so as not, said Douglass in his most tantalizing style, to "induce greater vigilance on the part of slaveholders" – was compared to Dickens's *Oliver Twist* and Eugène Sue's *Mysteries of Paris* as an example of how gothic writing could flourish in a real-life American setting.[61] The racial milieu of the United States, as Richard Wright was to observe in the introduction to his novel *Native Son* (1940), provided a situation "dense and heavy enough to satisfy even the gloomy broodings of a Hawthorne," with Wright going on to observe that "if Poe were alive, he would not have to invent horror; horror would invent him."[62] The intertwining of slave narratives with this gothic style suggests how some of the commercial success of these narratives among nineteenth-century readers was linked not so much to virtuous abolitionist sentiment but to the entertainment value typically associated with lurid representations of violence and bondage.

The sense of distance associated with the gothic genre can be seen as a parallel to the strategic distance employed by African American writers so as to gain perspective on their native territory. For example, William Wells Brown wrote and published *Clotel; or, The President's Daughter* (1853), the first published novel by an African American, during a series of anti-slavery lectures in England, with the author signing his preface to the novel from "22, Cecil Street, Strand, London." Brown's novel addresses cultural and economic circuits linking France to "the slave-market" of New Orleans, where Mary is purchased by a "French gentleman" who takes her away to Europe: "We can but blush for our country's shame," concludes the narrator, "when we recall to mind the fact, that while George and Mary Green, and numbers of other fugitives from American slavery, can receive protection from any of the governments of Europe, they cannot return to their native land without becoming slaves."[63] By using France as a site for the reunion of George and Mary in *Clotel*, Brown inverts the transatlantic paradigm of French aristocrat Alexis de Tocqueville, who in the two volumes of his *Democracy in America* (1835, 1840) extolled a certain slanted version of New World democracy. Whereas de Tocqueville idealized American liberalism, the African American radical Brown conversely looked to France as a guarantor of basic human liberties. As Bill Marshall has noted, New Orleans itself became a "haven" for various groups of French political exiles at various times in the post-Revolutionary era – royalists in the 1790s, anti-bonapartists after 1799, bonapartists after 1815, republicans after 1848 – and this again suggests how the new United States not only located itself within transatlantic horizons but responded in distinctively transnational ways to political events as they unfolded.[64]

In this way, the African American narratives of Brown and Frederick Douglass, no less than the canonical novels of Hawthorne and Melville, appropriate the European cultural landscape as a kind of mirror site, an alternative space in both a literal and a figurative sense, where social patterns are organized differently.[65] In his introduction to *Clotel*, Brown mentions how it "has been for years thought desirable and advantageous to the cause of Negro emancipation in America, to have some talented man of colour always in Great Britain, who should be a living refutation of the doctrine of the inferiority of the African race." The inverse dynamics of these British colonial scenes enable such American authors to highlight, by contrast, the specificity of their US cultural experience. The self-consciously intertextual aspects of these transatlantic parallelisms serve simultaneously to align American literature with long-established cultural models and also to illuminate particular junctures at which these models diverge rather than converge. Susan Warner's novel *The Wide, Wide World* (1850), true to the global proclivities of its title, has scenes where the American heroine Ellen Montgomery visits Scotland, thereby allowing Warner to play off the aristocratic Lady Keith's snobbish attitude towards "thick-headed and thicker-tongued Yankees" against the more democratic virtues of American fellow feeling. Warner thus contrasts European obfuscations of sentiment, epitomized in the novel by the "crooked ways" of the Edinburgh urban landscape, with American openness and transparency, as if again to reinforce the virtues of American domestic security by contrasting it with the more sinister dimensions of global space.[66]

Contrary to the kind of compartmentalized literary scholarship that has emphasized the establishment of separate national traditions, then, the cultural links between different sides of the Atlantic during the nineteenth century should be seen as amorphous and free-flowing. The farcical drama *Our American Cousin*, which was written by English dramatist Tom Taylor and which features an American going to England to claim his family estate, was premiered in 1858 not in London but in New York, with the play subsequently achieving notoriety when Abraham Lincoln was assassinated in 1865 during a performance at Ford's Theater in Washington DC. The broad popularity of this play's leading character, the dim-witted aristocrat Lord Dundreary, exemplifies the extent to which transatlantic cultural relations became a fixed point of reference within US popular consciousness during this era. Victorian Americans often experienced a love-hate relationship with the apparatus and iconography of the British establishment, taking delight in mocking them, but also bound up magnetically in their colonial (or postcolonial) orbit. Elisa Tamarkin has written of how many high-minded American abolitionists from the Boston area in the middle of the nineteenth century sought associations in England from motivations of pleasure as much as morality, traveling to the old country so as to combine "reforming zeal" with "having fun."[67] Indeed, on her trip to Britain in 1853, Harriet Beecher Stowe was entertained as a visiting dignitary at the Duchess of Sutherland's palatial country house, where the guests included all the great and the good from English society: Lord and Lady Palmerston, Lord John Russell, William Gladstone, and many others. Although she later wrote a famous indictment of Lord Byron's sexual misconduct, Stowe also admired the radical English poet – the reformist hero of her 1856 novel *Dred: A Tale of the Great Dismal Swamp*, Edward Clayton, is described there as "quite Byronic" – and Stowe herself in many ways shared Byron's appetite for public fame and recognition.[68]

Just as (much to the chagrin of the author himself) the works of Charles Dickens were reprinted cheaply in America because of the absence of an international copyright agreement, which was not signed until 1891, so Stowe's *Uncle Tom's Cabin; or, Life Among the Lowly* (1852) was an even bigger seller in Britain than in America, in part because the London publishers, owing no royalties to the author, could afford to offer it so cheaply. Indeed, when Stowe toured Britain in 1853, the suggestion surfaced that each reader should contribute one penny to compensate her for these lack of earnings, a scheme that eventually enabled her to return to America with more than $20000 in her pocket. On this 1853 London visit, Stowe was also guest of honor at a banquet hosted by the Lord Mayor of London, where she was seated opposite Dickens. The two celebrated novelists were held up in a toast at the banquet as "having employed fiction as a means of awakening the attention of the respective countries to the condition of the oppressed and suffering classes."[69] Although in an earlier 1843 essay Stowe had expressed some reservations about Dickens's tendency to make light of religion, the two authors shared a commitment to melodramatic forms of public address that garnered a wide readership, due in no small part to their skillful exploitation of commercial fictional forms. Particularly in *Dred*, where she delights in making fun of narrow-minded theologians who seek to justify the practices of slavery on philosophical grounds, Stowe internalizes a Dickensian property of burlesque whose aesthetic impulse is linked to the way it conjoins the commodified form of the serial novel – where, because of the structural discontinuities necessarily involved in the reading experience, the portrayal of characters has to be flattened to make them instantly recognizable – with a capacity for broad popular humor.

This comic style effectively differentiates Stowe from George Eliot, with whom the American author is more frequently compared, not only because of their shared gender but also because of their explicit mutual commitments to an ethics of social reform. Stowe and Eliot never actually met, but they corresponded over many years, with Stowe, as she recalled in her autobiographical *Life of Harriet Beecher Stowe* (1889), trying as late as the 1870s to persuade Eliot to pay a visit to the "orange shades" of her home in Florida. But although they both came from Nonconformist backgrounds and were concerned to subject society to intense moral scrutiny, these two authors approached their material in very different ways, with Stowe advising the English author that what *Middlemarch* fatally lacked was "jollitude," something the American writer claimed to be characteristic of "our tumble-down, jolly, improper, but joyous country." Stowe casts herself in this transatlantic correspondence as a proselytizer for American popular culture – "You write and live on so high a plane," she complains to Eliot – whereas Eliot herself holds to the cultural high ground by telling Stowe "that if a book which has any sort of exquisiteness happens also to be a popular, widely circulated book, the power over the social mind for any good is, after all, due to its reception by a few appreciative natures, and is the slow result of radiation from that narrow circle."[70] The English author was consequently wedded to an unabashedly elitist conception of metropolitan influence filtering slowly into the wider community, while Stowe was far more immersed in, and committed to, a broader domain of market forces, whose circulation she understood in traditional American terms as a power for good.

George Eliot nevertheless reviewed *Dred* very positively in the *Westminster Review* in 1856, calling it "a great novel" even while specifically declining to comment on its "political" pertinacity. What Eliot admired about *Dred* was not its position on what she called "the terribly difficult problems of Slavery and Abolition," but the fact that it retained a "keen sense of humor" and a strong "dramatic interest," something she found "all the more remarkable" given that the novel was clearly "animated by a vehement polemical purpose." In this sense, Stowe's "rare genius," in Eliot's eyes, lay in her capacity for encompassing "a national life in all its phases – popular and aristocratic, humorous and tragic, political and religious."[71] It was *Dred*'s multifaceted quality, rather than its narrowly evangelical spirit, that appealed to Eliot's artistic and critical imagination. Her recognition of Stowe's versatility as a novelist is commensurate with a key attribute of *Dred*, which is the way its author reconfigures the American South within a comparative context. The novel is set largely on a plantation in North Carolina, but Stowe is generally sympathetic towards her fictional slave-owning family, the Claytons, who are represented here as well-meaning reformers. Of course, such sympathy also goes along here with vituperative satire, with the vicious young white master, Tom Gordon, being treated by the author as harshly as he himself treats his own slaves. But, as Eliot observed, it is the "genius" of Stowe to enter into the spirit of her various characters and to allow us as readers to see the world through their eyes.

This is why a comparative aesthetic was entirely consistent with Stowe's overall moral design, which involves exposing enclosed minds and entrenched conventions to alternative points of view. The behavior of Tom Gordon, remarks the author, has suffered over the years from "the secluded nature of the plantation" on which he was born and bred.[72] Consequently, one significant trajectory of *Dred* is linked to the novel's ever-expanding geographical range, starting from the "secluded" plantations of the South but subsequently bringing into play Canada, to where Edward Clayton eventually emigrates, and New York, to where he helps his former slaves escape. In *Uncle Tom's Cabin*, published four years earlier, Stowe had suggested a migration of African Americans to Liberia as a possible long-term solution to the nation's racial problems, whereas in the more legalistic and politicized world of *Dred* no such general exodus or utopia is envisaged. Indeed, the outlaw Dred himself raises in this latter book a more overt prospect of insurrectionary violence, and in this sense the novel projects a distinctly darker vision of American racial affairs on the eve of the Civil War.

Conceptually, however, what is most noticeable about *Dred* is its receptiveness to the possibility of transformation of every kind, its acknowledgment of how the current history and geography of the United States comprise only contingent narratives. Edward Clayton's friend Frank Russel, for example, talks of the Southern aristocracy's plan to extend their slave-holding empire by annexing Cuba and the Sandwich Islands, while he also describes the idea of American liberty as one of those "agreeable myths" which "will not bear any close looking into," since "Liberty has generally meant the Liberty of me and my nation and my class to do what we please."[73] While *Dred* does not entirely endorse Russel's cynicism, it is, in its textual openness to displacement, generally hospitable to his capacity for envisaging the encrusted state of the material world from radically different perspectives.

Although there has been widespread scholarly concern over the past 50 years to renew the visibility of both slavery as a phenomenon and the place of African American literature within the US literary canon, this has not always been associated with the ambition to relocate American literature within a wider world. The initial impetus to institutionalize Frederick Douglass in the American literary canon in the 1970s was linked primarily to the renewed visibility and popularity of his first autobiography, *Narrative of the Life of Frederick Douglass* (1845). For critics in the Civil Rights era still working within the academic framework established by Matthiessen's *American Renaissance*, it became relatively easy to establish Douglass as the missing racial element within the orbit of an American literary nationalism thought to be centered on the masculine genius of a heroic transcendentalism. We know that Douglass read and admired Emerson, and there are indeed many structural parallels between the writings of Emerson (and Thoreau) and Douglass's 1845 *Narrative*.[74] There is a similar stress on self-reliance, on a quest for personal freedom; there is an emphasis on oratorical power and emotional authenticity, generated in part by Douglass's performances on the abolitionist lecture circuit in the early 1840s under the patronage of the white reformer William Lloyd Garrison; there is a philosophical temper of idealism, whereby, in dramatically dualistic terms, the "dark night" of slavery is contrasted with an image of unfettered freedom, sailing ships "robed in purest white, so delightful to the eye of freemen."[75] Although the *Narrative* of course inflects racial politics differently than transcendentalism, its underlying rhetorical strategies involving a passage from bondage to freedom are curiously similar, and, not surprisingly, various critics have commented on how this work appropriates familiar tropes of the American literary tradition. Joseph Fichtelberg has compared it to a "Christian conversion" narrative, whereby the narrator's physical battle with his slave-breaker, Covey, is presented as "the turning-point in my career as a slave" (p. 65), while Henry Louis Gates Jr has associated Douglass's depiction of his flight and passage to self-realization with US black literature's seemingly "great, unique theme" of escape from bondage.[76]

It is, then, easy to see why Douglass's first autobiography should have been quickly canonized as the most representative of the slave narratives, an African American version of a literary declaration of independence. The fact that the *Narrative* also sold very well – 11 000 copies between 1845 and 1847, with nine editions in Britain during these first two years of its publication – also helped to consolidate its representative status, since it could be said to bridge the more abstract, philosophical discourses characteristic of transcendentalism with the broader appeal of a more sentimental literary tradition that, thanks in no small part to changes in modes of production and a dramatic increase in the number of mass-market paperbacks, was beginning to flourish during the 1840s. Douglass, like Susan Warner and Fanny Fern a few years later, skillfully manipulated his rhetoric so as to engender emotional pathos and affect, and these melodramatic aspects helped to ensure the general accessibility and popularity of the 1845 *Narrative*, its appeal to a wide range of readers, including of course those who enjoyed tales of plantation life for prurient rather than purely political purposes.

Douglass had been since 1841 a paid lecturer for Garrison's American Anti-Slavery Society (AASS), which financed the publication of his first autobiography; however, the AASS expressed a fear that the publicity generated by this work might imperil Douglass's own personal safety since, as an escaped slave, he was still liable to be legally reclaimed by his master in Maryland. The AASS consequently decided to send Douglass on a lecture tour to Britain, and it was there that, away from the immediate influence of the New England abolitionists, Douglass came to realize how tired he was of his enforced role as a theatrical performer tied to Garrison's bidding. "Instead of the bright, blue sky of America," Douglass wrote to Garrison on 1 January 1846, "I am covered with the soft, grey fog of the Emerald Isle. I breathe, and lo! The chattel becomes a man" (p. 374). Douglass had moved from being the property of a plantation owner to the property of abolitionists, and, despite his representative status within the American literary tradition, it was in fact Europe that first gave him the taste of a different kind of freedom.

Douglass left Boston on 16 August 1845 for Ireland, where he spent five months before beginning a lecture tour of Scotland in January 1846. He then toured England, joined for part of the time by Garrison, before returning to America in April 1847. During his travels, Douglass encountered a whole range of political scenarios that impelled him to think through issues of freedom and oppression within a more expansive transnational framework. Garrison saw his mission as fundamentally to change people's hearts on the slavery question, and he therefore opposed any attempt to vitiate what he perceived as the horrific impact of the slave experience by any confusion of the politics of abolition with wider issues. For Douglass, however, such forms of moral purity seemed increasingly narrow and difficult intellectually to sustain. His first lecture on foreign soil, in Dublin on 31 August 1845, was on the evils of alcohol rather than slavery, and while in Ireland he visited the jail where Daniel O'Connell had been held a couple of years earlier, as a gesture of solidarity with the Irish patriot leader who had campaigned openly against slavery. Douglass also profited financially from a second edition of his *Narrative*, published in Dublin by Webb and Chapman in 1846, with a new preface and appendix. In the latter, the author took delight in publicly ridiculing letters by A.C.C. Thompson, a native of Delaware, who had insisted that Douglass's *Narrative* was so well written it must be fraudulent, since the escaped slave with whom he was acquainted in that vicinity was called "Frederick Baily" and was "unlearned"; only an "educated man," averred Thompson solemnly, "one who had some knowledge of the rules of grammar, could write so correctly."[77] This mordant irony, which of course served to validate the authenticity of Douglass's story, helped further to boost his sense of autonomy, and he became particularly irked to learn in Dublin that Maria Weston Chapman, a doyenne of the Boston Anti-Slavery Society, had written to Dublin publisher Richard

D. Webb asking that he "keep an eye" on Douglass to make sure he would not be won over by those in the English anti-slavery movement who did not support Garrison. Douglass wrote Chapman a sharp reply, saying that he would not "tolerate any efforts to supervise and control" his activities.[78]

When Douglass moved on to Scotland, he found himself engaged in controversy, with the Free Church of Scotland, which had the previous year sent representatives to the American South on a fund-raising mission. Since the American Presbyterian Church was one of the most popular congregations in the slave states, they managed to collect for their friends and allies in the Free Church some £3000. At a meeting in Arbroath in February 1846, however, Douglass chastised the Free Church for "wallowing in the filth and mire of slavery," and he skillfully presented the argument so that "SEND BACK THE MONEY" became a familiar slogan in every town he visited in Scotland, one daubed on city walls and chanted at meetings.[79] For Douglass, this episode was an insight into the transnational tentacles of slavery, the way in which, like apartheid 100 years later, it could be implicitly sanctioned and financially supported by those who were not directly involved in its practice. While Douglass flattered his audience in Paisley, Scotland, on 18 March 1846 by asserting that "[l]iberty is commensurate with and inseparable from British soil," he also acknowledged in the same address how "slavery is such a gigantic system that one nation is not fit to cope with it," thereby suggesting again his recognition of the politics of slavery as a complicated transnational business.[80] Indeed, as he moved through Britain on his speaking tour Douglass became increasingly aware of the complex, interlocking nature of social and economic power, the ways in which slavery could not always be reduced simply to a question of what Garrison liked to call "moral suasion." In Ireland, Douglass associated slavery with the murderous poverty he witnessed there, and he also spoke at Bristol in 1846 of "political slavery in England," using the term metaphorically in association with practices in the army and navy: "Why does not England set the example by doing away with these forms of slavery at home," Douglass asked, "before it called upon the United States to do so?"[81]

All of this further alienated Douglass from Garrison, for whom the evils of racial slavery transcended everything else. Garrison was similarly hostile to the friendship Douglass struck up with the white English woman Julia Griffiths, whom he first met at a speaking engagement at her home town of Newcastle-upon-Tyne, and who, under the spell of Douglass's not inconsiderable personal charm, subsequently moved to Rochester, New York, to assist him with his work. Griffiths remained in Rochester for seven years, staying at first in the Douglass household, and there has been much (inconclusive) speculation about the exact nature of the relationship

between them. What is clear, though, is that Griffiths was extremely effi-
cient on a practical level, assuming responsibility for the financial management of Douglass's journal *North Star*, whose first issue appeared in
December 1847. The launch of the *North Star* was itself financed by
Douglass's British abolitionist friends, who between them raised $2175 to
enable him to purchase a printing press, with the journal's title deliberately evoking Feargus O'Connor's *Northern Star*, the leading paper of the
Chartist movement. Again, the Chartists were a group Douglass had
encountered while in England, and he collaborated with Chartist leaders
William Lovett and Henry Vincent in 1846 to launch publicly the new
Anti-Slavery League. Garrison was also present on that occasion, but he
objected to the practical assistance offered by British abolitionist sympa-
thizers, led by Ellen and Anna Richardson of Newcastle, who raised the
funds in 1847 to purchase Douglass's freedom from his owner, Hugh Auld
of Maryland. For Garrison and other American radicals, this amounted to
an implicit recognition of property rights in humans, something that was
anathema to their Christian conscience.

On one level, this difference of approach exemplifies the division
between Garrison's party, dedicated as it was to an eradication of slavery
in accordance with higher law, and Douglass himself, who tended politically to take more pragmatic lines. For Douglass, the end tended to justify
the means, and he had no compunction about manipulating the engines
of publicity to achieve his goals. We see this in his great admiration for
Dickens's *American Notes* (1842), to whose anti-slavery sentiments
Douglass referred during several of his speeches in England in 1846, and
later on in his admiration for Stowe's *Uncle Tom's Cabin*.

As he grew older, Douglass became above all a realist in politics, experienced at operating the levers of power, and his time in England and
Ireland helped to hone these skills by alerting him to ways in which the
ideologies of national romance – in this case, the romantic myth of
Britain as a cradle of liberty – tended to go hand in hand with a more
coercive social system, within which forces of domination and control
were played out on a more surreptitious basis. Although African
Americans such as himself were legally free in Britain in a way they were
then not in the United States, Douglass was all too aware of how British
public intellectuals such as Thomas Carlyle were linking the maintenance
of slave labor in the Caribbean to the preservation of established social
order at home, so that Douglass became sharply aware of the rhetorical
gap between words and action, between the myth of British "liberty" for
all and the realities of the country's participation in the so-called "coolie"
trade. Douglass himself was never averse to appropriating romantic
myths for useful purposes, and indeed in 1838 he had adopted his own
name from that of a heroic warrior in Walter Scott's poem *The Lady of*

the Lake (1810), apparently simply because he liked how it sounded. But whereas the 1845 *Narrative* is driven primarily by oratorical energy and sentimental affect, Douglass's writing from the 1850s onwards correlates these emotional dynamics with a more critical and reflexive understanding of the multifaceted nature of social relations.

Towards the end of his second autobiography, *My Bondage and My Freedom* (1855), Douglass looks back to what he calls his "two years of semi-exile in Great Britain and Ireland" (p. 389). That notion of "semi-exile," betokening a condition half in and half out of the United States, is significant to the larger trajectory of his later works. *My Bondage and My Freedom*, which is nearly four times as long as the earlier *Narrative*, seeks deliberately to gain more distance and perspective upon Douglass's experiences as a slave, offsetting its initial binary opposition between bondage and freedom against a much broader sense of how both these terms permeate society in different ways. It is true that *My Bondage* goes over much of the same ground as the 1845 *Narrative*, but it tends to treat its material in a more analytical and less directly personal fashion. Thus, for example, Douglass writes of how "[t]he slaveholder, as well as the slave, is the victim of the slave system" (p. 171), even if "[t]he slave is a subject subjected by others," while "the slaveholder is a subject, but he is the author of his own subjection" (p. 189). There is more political consciousness in this later autobiography – the narrator says he is not just the slave of Master Thomas, but "the slave of society at large" (p. 247) – and also more recognition of how notions of legitimacy depend upon the establishment of particular points of view: "Every slaveholder," he writes, "seeks to impress his slave with a belief in the boundlessness of slave territory, and of his own almost illimitable power" (p. 310). There is also a conceptual link between this 1855 work and what Carla Peterson has described as a general shift from first-person to third-person narrators in African American prose works written during the 1850s, when authors such as Delany and William Wells Brown sought to describe a wider social canvas by moving away from the sometimes claustrophobic confines of an autobiographical aesthetic form.[82]

All of this signaled a further move away in Douglass's writings of the 1850s from the position of Garrison and the New England radicals, who placed less emphasis on slavery as a social or institutional problem, preferring to present it in more direct personal terms as a question of individual moral choice.

Despite, then, frequent critical attempts to find points of overlap between Douglass and the transcendentalists, after the mid-1840s there were increasing points of divergence between their respective positions and projects. It is no surprise to find that when James Russell Lowell proposed Douglass as a member of Boston's Town and Country Club in

1849, he found Emerson among those reluctant to support him, since Douglass's penchant for increasingly flashy forms of self-publicity, no less than his skepticism about the ethical dimensions of politics, would have alienated him from many in the Boston intellectual firmament.[83] Conversely, Douglass became an increasingly visible and recognized leader of the African American community in the years leading up to the Civil War, and when the conflict began he kept President Lincoln under pressure to issue the Emancipation Proclamation, which finally arrived in September 1862 (to be effective from 1 January 1863). Lincoln met with Douglass three times in the White House, lauding him as "one of the most meritorious men, if not the most meritorious man, in the United States," and, in one of the last eras before the advent of electronic mass media, both leaders shared a canny proclivity and expertise in polishing their public images to ensure the widest possible exposure.[84] Like Lincoln, Douglass had by this time grown into a sophisticated political thinker, perhaps less akin in style to Emerson than to John Stuart Mill, whose seminal work *On Liberty* (1859) addressed the problem of individual freedom and social coercion within a different but parallel context. Many American slaves had fled to England after the passage of the Fugitive Slave Act in 1850, so the whole question of personal liberty and how it related to the authority of state power was a burning issue at this time on both sides of the Atlantic.

Douglass's second trip across the Atlantic came in November 1859, when a visit to England for six months had the beneficial effect of enabling him to avoid extradition to Virginia for his alleged involvement in John Brown's attack on Harpers Ferry. Like other African Americans of his time, Douglass always looked on Britain as a safe haven in legal terms, even if he believed that country's forms of social and racial oppression to be more insidious than some of those holding a candle to the memory of William Wilberforce would have cared to admit. Gilroy, whose *Black Atlantic* has strongly influenced the reconsideration of Douglass within a transatlantic context, argues that he "played a neglected role in English anti-slavery activity" but it is important to recognize how Douglass used Britain primarily to gain an alternative perspective on US society, rather than seeking to identify with British culture itself.[85]

During the second half of his career, Douglass became adept at skillfully appropriating nationalist iconography for specific political purposes. This rhetorical manipulation began with his famous "change of opinion" on the US Constitution, which Douglass announced in May 1851, and it reverberated through his speech in Rochester a year later, "What to the Slave is the Fourth of July?" (1852). In both of these instances, Douglass was seeking not simply to take an oppositional stance toward the United States, but to rotate the axis of its master narratives so as to bring patriotic narratives into alignment with African American interests. Just as Douglass was quick in the 1860s to recognize the symbolic potential of Abraham Lincoln, so in his later career he became an astute operator in the fluid world of public rhetoric.[86]

These chameleonic aspects to Douglass's life and work, however, also ensure that his specific positions on particular issues are often hard to pin down. On the question of Ireland, most notoriously, he shifted his line of argument throughout his career. During his own trip to Ireland, he expressed considerable sympathy with Daniel O'Connell and the Fenians, a group campaigning for Irish national independence, and in 1871 he remarked approvingly on the way the British Royal Family had been hissed on a visit to Dublin. The following year, he even went so far as to describe himself as "something of an Irishman as well as a negro."[87] But such equations between "Irishman" and "negro" are held firmly in check in Douglass's final autobiography, *Life and Times* (1881, revised in 1892), where he insists on dissociating civil equality (which he supported) from social equality (which he did not). Although Douglass continues here to indict British policy for the "injustice and oppression" which has reaped "bitter consequences," he also declares that any notion of an underclass, what he calls a "black Ireland in America," would be disastrous (p. 973). While continuing to honor the memory of O'Connell – whom he calls a true "transatlantic statesman" (p. 683) – Douglass is critical of a later generation of Irish leaders who, he says, tended more chauvinistically to campaign for liberty for the Irish, but not for other races. In particular, he sharply criticizes John Mitchell, an Irish emigrant who expressed pro-slavery sentiments on his arrival in America, while he also describes as one of the darkest chapters in the Civil War the riots by an Irish mob in New York in July 1863 against enlistment in the Union army, a reaction which also manifested itself here in the lynching of African Americans.

Douglass always maintained an interest in Irish affairs, hearing Prime Minister William Gladstone discuss the Irish question in Parliament during his final visit to England in 1887, and subsequently speaking himself at a meeting in Washington in support of Irish Home Rule. But, opposed as he generally was to ideas of racial essentialism, Douglass recognized how the Irish in Ireland and the Irish in America were two quite different phenomena, working within a quite different set of social circumstances and expectations.

While in principle Douglass was sympathetic to the idea of solidarity between oppressed ethnic groups, in practice he found himself forced to recognize the mutual antagonism and hostility between the Irish American and African American communities. For Douglass, different circumstances brought different political challenges, and such openness to contradiction, to a recognition of the disjunction between theory and practice, testifies to the way Douglass increasingly became a political pragmatist, with affinities in temperament and tone to Booker T. Washington. Indeed, Douglass, like Washington, became a stalwart of the Republican Party in his later years, being appointed by President Rutherford Hayes as US Marshall for the District of Columbia, where his primary task was to enforce federal court orders within the nation's capital. Douglass later held government posts in Haiti and Santa Domingo, and, although of course in the nineteenth century the Republican party was the more progressive on racial issues, it is nevertheless an oddity of cultural history that such a die-hard Republican politician was to become so closely associated with the academic agendas of multiculturalism at the end of the twentieth century. This anomaly has been generated partly by the excessive concentration on Douglass's earlier rather than his later work. *Life and Times*, in particular, is in general a philosophically conservative book, where the narrator recounts his feeling that he "had on my side all the invisible forces of the moral government of the universe" (p. 896), but where he also associates such "moral government" with a spirit of desperate struggle. Gilroy has floated the name of Nietzsche in conjunction with the later work of Douglass, and its edgy ambience would certainly appear to have more in common with the harsh world of the naturalist philosophers – Charles Darwin is mentioned in this text (p. 939) – than with the evangelical Christian faith of African American preachers such as Sojourner Truth. *Life and Times* is nearly twice as long as *My Bondage and My Freedom*, and six times as long as the 1845 *Narrative*, but that is not the only reason it has not been so frequently assigned in the American college classroom.

In the latter part of his career, then, Douglass moved further away from recycling the pieties of freedom, and more toward a recognition of race as an element within a brutal *realpolitik*, something derived in part from European cultural influences. Although there is no direct evidence that Douglass was familiar with Nietzsche or Hegel, we know that he had been introduced to the world of German philosophy by Ottilie Assing. Assing, who regarded herself as what her biographer calls Douglass's "natural" wife, came upon Douglass by reading *My Bondage and My Freedom*, and she probably began an affair with him in the 1850s, although details of this are now difficult to establish because most of Assing's letters were burnt in a fire at Douglass's house in Rochester in 1872, while his letters to her were destroyed under the terms of Douglass's will.[88] Assing, born in Hamburg, began working as an American correspondent for the German newspaper *Morgenblatt* in 1851, sending back articles on American art and culture to be published in German in Germany, and it was she who introduced Douglass to Ludwig Feuerbach, David Friedrich Strauss, and other German advocates of "Higher

Criticism," which treated Biblical narratives as myth. After reading Feuerbach's *Essence of Christianity* (1841) with Douglass, Assing wrote to the German philosopher about "the satisfaction ... of seeing a superior man won over for atheism."[89] Douglass subsequently kept busts of Feuerbach and Strauss in his study, doubtless gifts from Assing, along with portraits of abolitionist friends and heroes such as Wendell Phillips, John Brown, Abraham Lincoln, and Toussaint L'Ouverture. Assing herself translated *My Bondage and My Freedom* into German, publishing it in 1860 as *Sclaverei und Freiheit*. She and Douglass remained close friends until the 1870s, and the significance of her influence as what Christoph Lohmann calls "an atheist and freethinker" on Douglass has probably been underestimated.[90]

In his later writings, Douglass, despite his religious skepticism, follows Feuerbach and Strauss in continuing to manipulate and exploit the residual power of religious metaphors, even while emptying out their metaphysical connotations. "Men have their choice in this world," he declared in a lecture delivered at the Zion Church in Rochester on 16 June 1861: "They can be angels, or they may be demons ... The slaveholders had rather reign in hell than serve in heaven."[91] Douglass's refurbishment here of Milton's language in *Paradise Lost*, like the way he held up the language in the Declaration of Independence and the US Constitution, suggests again how he exploits the cultural force of symbolic capital without himself having any specific commitment to it as a form of positive truth. Although over the past 40 years there has been a massive critical sentimentalization of Douglass within the US academy, and appropriation of him as a spokesperson for liberal versions of identity politics, he remains in many ways a much more enigmatic and elusive figure.

The interest of Douglass's later writing, then, lies in its increasingly complicated and problematic relation to US national narratives. Whereas in the 1845 autobiography liberty is presented as antithetical to slavery, from the 1855 *My Bondage and My Freedom* onward, it is more the capacity to switch positions, to show ways in which "legally sanctioned bondage emerges as the undeniable twin of freedom," as Russ Castronovo puts it, that forms the nexus of Douglass's bifocal vision.[92] There are, of course, many conceptual corollaries for this kind of irony, including Douglass's own mixed race provenance, along with those institutional forms of repression that remained blind for so long to ways in which the American mythology of a self-made man was not only racially inflected but depended crucially upon the systematic exclusion of African Americans. In this sense, some of the power of Douglass's rhetoric derives from something like parody, from the way he sets up familiar American icons and images and forces his audience to reimagine them from an unfamiliar perspective. We see this in his famous address where he asks "[w]hat to the American slave is your Fourth of July?" (p. 434), and also in a speech delivered in New York on 4 August 1857 to commemorate the 23rd anniversary of emancipation in the British West Indies, where he travesties John Winthrop's famous sermon of 1630 by relocating the Biblical city on a hill from New England to Old England: "The day and the deed are both greatly distinguished. They are a city set upon a hill ... It has made the name of England known and loved in every Slave Cabin, from the Potomac to the Rio Grande."[93]

Although Douglass himself was famous for his parodic imitations of slave masters and pro-slavery preachers, he probably would not have been very happy with this notion of parody as a structural component of his work, since it might seem to imply a form of negativity, an undermining of conventional value, which he as a staunch American patriot would have wished to avoid. Nevertheless, it is clear that the power of Douglass's oratory depends upon an esthetic of defamiliarization, a reassignment of established ideas so that they are recast in a parallel but alien light. This is the classic type of parody as Linda Hutcheon described it, a form of "repetition" and "authorized transgression" involving "difference rather than similarity ... a method of inscribing continuity while permitting critical distance."[94] This is also the basis for the significance of Britain within Douglass's imaginative world; not only did Britain furnish him with practical assistance for his manumission and publishing projects, it also provided the metaphorical "distance" that offered a symbolic example of how the Atlantic world might be organized differently. The politics of Chartism and the question of Irish emancipation were problematic issues in themselves for all kinds of reasons, but their central importance was the way they forced Douglass to assume a position of estrangement toward the plantation culture of the Old South. The viability of the plantation, as Douglass remarked in an 1853 essay on Stowe, depended on its power systematically to exclude the outside world, to imagine itself as "a little nation of its own." Slavery wants "just to be let alone," whereas the "exposure" of its ignominies depends upon a capacity to "drag slavery out of its natural darkness" into "the light."[95] For Douglass, this process of enlightenment involved the inscription of an alternative conceptual space within which the antiquated customs of the plantation could be understood as contingent and, therefore, as reversible.

Douglass further explored this kind of relativity of perspective on his final trip to England in 1886–1887, which included side trips to Paris, Rome, and Egypt. In Avignon, he ironically commends the old papal palace for its material rather than spiritual riches, its "large and beautiful grounds" and "very pleasant" aspect, all of which in his eyes exemplify "the German proverb, 'They who have the cross will bless themselves'"

(p. 992). In Rome, Douglass talks of his "curiosity in seeing devout people going up to the black statue of St Peter," adding wryly: "I was glad to find him black, I have no prejudice against his color" (p. 1004). Douglass's grim humor here involves another example of cultural transposition; as Robert S. Levine remarks, the anecdote "speaks to his effort to 'blacken' traditional accounts of European and Christian history by questioning assumptions of whiteness."[96] The kind of parodic transvaluation apparent in Douglass's invocation of a black St Peter testifies to his proclivity for racial hybridity and mixing, and it also helps to explain his uneasiness in Egypt, where he finds acute poverty and degradation: "Egypt may have invented the plow," he observes sardonically, "but it has not improved upon the invention. The kind used there is perhaps as old as the time of Moses" (p. 1011). Constitutionally suspicious of the idea of origins, Douglass was uncomfortable with any notion of Egypt as a natural home or point of reference for African American civilization. As in his other travels, the landscapes of Africa provide a horizon of alterity against which Douglass's sense of himself as a patriotic American can be calibrated.

The alterity associated with such transnational perspectives can be correlated with Douglass's assumptions about hybridity within the African American cultural experience, which in turn might be associated with his discourse of hybridity in a stylistic sense. As Stephen Railton has argued, one of the characteristics of nineteenth-century American literature in general was the way in which, in its emphasis on the variegated skills of rhetorical "performance," it tended to draw eclectically upon the formal conventions of sermons, journals, and autobiography.[97] Douglass, like other American writers of his time, accommodated these various elements in a new generic mix. In a manuscript that John W. Blassingame dates to about 1865, Douglass discusses Emerson's comments on creative producers and poets, and he specifically asserts his interest in the "philosophy of art," refuting the claim that this is a subject "Negroes know nothing about."[98] In this sense, Douglass's art of estrangement, the way he recombines his own life story in relation to different social and philosophical dimensions, is no less consciously arranged than that of his literary contemporaries, both black and white. There is a similarity between Douglass's autobiographical idiom and Brown's novel *Clotel*, which also follows a generically mixed style in the way it blends a personal slave narrative with a parallel account of American history, reinterpreting the *Mayflower* and the presidency of Thomas Jefferson in the light of stories about his illegitimate slave children.

Clotel brings together lecture, fiction, and history in equal measure, and Douglass's writings from the same period have a similar kind of esthetic momentum in the way they project the speaker's rhetorical voice into ever more complicated, self-alienating scenarios. Rather than simply repeating his life story, Douglass continued to experiment by situating his persona within a range of intellectual contexts, to explore different ways in which the African American subject might appear if slavery were to be represented in relation to violence, or eroticism, or politics, or (especially in *Life and Times*) questions of social power and naturalistic determinism. His writing depends upon a constantly shifting relationship between subject and object, between the articulation of a speaking position and the establishment of a more exigent social framework. In this sense, the trope of the black Atlantic becomes less a topographical element than a formal characteristic within Douglass's writing, since the imaginative rotation of his world upon a transatlantic axis manifests itself as a crucial element within his entire intellectual project.

Douglass's only work of fiction, "The Heroic Slave" (1853), chronicles in fictional terms a mutiny that had taken place 12 years earlier on the *Creole* slave ship, and it portrays in some ways a more multifaceted picture of slavery than emerges through Douglass's more picaresque autobiographies. In "The Heroic Slave", Douglass's hero Madison Washington chronicles his escape to Canada by writing of how he "nestle[s] in the mane of the British lion, protected by his mighty paw from the talons and the beak of the American eagle."[99] The *Creole* subsequently sails into the British port of Nassau in the Bahamas, where all the slaves are set free, an episode which refers back pointedly to the Slavery Abolition Act of 1833, which made slavery illegal throughout the British Empire. And yet, as Ivy G. Wilson has observed, the implicit analogies in "The Heroic Slave" between Madison Washington and George Washington, and the ways in which the author clearly links his hero with other American patriots such as James Madison, ensure a more complex series of cross-currents whereby this narrative suggests how "permitting slavery to exist amounts to returning the United States to the status of a colony of the British empire."[100] Douglass thus idealizes Britain here for the paradoxical purpose of encouraging African Americans to recapitulate their country's revolutionary gesture; he wants slaves to liberate themselves in the same way as Americans in the 1770s and 1780s threw off the British yoke. Just as Wilson Moses has shown how African Americans have simultaneously identified with the children of Israel in Egyptian bondage and with an Afrocentric mythology of pharaonic Egypt, so Douglass here exploits the contradiction whereby his African American fictional hero both idealizes and rejects Britain simultaneously.[101]

"The Heroic Slave" was first published in *Autographs for Freedom* (1853), an anti-slavery anthology created as an aid to fundraising by Julia Griffiths. Whereas Douglass's own autobiographies focus on himself as the central protagonist, "The Heroic Slave" is curiously dispersed in form, since it does not actually portray Madison Washington's revolt on the *Creole* upon which this story is based. Perhaps, as Levine has suggested, this involved on the author's part a strategic attempt to tone down the representation of insurrectionary violence in an attempt to appeal, like Harriet Beecher Stowe, to the sympathies of a wider readership.[102] But this displacement of Madison Washington also testifies on Douglas"s part to what Carrie Hyde has called an "insistent downplaying of human agency," whereby the narrative moves backward and forward across space and time, charting Washington's encounter with the abolitionist Listwell in Virginia, their subsequent meeting at Listwell's home in Ohio, Washington's account of his flight to Canada and then, in the final section, a "conversation" between the "*ocean birds*" Jack Williams and Tom Grant that "throws some light on the subsequent history, not only of Madison Washington, but of the hundred and thirty human beings with whom we last saw him chained."[103] For readers who might recall the vivid intensity of Douglass describing his fight with the overseer, Covey, in his first *Narrative*, this structure of "The Heroic Slave" might seem curiously distant or deliberately anticlimactic, yet it speaks aptly to Douglass's increasing understanding in the 1850s of slavery as a complex, multidirectional phenomenon, one where human heroism necessarily circulates around an international axis.

Although the "manly form" and "mesmeric power" of Washington in "The Heroic Slave" is characteristically idealized, and though the narrative cites Byron's *Childe Harold* to justify its stance of active rebellion, the narrative tone here is more one of absence and enigma, where the relation between traditional heroism and ultimate deliverance is problematized rather than validated. This quizzical pattern extends from the first page of Part One – "Curiously, earnestly, anxiously we peer into the dark, and wish even for the blinding flash, or the light of northern skies to reveal him. But alas! He is still enveloped in darkness" – to the retrospective rumination of the old salts in the final Part Four. But such a displacement of subjective perspective accords with the larger way in which Douglass's story works itself out across a hemispheric trajectory, situating the United States against Canada to the north and a "British port" to the south, and emphasizing how the laws relating to slavery vary according to jurisdiction.[104] Whereas Douglass's first autobiography presented freedom more as a "self-evident" right, "The Heroic Slave" implies, as Wilson acknowledged, how rights are "politically rather than naturally endowed," being legal entities defined by particular local situations; indeed, the very last paragraph of "The Heroic Slave" returns to this legal question, with Grant recalling how he told the British consul in Nassau how "by the laws of Virginia and the laws of the United States, the slaves on board were as much property as the barrels of flour in the hold."[105] In this context, Tom Grant's differentiation of land and water – "It is one thing to manage a company of slaves on a Virginia plantation, and quite another to quell an insurrection on the lonely billows of the Atlantic, where every breeze speaks of courage and liberty" – highlights Douglass's recognition of how the prospect of slave rebellion was facilitated by the deterritorializing impulse of transnational ocean space.[106]

Douglass became a militant advocate of violence against the state only after the passage of the Fugitive Slave Law in 1850, and it is true that "The Heroic Slave" eschews a more passive belief in the inevitability of deliverance, as recommended by the likes of Sojourner Truth, in favor of a somber recognition of the need for more brutal resistance. But it also adumbrates a sense of how the larger circumference of global politics in relation to the slavery issue was changing, of how, as Lydia Maria Child put it in 1842, "*events* are closing upon it [slavery] with tremendous power."[107] Hence the very title "The Heroic Slave" might be understood as a typical Douglass form of ironic paradox or reversal, whereby the exceptionalist nature of the individual slave becomes of less moment than the larger "circum-Caribbean" circuits that serve to position this protagonist within a more variegated framework.[108] The opportunity for Madison Washington to achieve liberation derives from a strategic juxtaposition of protagonist and milieu, where (as in Marx's formula) men make history but not under conditions of their own choosing, rather than from an older style of personal regeneration based upon quasi-religious principles.

The novel in which this threat of violent slave rebellion manifests itself most clearly is Martin Delany's *Blake, or The Huts of Africa*. The incendiary nature of Delany's narrative meant that it was difficult for him to find a publisher – Garrison pointedly ignored the author's request for help in this matter – and the novel did not in fact appear in book form until 1970, although its two parts were published in consecutive weekly installments, in *The Anglo-African Magazine* in 1859 and then in *The Weekly Anglo-African* in 1861.[109] As a black man born free in Virginia whose grandparents were African, Delany took exception to the ingrained racialism that he associated with *Uncle Tom's Cabin*, and *Blake* portrays a country teetering on the brink of violence, with the author drawing upon the simile of a volcano to describe Georgia as being "like a city at the base of a burning mountain, threatened with destruction by an overflow of the first outburst of lava from above." The word *insurrection* is used frequently in *Blake* to denote this imminent threat of slave uprising, and it is associated here with a condition of dream or nightmare: "A sleeping wake or waking sleep," involving a "dreamy existence of the most fearful apprehensions."[110] This attention to subliminal states exemplifies how, as in Poe's "Masque of the Red Death," Delany's narrative evokes a state of disorder and disorientation lying in wait just beneath the general level of everyday consciousness. The protagonist visits the "region of the Dismal Swamp" in North Carolina, where the names of leaders of slave rebellions such as "Nat Turner, Denmark Veezie, and General Gabriel were held ... in sacred reverence," and, having rescued his wife who has been sold from a Mississippi plantation to a slave owner in Cuba, Delany's hero presents himself as "Leader of the Army of Emancipation," vowing "war upon the whites."[111] The novel presents American slaves as conditioned by Christianity to be docile and passive, as if "their right to freedom by self-resistance ... was forbidden by the Word of God," and part of Blake's insurrectionary manner consequently involves an attempt to raise African American consciousness: the "old man" Maudy Ghamus claims "the blacks" have "sufficient number to take the whole United States; the only difficulty in the way being that the slaves in the different states could not be convinced of their strength."[112]

Blake is also unusual among American novels of this time in the way it incorporates the United States so explicitly within a hemispheric trajectory. The book mentions in its very first paragraph how the slave trade rotates on a commercial axis between Baltimore and Cuba, and it presents the plantations of Mississippi and Louisiana as deeply imbricated within a financial system of transnational exchange, with slaves being routinely transported between New Orleans and Havana, in a continuation of the notorious "Middle Passage" route across the Atlantic from Africa that is also described here.[113] The complicated political landscape of this novel involves white Americans trying to annex Cuba because of the likelihood there of a slave uprising and thus the prospect of a black republic "almost in sight of our shores," as the Louisiana state legislature warned in 1854, and this leads in Delany's novel to white American *agents provocateurs* trying to spread rumors of a "general insurrection" by the "Negroes of Cuba," so as to deflect the attention of Cuban authorities away from US attempts to destabilize the island.[114] In this sense, the multiple identities endemic to Delany's characters – Henry Gilbert is transmogrified into Henry Blake, which he says is an anglicization of his Spanish name "Henrico Blacus" – are commensurate with the shifting positions linked to the narrative's frequent shifts of geographical perspective. George Royer, American second officer on the *Vulture*, feels while en route to Africa that "the only place where a white man was safe and a Negro taught to know his place, was the United States," and *Blake*'s perpetual disruptions of the idea of *place*, in relation to both geographical location and racial hierarchy, highlight the unsettling nature of this process of criss-cross dislocation for the US body politic.

Rather than adumbrating a country demarcated into two distinct blocks – North versus South, white versus black – Delany thus

chronicles a multidirectional world where allegiance is elusive and
where local landscapes are complicated, often in opaque ways, by more
distant factors. Judge Ballard, an "eminent jurist of one of the Northern
States," is said to own a large estate in Cuba and to be also seeking to
buy "a Mississippi cotton place," and this transverse pattern implies
how in Delany's world the complicated mesh of vested financial and
political interests, like the networks of slave resistance, are partially
concealed from public view.[115] The fact that Delany left *Blake* unfin-
ished in some ways corroborates this inchoate or enigmatic quality, in
which any resolution might seem arbitrary and premature; as Eric J.
Sundquist remarks, the book "concludes in a state of paralysis," one that
"brings rebellion to the point of outbreak without actualizing it,"
although in fact this inconclusive strain of potential violence is one of
the most powerful aspects of this novel.[116]

Frederick Douglass's 1846 *Narrative* has generally been popular with
students, particularly in the United States, not only because it ultimately
resolves the protagonist's dilemmas in an uplifting manner, but also
because it is stylistically clear, offering a model of transparent self-reliance that can be accommodated all too readily within a conventional
Emersonian paradigm. By contrast, the issue of how slavery was represented within the broader transatlantic and transhemispheric world
tended to raise disconcerting questions about an absence of authenticity,
a systematic lack of resolution, and the troubling dispersal of American
cultural politics across a more opaque and amorphous sphere.

3.3 Planetary Space and Intellectual Distance

The engagement of nineteenth-century American literature with Latin
America, the borderlands culture of the Rio Grande, and the Caribbean
has been particularly well examined by Anna Brickhouse, who has discussed ways in which New England authors such as Hawthorne and
Longfellow were involved in various ways with the different climate and
culture of Mexico. Brickhouse also described how *Uncle Tom's Cabin* was
reimagined in a Haitian context by Pierre Faubert in his historical drama
Ogé, ou, Le préjugé de couleur (Ogé, or Color Prejudice), which represents the Haitian declaration of national independence in 1790 through
the comparative framework of what Faubert, writing from a situation of
exile in Paris, calls *L'Oncle Tom.*[117]

Although the question of slavery in the United States has conventionally been related to the domestic context of the American Civil War, it
clearly had an international resonance at this time, and there has been
increasing attention over recent years to ways in which Haiti and the

Caribbean offered a wider continental framework within which the conflicts associated with the politics of American slavery were acted out. A poem taking its title from the Haitian insurrectionary leader Vincent Ogé was published by African American attorney George B. Vashon in a revised 1854 edition of the *Autographs for Freedom* volume where Douglass's "Heroic Slave" had first appeared the previous year.[118] Vashon was the first black graduate from Oberlin College and then the first black lawyer in New York, and his "Vincent Ogé" is particularly interesting for the way it poetically frames Ogé's revolt within the formal rhyme scheme of a Pindaric ode, with a set meter and rhyme pattern defined by three triads: strophe, antistrophe, and epode. This has the effect of linking events on the French colony of Saint-Domingue not with mere disorder, as Carlyle and other political opponents of slave insurrection claimed, but with an epic tradition extending back to classical times. By integrating carnage with Greek pastoral forms, Vashon implies ways in which violence can become emancipatory. He thus uses classical parallels to defamiliarize recent political events, achieving a discursive distance that effectively overcomes Ogé's sense of both personal and historical isolation by portraying him in relation to a distinguished republican ancestry.

The international ramifications of slavery were also remarked upon by Mark Twain during his 1895 Australian trip, where he draws overt parallels between the cultures of Queensland and the American South as he describes how "[f]rom the multitudinous islands in these regions the 'recruits' for the Queensland plantations were formerly drawn; and are still drawn from them, I believe. Vessels fitted up like old-time slavers come here and carried off the natives to serve as laborers in the great Australian province."[119] The British government of the late nineteenth century refused to uphold Queensland's attempt to annex New Guinea, and indeed Queensland joined the political process of Australian federation in the 1890s only reluctantly, knowing that such a federal framework under British dominion would require the big sugar companies to end their black labor system, a process that essentially involved kidnapping natives of the Polynesian islands to work in Queensland's cane fields. Complaints about the seizure of these islanders by agents working on behalf of plantation owners in Queensland and Fiji had been going on for many years, with Fiji, according to Australian missionary Daniel Macdonald in 1878, being notoriously considered "the Australian West Indies." The British consul in Fiji was himself a known ringleader in a group of white men who banded themselves together into an offshoot of the Ku Klux Klan, and Gerald Horne has commented on the grim parallel whereby "just as the Ku Klux Klan was rising in the U.S. South to administer an unyielding admonition to those so bold as to resist the logic of white supremacy, a similar need arose at precisely the same moment in the South Seas."[120]

Such a clear echo in Australia of the American internecine conflict between federal government and the rights of individual states effectively undermines the narrower New Historicist critical focus on domestic slavery within the United States by illustrating how, for Twain, the whole question of race could be understood only across a global axis, within which coercive imperial and economic interests were fighting for dominion. But the more general point to emphasize is how, for Twain, this racial and imperial logic unfolds according to a harsh cycle of determinism, from which the potentialities of agency have been erased. From this angle, Twain's writing does not properly fit within a Christian or moralistic framework of antiracism; instead, he adumbrates a more pessimistic, Darwinian world of struggle, where "[t]he Whites and the Blacks hunted each other, ambushed each other, butchered each other."[121] Twain's satirical essays on empire in the early years of the twentieth century – *To the Person Sitting in Darkness* (1901), which was published as a pamphlet by the Anti-Imperialist League of New York, and *King Leopold's Soliloquy: A Defense of His Congo Rule* (1905) – similarly travesty the pretensions of imperialism without proposing the comfort of any radical alternative, and this suggests a more pessimistic view of Twain than is normally recycled through the process of what Jonathan Arac called the "hypercanonization" of *Huckleberry Finn* (1884) in the American classroom.[122] The traditional nationalist line in *Huckleberry Finn* criticism was predicated not only upon what Leo Marx in 1964 called its "vernacular narrator" with his "freshness and lyricism unmatched in American writing," but also upon a sense of Huck belonging so intimately to his locale that "his language is native to it." As Marx went on to admit, this was essentially a nostalgic vision of antebellum America, and it was Twain's own awareness of how "the noble but extravagant ideal of freedom associated with the raft" could not be "reconciled with the facts" of society that leads to the smashing of the raft in Chapter 16 of the novel and the characters' subsequent return to those "patterns of contradiction" endemic to the political conditions of mid-nineteenth-century America.[123]

Nevertheless, Twain was generally represented in twentieth-century American criticism as an incarnation of national values, with Ernest Hemingway in 1935 declaring that "[a]ll modern American literature comes from one book by Mark Twain called *Huckleberry Finn*," and Norman Podhoretz in 1959 calling Twain "the quintessential American writer."[124] Yet Twain resided not in the United States but in London and various other parts of Europe throughout most of the 1890s, and many of his later books, in particular, are set outside the territorial boundaries of the United States. In one of Twain's last works, *Extract from Captain Stormfield's Visit to Heaven* (1909), the celestial underclerk asks the recently deceased captain where he comes from, and when Stormfield tells him that he's "from America – the United States of America," the clerk responds: "There ain't any such orb." *Extract* is about remapping the solar system in the light of modern astronomical science; planet Earth is described here as "in one of the little new systems away out in one of the thinly worlded corners of the universe."[125] The spatial disorientations and reconfigurations of this metaphysical fantasy operate as a corollary to *Following the Equator* (1897), Twain's account of his round the world voyage that similarly involves geographically resituating American culture, albeit here within an international rather than cosmic dimension. Although Twain was driven to this exhausting international travel because of financial exigency after his business investments in James Paige's typesetting machine had failed, his perception of the world at a fraught moment of imperial politics – just before the Boer War and Australian federation, and when the independence movement in India was beginning to gain momentum – enabled him to reposition his vernacular American idiom within a global setting. The pessimism of Twain's later writing thus derives from a profound sense that human nature is more or less the same the world over, that noble aspirations are brought low by the Darwinian energies associated with power struggles both evolutionary and political. This serves to decenter both the human consciousness from a wider discursive circumference and also, simultaneously, the United States from its centripetal position within the planetary sphere.

To consider how American literature relates to world literature within a nineteenth-century context thus involves a whole series of paradoxical reversals and conundrums. There is no doubt that the universalist dimensions of transcendentalism tried to position the United States at the center of a sphere that it imagined radiating outwards from the American homeland, and in this sense Emerson's appropriation of Kantian idealism for domestic purposes can be seen as commensurate with Whitman's reconfiguration of Manifest Destiny in "A Passage to India," as he attempts ebulliently to incorporate the American Pacific as a fulcrum of global trade. The political rhetoric of immigration and assimilation, predicated as it was upon the notion of making the United States home to all nations, also served to elide divisions between America and the world, as if the American scene could henceforth become the template for a new world order. But other forces operated in an inverse direction, so that the relation between American literature and global space at this time should not be understood simply as a trajectory working from the inside out, as if the American imagination could co-opt the whole planetary sphere.

Twain, as we have seen, was exercised by a more unsettling consciousness of the wider world impacting in significant ways upon the American domestic domain, with the racial and colonial conflicts in India and Australia holding up an uneasy mirror to the trauma of both the War of Independence and the US Civil War, thereby suggesting how American cultural history itself formed part of a larger deterministic pattern. As with other US writers at the turn of the twentieth century such as the African American fiction writer Pauline Hopkins and Californian novelist Frank Norris, the fictional narratives of Twain are shadowed by an uneasy sense that the reinforcing rhetoric of American exceptionalism might be exposed as illusory, with the United States being reduced, as Captain Stormfield uncomfortably discovers, to a remote speck in cosmic space.

The poetry of Emily Dickinson is interesting to consider in this regard, not least because she has been understood in both traditional and popular terms as a quintessentially American poet, one whose style was linked inextricably to a specific genius of place. Dickinson herself plays with this prospect in her poem "The Robin's my Criterion for Tune," where she acknowledges how her vision is constructed by her local angle of vision.[126] Yet this becomes for Dickinson not a valorization of provincialism but, rather, an epistemological paradox, one that insists that even royalty's gaze is framed within a particular line of sight:

> Because I see—New Englandly—
> The Queen, discerns like me—
> Provincially—

Although Dickinson is sometimes celebrated rather sentimentally in terms of her interest in the folk culture of her time, her work also reveals a much more austere intellectual concern to correlate American landscapes with the scientific theories of evolution and geology that were linking US scenes to a much more expansive circumference during the nineteenth century. Dickinson was strongly influenced by transcendentalism – with which she nevertheless quarreled intellectually, rejecting Emerson's Olympian faith in the poet's "transparent eye-ball," his ambition to see through the world and reduce it to order – and her poetry is also marked by nineteenth-century technological developments and political events, such as the telegraph and the Civil War.[127] Yet earthquakes, volcanoes, oceans, and other natural phenomena play a crucial part in Dickinson's poetic landscape, and the overall effect of her work is to induce a radical displacement of American consciousness, a resituation of her domestic figures within a world whose expanse radically exceeds the spatial and temporal constraints of any given nation.

To take just one example of this, the poem "A Still – Volcano – Life" deliberately evokes a posthuman environment, one where the oceanic life of coral reefs throws the conventional human system of measurement into sharp relief:

A still—Volcano—Life—
That flickered in the night—
When it was dark enough to do
Without erasing sight—

A quiet—Earthquake Style—
Too subtle to suspect
By natures this side Naples—
The North cannot detect

The Solemn—Torrid—Symbol—
The lips that never lie—
Whose hissing Corals part—and shut—
And Cities—ooze away—[128]

Dickinson is not normally thought of as an "environmental" writer in the same way as (for example) Thoreau or Aldo Leopold, because she does not directly describe the scenes of American flora and fauna that lie around her. What she does instead is to contrast the movement of the planet with more conventional social designs, portraying the "Earthquake Style" here as too "quiet" and "subtle" for human senses to "detect," and in this way she sets up a disturbing dialectic where the way the volcano "flickered" creates an enigmatic scenario in which the subterranean currents of the earth are only partially visible. By dislocating the routines of daily life through the way she juxtaposes them with a metaphysical sense of distance that remains partly "dark," Dickinson's fractured poetic idiom sunders the regularly conjoined space of the nation and exposes it to a disintegrating fabric. Dickinson's "hissing Corals" create a sinister landscape, one in which the relation between human order and natural entropy is reversed, since in the deliquescent vision of this poem it is the human "Cities" that become subject to environmental depredation as they "ooze away."

In *The Limits of Critique* (2015), Rita Felski complained of an analytical obsession among scholars with deconstructing fictional narratives so as to expose the power relations informing them, and she claimed this has the negative effect of turning students away from the imaginative power of literary works, obscuring ways in which "critique is as much a matter of affect and rhetoric as of philosophy or politics."[129] However, it might be argued that framing American literature of the nineteenth century through discursive strategies of distance, both geographic and intellectual, actually serves to highlight its fictional force and imaginative impact. The transcendentalism of Emerson and Whitman engenders not Biblical truths but forceful fictions, and reading the works of these writers for their aesthetic rather than moral qualities – as projections of the world deriving from a particular time and place, rather than as scriptural truth or a guide to ethics – might have the beneficial effect of licensing such texts for the efficacy of their fictive dimensions. Matthew Arnold, who did not in any sense share Emerson's world view and who thought that his prose style "wants the requisite wholeness of good tissue," nevertheless concluded that "as Wordsworth's poetry is in my judgment the most important work done in verse, in our language, during the present century, so Emerson's *Essays* are, I think, the most important work done in prose." Arnold credits Emerson's prose as "more important than Carlyle's" because of the way he "holds fast to happiness and hope," and while Arnold does not necessarily believe in "happiness and hope" as principles to live by, he nevertheless admires the way Emerson gives them life as imaginative formulations.[130]

Nineteenth-century American literature has been diminished in various ways by excessively narrow pedagogical perspectives that have tried to claim authors from Emerson through Dickinson to Twain as homegrown products, as if they were merely spokespersons for an established set of social values. But to relocate these figures within a wider global sphere is not only to elucidate the multidimensional ironies that permeate the visions of these American writers, but also to appreciate the complexity and variety of their artistic works. Rather than being categorized merely within the curriculum of American literature, such writers can consequently be understood in productive ways as exponents of world literature.

References

1 Phillips, C. (2001). Marvin Gaye. In: *A New World Order: Selected Essays*, 35. London: Secker and Warburg.
2 Kroes, R. (2005). European Anti-Americanism: What's New?. European Perspectives in American Studies: Histories-Dialogues-Differences. JFK Institute for North American Studies, Free University of Berlin, 12 Febuary 2005.
3 Matthiessen, *American Renaissance*, xii.
4 Gioia, D. (1993). Longfellow in the Aftermath of Modernism. In: *The History of American Poetry* (ed. J. Parini), 65. New York: Columbia UP.
5 Matthiessen, *American Renaissance*, 174, 34.

6 Goddu, T. (1997). *Gothic America: Narrative, History, and Nation*, 73–93. New York: Columbia UP.

7 Poe, E.A. (1967). The Masque of the Red Death. In: *Selected Writings* (ed. D. Galloway), 254, 260, 256–257. London: Penguin.

8 Bercovitch, S. (1993). *The Rites of Assent: Transformations in the Symbolic Construction of America*. New York: Routledge.

9 Heimert, A. (1963). *Moby-Dick* and American Political Symbolism. *American Quarterly* 15(4): 499.

10 Simms, W.G. (2003). In: *The Cassique of Kiawah: A Colonial Romance* (1859) (ed. K. Collins), 381. Fayetteville: U of Arkansas P.

11 Lincoln, A. (1940). Annual message to congress (1862). In: *The Life and Writings of Abraham Lincoln* (ed. P. Van Doren Stern), 736. New York: Modern Library; Opinion of the draft (1863), in *Life and Writings*, 770; letter to Albert G. Hedges, 4 April 1864, in *Life and Writings*, 807.

12 Samuels, S. (2004). *Facing America: Iconography and the Civil War*, 34. New York: Oxford UP.

13 Lincoln. *Life and Writings*, 649.

14 Lincoln, *Life and Writings*, 657; Brogan, H. (ed.) (1975). *The American Civil War: Extracts from* The Times, *1860–1865*, 86. London: Times Books; Blackett, R.J.M. (2001). *Divided Hearts: Britain and the American Civil War*, 226. Baton Rouge: Louisiana State UP.

15 Whitman, W. (1973). *Leaves of Grass* (ed. S. Bradley and H.W. Blodgett), 330, 337, 333. New York: Norton.

16 Fisher, P. (1988). Democratic social space: Whitman, Melville, and the promise of American transparency. *Representations* 24: 60–101.

17 Warrior, R. (2005). *The People and the Word: Reading Native Nonfiction*, 181. Minneapolis: U of Minnesota P, and (2009). Native American scholarship and the transnational turn. *Cultural Studies Review* 15(2): 119–130.

18 Byrd, J.A. (2011). *Transit of Empire: Indigenous Critiques of Colonialism*, xxi, 19. Minneapolis: U of Minnesota P.

19 Carr, H. (1996). *Inventing the American Primitive: Politics, Gender, and the Representation of Native American Literary Traditions, 1789–1936*, 140. New York: New York UP.

20 Mielke, L.L. (2008). *Moving Encounters: Sympathy and the Indian Question in Antebellum Literature*, 21, 28. Amherst: U of Massachusetts P.

21 Thoreau, H.D. (1971). *Walden; or, Life in the Woods*, 156. Princeton: Princeton UP.

22 Calloway, C.G. (2011). 2008 Presidential Address: Indian history from the end of the alphabet; and what now?. *Ethnohistory* 58(2): 200.

23 Mizruchi, S.L. (1988). *The Power of Historical Knowledge: Narrating the Past in Hawthorne, James, and Dreiser*, 11. Princeton: Princeton UP.

24 Cooper, J.F. (1985). The Pathfinder; or, The Inland Sea. In: *The Leatherstocking Tales II*, 41, 140. New York: Library of America.

25 Cooper, *The Pathfinder*, 79, 155, 178.

26 Cooper, *The Pathfinder*, 436; Cooper, J.F. (1997). *The Spy* (ed. W. Franklin), 33. New York: Penguin.

27 Cooper, *The Spy*, 50, 89.

28 Cooper, *The Spy*, 92, 356, 397, 377.

29 Cooper, J.F. (1982). *Gleanings in Europe: England* (ed. D.A. Ringe and K.W. Staggs), 1, 11. Albany: State U of New York P.

30 Cooper, *Gleanings in Europe: England*, 71, 46.

31 Cooper, *Gleanings in Europe: England*, 145–146, 121.

32 Cooper, J.F. (1855). *The Headsman; or, The Abbaye de Vignerons: A Tale*, 259. London: Routledge.

33 Cooper, *The Headsman*, 236, 251, 286.

34 Cooper, *The Headsman*, 6.

35 Philbrick, T. (1961). *James Fenimore Cooper and the Development of American Sea Fiction*, 262. Cambridge: Harvard UP.

36 Cooper, J.F. (1963). *The Crater; or, Vulcan's Peak: A Tale of the Pacific*, 299, 381. New York: Gregory.

37 Cooper, J.F. (1860). *The Sea-Lions; or, The Lost Sealers*, 401, 346, 360, 261. New York: Townsend.

38 Cohen, M. (2010). *The Novel and the Sea*, 233. Princeton: Princeton UP.

39 Emerson, R.W. (1969). *The Journals and Miscellaneous Notebooks of Ralph Waldo Emerson*, vol. VII (ed. A.W. Plumstead and H. Hayford), 200. Cambridge: Harvard UP. (26 May 1839).

40 Ferguson, R.A. (1984). *Law and Letters in American Culture*, 158. Cambridge: Harvard UP.

41 Leary, L. (1963). *Washington Irving*, 41. Minneapolis: U of Minnesota P.

42 Irving, W. (1981). The Life and Voyages of Christopher Columbus. In: *Complete Works, XI* (ed. J.H. McElroy), 67. Boston: Twayne.

43 Emerson, R.W. (2007). Society and Solitude. In: *The Collected Works of Ralph Waldo Emerson, VII* (ed. R.A. Bosco and D.E. Wilson), 14. Cambridge: Harvard UP.

44 Emerson, R.W. (1971). The American scholar. In *The Collected Works of Ralph Waldo Emerson, I: Nature, Addresses, and Lectures* (ed. R.E. Spiller and A.R. Ferguson), 69, 64. Cambridge: Harvard UP.

45 Emerson, R.W. (1959). Chaucer. In: *The Early Lectures of Ralph Waldo Emerson, I: 1833–1836* (ed. S.E. Whicher and R.E. Spiller), 284–285. Cambridge: Harvard UP).

46 Emerson, R.W., "The Age of Fable," in *Early Lectures*, 253.

47 Whitman, *Leaves of Grass*, 88.

48 Berlant, L. (1991). *The Anatomy of National Fantasy: Hawthorne, Utopia, and Everyday Life*. Chicago: U of Chicago P.

49 Hawthorne, N. (1962). *The Scarlet Letter*, 232, 105, 120. Columbus: Ohio State UP.

50 James, H. (1967). *Hawthorne* (ed. T. Tanner), 54. London: Macmillan.

51 Hawthorne, N. (1968). *The Marble Faun; or, The Romance of Monte Beni*, 26, 463. Columbus: Ohio State UP.

52 Hawthorne, *The Marble Faun*, 410.

53 James, H. (1989). Nathaniel Hawthorne (1879). In: *The American Essays*, rev. ed. (ed. Edel, L.), 22. Princeton: Princeton UP.

54 Hawthorne, N. (1970). *Our Old Home: A Series of English Sketches*, 60, 59, 309. Columbus: Ohio State UP.

55 Twain, M. (1996). *The Innocents Abroad*, 165. New York: Oxford UP.

56 Hawthorne, *Our Old Home*, 10.

57 Phillips, D. (1994). Nineteenth-century racial thought and Whitman's 'Democratic Ethnology of the Future'. *Nineteenth-Century Literature* 49(3): 290; Whitman, *Leaves of Grass*, 147–148.

58 Lauter, P. (1994). Melville climbs the canon. *American Literature* 66(1): 10.

59 Melville, H. (1988). *Moby-Dick; or, The Whale* (ed. H. Hayford, G. Thomas Tanselle, and H. Parker), 6. Evanston: Northwestern UP.

60 Dana, R.H., Jr. (1981). *Two Years Before the Mast: A Personal Narrative* (ed. T. Philbrick), 125, 177, 130. New York: Viking Penguin.

61 Douglass, F. (1994). *Narrative of the Life of Frederick Douglass, an American Slave*, in *Autobiographies*, 84. New York: Library of America. Subsequent page references to this edition are cited in parentheses in the text.

62 Wright, R. (1991). How 'bigger' was born. In: *Early Works*, 881. New York: Library of America.

63 Brown, W.W. (1969). *Clotel; or, The President's Daughter* (ed. W.E. Farrison), 16, 239, 241, 244. New York: University Books.

64 Marshall, B. (2007). New Orleans, nodal point of the French Atlantic. *International Journal of Francophone Studies* 10(1 and 2): 40.

65 Brown, *Clotel*, 45.

66 Warner, S. (1987). *The Wide, Wide World*, 505, 500. New York: Feminist Press.

67 Tamarkin, E. (2008). *Anglophilia: Deference, Devotion, and Antebellum America*, 215. Chicago: U of Chicago P.

68 Stowe, H.B. (2000). *Dred: A Tale of the Great Dismal Swamp* (ed. R.S. Levine), 9. Chapel Hill: U of North Carolina P.

69 Hedrick, J.D. (1994). *Harriet Beecher Stowe: A Life*, 243. New York: Oxford UP.

70 Stowe, H.B. (1890). *The Life of Harriet Beecher Stowe* (ed. C.E. Stowe), 468, 471. (1889; rpt.). Boston: Houghton Mifflin.

71 Eliot, G. (1967). *Essays of George Eliot* (ed. T. Pinney), 326–327. New York: Columbia UP.

72 Stowe, *Dred*, 39.

73 Stowe, *Dred*, 535.

74 Stauffer, J. (2007). Frederick Douglass's self-fashioning and the making of a representative American man. In: *The Cambridge Companion to the African American Slave Narrative* (ed. A. Fisch), 205. Cambridge: Cambridge UP.

75 Douglass, F. (1994). Narrative of the Life of Frederick Douglass, an American Slave. In: *Autobiographies*, 58–59. New York: Library of America. Subsequent page references to this edition are cited in parentheses in the text.

76 Fichtelberg, J. (1989). *The Complex Image: Faith and Method in American Autobiography*, 132. Philadelphia: U of Pennsylvania P; Gates, H.L., Jr. (1985). Introduction: the language of slavery. In: *The Slave's Narrative* (ed. C.T. Davis and H.L. Gates, Jr.), xviii. New York: Oxford UP.

77 Douglass, F. (1846). *Narrative of the Life of Frederick Douglass*, 2e, cxxiv. Dublin: Webb and Chapman.

78 Ferreira, P.J. (2001). Frederick Douglass in Ireland: the Dublin edition of his narrative. *New Hibernia Review/Iris Eireannach Nua* 5(1): 61.

79 Douglass, F. (1979–92). The free Church connection with the slave Church: an address delivered in Arbroath, Scotland, on February 12, 1846. In: *The Frederick Douglass Papers: Series One – Speeches, Debates, and Interviews* (ed. J. Blassingame et al.), 5 volumes, I:156. New Haven: Yale UP).

80 Douglass, F. (1950–1975). *The Life and Writings of Frederick Douglass* (ed. P.S. Foner), 5 volumes, V, 29. New York: International Publishers.

81 McFeely, W.S. (1991). *Frederick Douglass*, 141. New York: Norton.

82 Peterson, C.L. (1992). Capitalism, black (under)development, and the production of the African American novel in the 1850s. *American Literary History* 4(4): 562–563.

83 Wortham, T. (1992). Did Emerson blackball Frederick Douglass from membership in the Town and Country Club?. *New England Quarterly* 65(2): 297–298.

84 Douglass, *Life and Writings*, 3:45.

85 Gilroy, *The Black Atlantic*, 13.

86 Wald, P. (1995). *Constituting Americans: Cultural Anxiety and Narrative Form*, 73. Durham: Duke UP.

87 McFeely, *Frederick Douglass*, 280.

88 Diedrich, M. (1999). *Love Across Color Lines: Ottilie Assing and Frederick Douglass*, 188. New York: Hill and Wang.

89 Diedrich, *Love Across Color Lines*, 225.

90 Lohmann, C. (ed.) (1999). *Radical Passion: Ottilie Assing's Reports from America and Letters to Frederick Douglass*, xxix. New York: Peter Lang.

91 Douglass, *Life and Writings*, III: 119–120.

92 Castronovo, R. (1995). *Fathering the Nation: Genealogies of Slavery and Freedom*, 213. Berkeley: U of California P.

93 Douglass, *Life and Writings*, II:426.

94 Hutcheon, *A Theory of Parody*, 6, 26, 20.

95 Douglass, F. The Key to *Uncle Tom's Cabin*. In: *Life and Writings*, vol. II, 240–241.

96 Levine, R.S. (2000). Road to Africa: Frederick Douglass's Rome. *African American Review* 34(2): 223.

97 Railton, S. (1991). *Authorship and Audience: Literary Performance in the American Renaissance*, 3–22. Princeton: Princeton UP.

98 Douglass, *Frederick Douglass Papers*, III: 620.

99 Douglass, F. (1993). The Heroic Slave. In: *Violence in the Black Imagination: Essays and Documents*, 2e (ed. R.T. Takaki), 56. New York: Oxford UP.

100 Wilson, I.G. (2006). On native ground: transnationalism, Frederick Douglass, and 'The Heroic Slave'. *PMLA* 121(2): 458.

101 Moses, W.J. (2004). *Creative Conflict in African American Thought: Frederick Douglass, Alexander Crummell, Booker T. Washington, W. E. B. Du Bois, and Marcus Garvey*, xiii. Cambridge: Cambridge UP.

102 Levine, R.S. (1997). *Martin Delany, Frederick Douglass, and the Politics of Representative Identity*, 83–84. Chapel Hill: U of North Carolina P.

103 Hyde, C. (2013). The Climates of Liberty: Natural Rights in the *Creole* Case and 'The Heroic Slave'. *American Literature* 85(3): 490; Douglass, F. (1996). The Heroic Slave. In: *The Oxford Frederick Douglass Reader* (ed. W. Andrews), 157. New York: Oxford UP.

104 Douglass, "The Heroic Slave," 134, 153, 157, 132, 160.

105 Wilson, "On Native Ground," 458; Douglass, "The Heroic Slave," 163.

106 Douglass, "The Heroic Slave," 158.

107 Child, L.M. (1997). The iron shroud. In: *A Lydia Maria Child Reader* (ed. C. Karcher), 216. Durham, NC: Duke UP.

108 Wilson, "On Native Ground," 453.

109 Miller, F.J. (1970). Introduction. *Blake; or, The Huts of America* (ed. M.R. Delany), xi. Boston: Beacon Press.

110 Delany, *Blake*, 109, 135.

111 Delany, *Blake*, 112–13, 251, 290.

112 Delany, *Blake*, 123, 113–14.

113 Delany, *Blake*, 224.

114 Levine, *Martin Delany*, 202; Delany, *Blake*, 266.

115 Delany, *Blake*, 201, 210, 4, 59.

116 Sundquist, E.J. (1993). *To Wake the Nations, Race in the Making of American Literature*, 184. Cambridge: Harvard UP.

117 Brickhouse, A. (2004). *Transamerican Literary Relations and the Nineteenth-Century Public Sphere*, 221–241. Cambridge: Cambridge UP.

118 Griffiths, J. (ed.) (1854). *Autographs for Freedom*, 54–60. Auburn: Alden Beardsley.

119 Twain, M. (1996). *Following the Equator: A Journey around the World (1897)*, in *Following the Equator and Anti-Imperialist Essays*, 81. New York: Oxford UP.

120 Horne, G. (2007). *The White Pacific: U. S. Imperialism and Black Slavery in the South Seas after the Civil War*, 69, 78. Honolulu: U of Hawai'i P.

121 Twain, *Following the Equator*, 256.

122 Arac, J. (1997). Huckleberry Finn *as Idol and Target: The Functions of Criticism in Our Time*, 3. Madison: U of Wisconsin P.

123 Marx, L. (1964). *The Machine in the Garden: Technology and the Pastoral Ideal in America*, 319, 333, 338. New York: Oxford UP.

124 Hemingway, E. (1977). *Green Hills of Africa* (1935; rpt.), 26. London: Granada; Arac, Huckleberry Finn *as Idol and Target*, 3.

125 Twain, M. (1996). *Extract from Captain Stormfield's Visit to Heaven*, 17, 23. New York: Oxford UP.

126 Franklin, R.W. (ed.) (1999). *The Poems of Emily Dickinson: Reading Edition*, 115. Cambridge: Harvard UP.

127 Emerson, R.W. Nature. In: *Nature, Addresses, and Lectures*, 10. For an ingenious argument linking Dickinson's elliptical style of poetry to the invention of the telegraph, see McCormack, J.H. (2003). Domesticating Delphi: Emily Dickinson and the electro-magnetic telegraph. *American Quarterly* 55(4): 569–601.

128 Franklin, ed., *Poems of Emily Dickinson*, 234.

129 Felski, R. (2015). *The Limits of Critique*, 3. Chicago: U of Chicago P.

130 Arnold, M. (1974). Emerson (1884). In: *Philistinism in England and America* (ed. R.H. Super), 182. Ann Arbor: U of Michigan P.

4

The Worlds of American Modernism

4.1 The American Novel and the Great War

In the early years of the twentieth century, American literature was generally regarded in academic terms as one of the branches of literature in English. American-born novelists such as Henry James and Edith Wharton lived for most of their working careers in Europe, as (slightly later) did American-born poets such as T.S. Eliot and Ezra Pound. This sense of reciprocity was compounded during the political turbulence in the 1930s that led to World War II, when many European writers moved to the United States. Exiles at this time included not only Germans (Thomas Mann, Bertolt Brecht) but also famous English figures such as W.H. Auden and Christopher Isherwood, while Hilda Doolittle "(H.D.)," born in Pennsylvania, wrote her most famous poem *Trilogy* (1944–1946) in the shadows of wartime London. This reinforced the general sense of modernism being by definition an international movement, one driven by cosmopolitan intellectuals who tended to be drawn magnetically to big capital cities. The presence of artists from many different national backgrounds in Paris, for example – James Joyce from Ireland, Pablo Picasso from Spain, Igor Stravinsky from Russia, Ernest Hemingway and Gertrude Stein from the United States – ran alongside a theoretical investment in the modernist city as a *topos* where various art forms (literature, music, painting, and others) could be brought into creative juxtaposition.

This was different in kind from postmodernist projections of space at the turn of the twenty-first century, when models of electronic communication were more advanced and intellectuals could happily live and work in dispersed geographical locations without necessarily feeling that they were cut off from key sources of cultural enrichment. Modernist writers also tended to look on exile from the familiar terrain of their home centers as what J. Gerald Kennedy called "an enabling exercise,"

American World Literature: An Introduction, First Edition. Paul Giles.
© 2019 John Wiley & Sons Ltd. Published 2019 by John Wiley & Sons Ltd.

one that empowered them to explore new forms of art without the inhibiting pressures of home comforts.[1] Henry Miller, whose *Tropic of Cancer* (1934) explicitly took issue with domestic circumstances, wrote buoyantly in that book: "I'm not an American any more, nor a New Yorker, or even less a European, or a Parisian ... I'm a neutral."[2]

Neil Smith has written of the period between 1898 and 1919 as the "first formative moment" of globalization in the United States.[3] World War I, which until the outbreak of the Second World War in 1939 was known simply as the "Great War," was a crucial influence in exposing the culture of middle America to the complexities of a wider world, with many films and other sources in mass culture testifying to the disruptive effect that war service overseas and the involvement of the United States in European political affairs exerted on the American imagination. The title of a 1919 song made popular by the Great War, "How Ya Gonna Keep 'em Down on the Farm (After They have Seen Paree?)," exemplifies this general sense of cultural disturbance, which cut across social hierarchies on both sides of the Atlantic. In "Within the Rim" (1917), an essay first published the year after his death, Henry James portrays himself walking along the coast near the "high-perched Sussex town" where he used to live and "staring at the bright mystery" across the English Channel: "Just on the other side of that finest of horizon-lines history was raging at a pitch new under the sun." In the same way that James in *The American Scene* (1907) represents himself as a displaced observer perturbed by the processes of modernization, so "Within the Rim" evokes an image of the author perplexed and disoriented by the prospect of change. He compares his sentiments to how a "quiet dweller in a tenement" might feel "when the question of 'structural improvements' is thrust upon him." James, with his typical candor and artistic openness to the unpredictable nature of experience, does not simply resist what he calls "the shock of events." Instead, he depicts himself as being disturbed by "the history of the hour addressing itself to the individual mind," along with the "degree of pain attached to the ploughed-up state it implied."[4]

James's response was not untypical of that of American writers to the Great War. However much they were appalled by the scenes of carnage and suffering, American writers also at some level tended to regard the war as an emblem of modernity, a necessary disruption of that state of ossified gentility which, by the second decade of the twentieth century, appeared to have become thoroughly anachronistic. Paul Fussell has written of how for English writers, this First World War operated as a kind of apocalyptic caesura, with the period before 4 August 1914 appearing in legend as a timeless Edwardian idyll, and the "Time After" a regrettable collapse into twentieth-century modernity. But Fussell's observation that "the Great War was perhaps the last to be conceived as taking place within a seamless, purposeful 'history' involving a coherent stream of time running from past through present to future" is an argument more readily applicable to English than to American writers: the English Georgian poet Rupert Brooke, for example, was nostalgically attached to a notion of "purposeful" tradition and "coherent" history in a way that American novelists such as John Dos Passos and Ernest Hemingway never were.[5] In this sense, as in many others, James's intellectual allegiance oscillates between different sides of the Atlantic, since his final essays imply a loyalty to the British fight against what he calls "the huge Prussian fist," while at the same time acknowledging, as do Dos Passos and Hemingway more explicitly, the various subtle ways in which contemporary conditions have the effect of "overscoring the image as a whole or causing the old accepted synthesis to bristle with accents."[6] There is an elegiac tone in James's farewell here to the "old accepted synthesis" of Edwardian Britain, but also an understanding that new "accents" have become inevitable.

Another difference between English and American cultural responses to the war derived from their discrepancies in their contributions to active military service. US President Woodrow Wilson held back from entering the conflict in 1915, when the British ship *Lusitania* was torpedoed with the loss of over 100 American lives, and it was only in April 1917, after significantly increased submarine warfare in the Atlantic, that the United States declared war against Germany. Since the Armistice was concluded in November 1918, this meant that American soldiers were engaged for only 19 months, as opposed to 48 months for troops from Britain and the Empire. Consequently, the fatality toll in America was 126 000 out of a total population of 100 million, a figure that in terms of brute statistics was quite small when compared with Britain's losses of 908 000 out of a population of 43 million. In addition, the forced centralization and increases in manufacturing technology associated with the war effort caused the US economy to forge ahead during the First World War, while the economies of Europe, which experienced the kind of widespread destruction of physical plants from which America was exempt, conversely lost ground and were significantly worse off than they had been at the start of the conflict.

In light of such anomalies, it is not altogether surprising that American writers were able to take what Malcolm Cowley in *Exile's Return* (1934) called a more "spectatorial attitude" towards wartime events.[7] Most American soldiers in 1917 were involved in peripheral military activities – training, driving ambulances and so on – rather than being caught up on the front line, so that the comment of Fred Summers, in John Dos Passos's novel *Nineteen Nineteen* (1932), about how "this ain't a war, it's a goddam Cook's tour" would have had a particular relevance to the situation of American servicemen in Europe.[8] Cowley's later description in *A Second Flowering* of the Great War as "the greatest spectacle in history" is oddly reminiscent of Jean Baudrillard's description of the Gulf War in 1990–1991 as marked by simulacra and an absence of direct conflict.[9] While there might be an element of intellectual truth in both cases, such curiously estranged, lop-sided perspectives tend to overlook how things often appeared quite differently from particular vantage points on the ground.

For American writers, nevertheless, the Great War was at least in part bound up with travel and exploration, the excitement of discovering Europe for the first time. In the eyes of Americans at the beginning of the twentieth century, Europe was associated with the allure of transgression in a way that is difficult to reconstitute fully within the media-saturated environment of 100 years later, when transcontinental travel has become much more commonplace. For Lambert Strether in James's novel *The Ambassadors* (1903), it is Paris itself that operates as the prime agent of the hero's increasing involvement in a field of moral ambiguity, a dangerous swerve away from the staid business values with which he had been surrounded in his home town of Woollett, Massachusetts. Similarly in E.E. Cummings's *The Enormous Room* (1922), there is a distinct focus on the French environment itself as opening the doors to perceptions of a new esthetic modernity. A war memoir which is related in the first person, with characters and events being dramatized in fictional terms, *The Enormous Room* was published some years after its author's wartime experiences, when he had been interned along with his friend William Slater Brown in a French military camp at La Ferté-Macé, a detention center for "undesirable persons" and suspected "spies." These somewhat farcical events are fused in Cummings's narrative into a kaleidoscopic portrayal of the military prison as an embryonic scene of modernity, with this picture of a world in a state of enforced immobility allowing the author to introduce weirdly oblique perspectives. In prison, Cummings remarks, events appear to exist independently of time: when an inmate realizes that no "speculation as to when he will regain his liberty" can hasten his release, he forgets the oppressive concept of "Time" altogether. In this sense, Cummings's representation through the French prison of an "actual Present – without future and past," where "each happening is self-sufficient," resembles his poetry of the interwar period, which similarly seeks to identify Neoplatonic patterns underlying the more positivistic concerns of human history. *The Enormous Room* thus recasts the French prison camp in the shape of modernist art, using caricature to frame its depictions of dehumanization within what the book calls a "somewhat cubist wilderness," while redescribing the French landscape in painterly, impressionist terms; he mentions, for example, "a very flourishing sumach bush ... whose berries shocked the stunned eye with a savage splash of vermillion."[10] Gertrude Stein, in *The Autobiography of Alice B. Toklas* (1933), remarked on how she was "much impressed" by *The Enormous Room*, and while Cummings here certainly ridicules authoritarian military structures, the book is also a notable example of the way in which American writers in the 1920s were seeking to requisition wartime landscapes as a harbinger of cultural modernism.[11]

In "The Ideology of Modernism" (1955), the Hungarian Marxist critic György Lukács argued that modernist esthetics involved a betrayal of the realist principles that had informed social consciousness in nineteenth-century literature, since modernism's fetishization of the eccentric and the abnormal caused it to lose sight of the broader historical dynamic linked to human agency. According to Lukács, the preference of modernist writers for focusing on the solitary, alienated condition of man tended to reify external reality as unalterable and thus to preclude the possibility of cultural or political change. It is true that American writers largely represent the First World War as an instrument of fate, but it would also be true to say that it is through the techniques of formal dislocation and strategic irony that they seek to reflect in narrative forms the historical conditions of wartime within their texts. Modernism itself was, in George Steiner's term, "extraterritorial," in that artists made a point of moving around among different locations to avoid provincial enclosure, and Paris was a site of initiation for American writers such as Cummings and Dos Passos, who first encountered the city through the exigencies of war.[12] Just as African American modernism, as Brent Hayes Edwards has shown, was formed by artistic experimentation in Paris as much as Harlem, so the masculine novel by white Americans in the early twentieth century rotated upon a transatlantic axis that operated, either literally or subliminally, as a memento of military conflict.[13]

Metaphorical equations between personal and cultural maturity are made explicit in Dos Passos's first novel, *One Man's Initiation: 1917*, which was first published in 1920. The book starts with an epigraph testifying to the authenticity of its narrative: "To the memory of those with whom I saw rockets in the sky, on the road between Erize-la-Petite and Erize-la-Grande, in that early August twilight in the summer of 1917." The hero, Martin Howe, says that he "never used to think that at nineteen I'd be crossing the Atlantic to go to a war in France." He continues, however, by stating that he has "never been so happy in his life," since for Martin the "initiation" of the book's title involves discovering the charms of French women as well as the chaos of the battlefield. Various overtly sexual references were censored when the book was first published in America, and one key theme of the work involves a turning away from ossified conventions and an embrace of modernity in all its confusions:

one of Martin's fellow soldiers says that "life was so dull in America that anything seems better."[14] At the same time, through one of the paradoxes of modernism in general, such an avant-garde sensibility also involves cultural regression, the acknowledgment of how contemporary events often echo ritualistic patterns of the past. Martin, in a nod to Dante's *Divine Comedy*, says he wants "to be initiated in all the circles of hell" – his colleague admits he would "play the part of Virgil pretty well" – while Martin also links the *danse macabre* of the Great War to the way "the people in Boccaccio managed to enjoy themselves while the plague was at Florence." Such a forced integration of the New World into medieval cycles serves to challenge the old idea of American exceptionalism, the notion that the United States enjoyed a sense of "freedom" from "the gangrened ghost of the past." Martin here specifically observes how his native country "has turned traitor to all that … now we're a military nation, an organized pirate like France and England and Germany."[15] In this sense, Dos Passos conscripts American literature into the wider conceptual framework of modernism, where, as in T.S. Eliot's *The Waste Land* or James Joyce's *Ulysses* (both published in 1922), esthetic modernity betokens a conscious attempt to reclaim the classical past, to disinter the archeological or atavistic framework underlying the superficial modernity of twentieth-century life.

Dos Passos's next novel, *Three Soldiers* (1921), extends this wartime scene into a more elaborate consideration of limitations on human freedom. The book again turns upon a transatlantic axis, starting off in San Francisco before following the fortunes of three American servicemen in France. Initially, Fuseli, like Martin Howe, enjoys the opportunities afforded by war – he says "It's great to be a soldier … Ye kin do anything ye goddam please" – but as the narrative progresses the forces of mechanization appear ever more brutalizing, and the romance of war is suppressed in favor of its "interminable monotony," with Fuseli coming to feel "full of hopeless anger against this vast treadmill to which he was bound."[16] In *Three Soldiers*, war is presented not so much as a site of physical carnage but as a gargantuan bureaucracy, a way of constraining human individuality "into the rigid attitudes of automatons in uniforms," all of which betokens "the hideous farce of making men into machines." The leading character in this novel, John Andrews, is a composer who comes to feel that serving his country in battle resembles the older forms of "slavery" that have disfigured history, and when he deserts from the army towards the end of the book he gives his name to a police officer as "John Brown," thereby deliberately affiliating himself with the nineteenth-century abolitionist, "a madman who wanted to free people."[17] In this way, Dos Passos extends his specific critique of war into a more general indictment of the coercive, corporate aspects of twentieth-century life. There is in this novel a deep romanticization of art as an antidote to such forms of dehumanization: Andrews himself idealizes Paris as a place "where one can find out things about music," while the book pays homage to composers Claude Debussy and Robert Schumann and to the writer Gustave Flaubert, whose "gorgeously modulated sentences" Andrews much admires. At the same time, the landscapes of Paris are frequently projected within an Impressionist esthetic: "the plane trees splotched with brown and cream color along the quais ... the Eiffel Tower with a drift of mist athwart it, like a section of spider web spun between the city and the clouds."[18]

Three Soldiers is characteristic of early Dos Passos in the way it sets up a binary opposition between artistic ideals and mechanized routines, an opposition that the later novels tend to disallow. By the time of *Manhattan Transfer* (1922), the author is more concerned with how the revolving glass doors of modern urban life create their own machine esthetic, while in his *USA* trilogy of the 1930s we witness what Michael Denning has called "a Tayloring of the novel" (after the pioneer of industrial efficiency, Frederick Winslow Taylor), where narrative scenes are organized in standardized typographic and media formats.[19] This is distinct from the style of merely following the world, as in the more traditional picaresque idiom of *One Man's Initiation*, through the eyes of an individual narrator. *Nineteen Nineteen*, the second novel in this *USA* trilogy, takes the Great War as one aspect of its global remit, but it also juxtaposes the events of war with other historical markers of the time: with Lenin and the Russian Revolution; with the general strike that took place in Seattle, and with the work of radicals in the art world, such as Picasso and Stravinsky in Europe and Charlie Chaplin in the United States. In this way, *Nineteen Nineteen* moves away from the more sentimental dimensions of *Three Soldiers* by inscribing a global esthetic where the shocks of war become analogous to the shocks of modernity in other cultural fields.

From James to Dos Passos, American novelists who wrote about the Great War pondered how its violence shaped a new esthetic world. But the question of how that world reverberated in the sphere of American letters, and in particular the relationship between cultural modernity and esthetic modernism, has remained a vexed one for literary studies. When the journal *American Quarterly* ran a special issue in 1987 on "Modernist Culture in America," the very idea of such a phenomenon appeared controversial, since the traditional narrative of literary history institutionalized by Alfred Kazin and others after the Second World War had worked on the assumption that European modernism developed in an abstruse and etiolated manner, while American novelists responded in a more robust, realistic fashion to changes they saw unfolding in the world around them. The attempts to define American literature as a separate field of study during the Cold War era often had the regrettable side effect of marginalizing European or transnational contexts, and in his contribution to this special issue, Malcolm Bradbury specifically called into question Hugh Kenner's version of American modernism as "a homemade world," in Kenner's 1974 book of that name, which Bradbury described as an act of intellectual "appropriation" that underestimated the involvement of American writers in more cosmopolitan artistic scenes.[20]

More recent critical work has suggested ways in which artistic modernism in general was not, as Lukács suggested, a principled rejection of historical modernity by its antagonists, but was rather enmeshed in complicated ways within it, and this speaks to what Frank Lentricchia has described as the typically "ambidextrous" quality of American modernism, where highbrow and lowbrow, mythology and realism are conflated in an often unobtrusive manner.[21] Unlike Eliot or Virginia Woolf, who flaunt their modernist complexities, Robert Frost presents his poem "After Apple Picking," from *North of Boston* (1915), as a much more oblique, down-home version of *Paradise Lost*, contemplating the disastrous consequences of eating forbidden fruit, but such double strands effectively undermine the conceptual dichotomy proposed by Kazin and Kenner between European allusiveness and American directness.

In *Modernism, Technology, and the Body*, Tim Armstrong has written of how the arts of modernism were implicated in numerous ways with the scientific, technological, and political shifts that characterize the modern era.[22] In this broader sense, one of the important legacies of the Great War was to raise awareness among American writers of the ethics and esthetics of the machine. "When everything is done by machines," asks Clara Butterworth in Sherwood Anderson's novel *Poor White* (1920), "what are people to do?"[23] Industrial development in the aftermath of the First World War introduced the same kind of anxieties that were to be seen at the end of the twentieth century around issues of information technology, and many writers of this earlier era address the issues of displacement, both psychic and geographic, that were associated with a general shift from an agrarian to an urban economy.

Some of these tensions were played out in the often hostile reception accorded in the United States to the alien figures of high modernist art, with the 1913 Armory Show in New York being the most egregious example of Americans accustomed to more traditional styles of representation finding it difficult to come to terms with Picasso paintings where human beings might be portrayed with two heads. But, as Paul K. Saint-Amour has shown, this kind of "syntax of rupture," where observers cannot give credence to the object that appears before their eyes, was not just a feature of cubist art but was also developed in common wartime technologies such as wireless telegraphy and aerial photography. Edward Steichen, who finished the war as chief of the US Air Service Photographic Section, was instrumental in developing the practice of overlapping aerial photographs for reconnaissance purposes, a technological shift which implicitly revealed the spatial and temporal contingency of human vision by emphasizing instead the kind of "vertigo of scale" associated with a stereoscope.[24] Dos Passos's esthetic idiom in *Nineteen Nineteen*, which is similarly designed to construct overlapping scenes so as to build up a "stereoscopic" vision of America's place in the world, might in this sense be linked to the kinds of reorganization of perceptual circuits that wartime technologies had helped to bring about.

There is also a more familiar equation between writing from the First World War and the esthetic strategies of modernist art, a link signaled by Ernest Hemingway in a 1922 newspaper article where he recalled looking down from an airplane on a field outside Paris: "It looked cut into brown squares, yellow squares, green squares and big flat blotches of green where there was a forest. I began to understand cubist painting."[25] Gertrude Stein, who was one of Hemingway's mentors in Paris, wrote in *The Autobiography of Alice B. Toklas* (which was to all intents and purposes her own autobiography) of the Great War as a specifically modern and American event, describing how she "always speaks of America as being now the oldest country in the world because by the methods of the civil war and the commercial conception that followed it America created the twentieth century, and since all the other countries are now either living or commencing to be living a twentieth century of life, America having begun the creation of the twentieth century in the sixties of the nineteenth century is now the oldest country in the world."[26] In this sense, war for Stein was represented as a conceptual equivalent to her understanding of abstract art, a historical correlative to the modernizing esthetics of Cézanne, a scenario where ornamental superfluity could be stripped away. It was Hemingway's similar elimination of the fustian associations of British literary tradition, along with his deliberate attempt to focus upon objects uncluttered by any kind of superfluous rhetoric, that first attracted Stein's attention. Hemingway's *In Our Time* (1924), which D.H. Lawrence called a "fragmentary novel," is a series of linked short stories that intercuts narratives set in America with scenes from the battlefront, with the book's title implying not only the hollowness of the prayer book's injunction – "give us peace in our time, O Lord" – but also ways in which the psychic disorientations of war extend across different times and places.[27] The author himself compared the dual perspective of *In Our Time* to watching the coastline from a ship first with the naked eye and then with binoculars, and this metaphor speaks again to the multilateral dimensions of American writing in the wake of the

Great War, its attempt self-consciously to encompass more than was ordinarily grasped within one particular person's field of vision.

Much of Hemingway's later work similarly seeks to understand the Great War not only journalistically but also within a larger framework of cultural modernism. *The Sun Also Rises* (1926), which John McCormick described as "the finest war novel we have," is actually set not on the front but in postwar Paris and Spain, with its hero, Jake Barnes, seeking to recover from the legacy of his wartime injuries by attending carefully to the present moment.[28] Jake insists on what he actually does think and feel, rather than what he is supposed to think and feel, and the novel harshly undercuts every kind of false sentiment in its effort to achieve a state of psychological integrity. Hemingway at a late stage lopped off the first 15 typed pages of *The Sun Also Rises*, omitting the biographies of Barnes and Lady Brett Ashley in an attempt to eliminate the cluttered verbiage of the old-fashioned novel of manners and to achieve instead a kind of minimalist grace. The bullfighting scenes in *The Sun Also Rises* also testify to ways in which wartime violence becomes sublimated for Hemingway's characters into other forms of ritualistic practice, while *A Farewell to Arms* (1929) treats this theme of First World War violence more explicitly, being set on the Italian front and told largely through the eyes of Lieutenant Frederic Henry, an American serving as an ambulance driver in the Italian army. Henry is wounded in the knee and sent to a hospital in Milan, and the subsequent development of his romance with Catherine Barkley, a nurse in the military hospital, is set against the backdrop of war. Part of the book's force involves its interrogation of patriotic clichés and its emphasis instead upon a phenomenological authenticity through which the facts of war come in themselves to attract a luminous esthetic force: "Abstract words such as glory, honor, courage, or hallow were obscene beside the concrete names of villages, the numbers of roads the names of rivers, the numbers of regiments and the dates."[29] As biographer Carlos Baker recounts, Hemingway himself was very critical of what he took to be the "fake" aspects of Willa Cather's war story "One of Ours" (1923) – he claimed Cather's war scenes were all "stolen" from D.W. Griffith's film *Birth of a Nation* (1915) – and the dominant effect of *A Farewell to Arms* is of a laconic knowingness, of characters in the modern world unsurprised by the violent events that surround them.[30]

At the same time, the belatedness that is endemic to Hemingway's war writing – as suggested by the title *A Farewell to Arms* – implies how elements of parody are inherent within Hemingway's literary project. In his attempt to achieve the emotional purity of what the title of one of his short stories calls "a clean well-lighted place," his work compulsively hollows out what it takes to be the calcified conditions of a superannuated culture. Just as Hemingway mocked the style of Sherwood Anderson and other modernist writers in *The Torrents of Spring* (1926) and spoofed the jargon of psychoanalysis in *The Sun Also Rises*, so the story "Soldier's Home," from *In Our Time*, turns upon a language of intertextual inversion and negativity: "There is a picture which shows him on the Rhine with two German girls and another corporal. Krebs and the corporal look too big for their uniforms. The German girls are not beautiful. The Rhine does not show in the picture."[31] In the same way that he indicts Cather for recycling wartime clichés, Hemingway also seems to express impatience towards his own narratives for the ways in which they are inevitably incarcerated in a metaphorical prison where the inherently reflexive quality of language always denies access to simple experiential truth. Hemingway's notorious violence, in other words, is incorporated into a psychological and philosophical world of self-immolation; for all of the author's stylistic innovations, his texts are haunted by specters of absence, by the wounds not only of wartime but also of ontological duality and a categorical loss of innocence.

One of the reasons why Hemingway was obsessed by wars and their "moral equivalents," as Harry Levin observed, was that his fiction came to represent life as being all about the fight to capture a state of plenitude or authenticity, something that for his narrators remains always elusive.[32] Consequently, the power of Hemingway's writing lies in its rhythms of perpetual anticlimax and disillusionment. He recapitulates the turbulence of the Great War that is explicit in his early writing in other kinds of conflict in his later work, whether in other military scenarios, such as the Spanish Civil War in *For Whom the Bell Tolls* (1940), or through more oblique forms of violent engagement, such as the scenes of big game hunting in *The Green Hills of Africa* (1935).

No group in America before 1918 had called itself a "generation," and one of the impacts made by the Great War was to identify people born at a certain point in history as shaped more by large-scale national or international trends rather than by older traditions of family or region. One of the authors who echoed Stein's observation that the First World War marked a generational shift was Edith Wharton, who wrote in her autobiography *A Backward Glance* (1934) how American social life had been changed abruptly by the United States entry into the war in 1917, when "what had seemed unalterable rules of conduct became of a sudden observances as quaintly arbitrary as the domestic rites of the Pharaohs."[33] Stein herself expresses admiration in *The Autobiography of Alice B. Toklas* for F. Scott Fitzgerald's very successful first novel, *This Side of Paradise* (1920), which she described as the "book that really created for the public the new generation," and which sold almost 50 000 copies in its first year.[34] Fitzgerald was fascinated by the structure of interpolated sketches that Hemingway devised for *In Our Time*, which he saw as characterizing the effects of war across a broad geographical spectrum, and his own fiction similarly embodies a choric quality, in the way it is designed self-consciously to tell the story of its era rather than just that of individual people within it. Amory Blaine in *This Side of Paradise* highlights this theme of temporal zones by describing how the war "certainly ruined the old backgrounds, sort of killed individualism out of our generation," and the novel suggests how in this new twentieth-century era even Leonardo da Vinci or Lorenzo de Medici could not have attained heroic status, since now "Life is too huge and complex." During his time at Princeton, Amory Blaine cannot be bothered with the war: "Beyond a sporting interest in the German dash for Paris the whole affair failed either to thrill or interest him." Nevertheless, the war's cultural ramifications are said to condition the lives of Amory's "generation" in both profound and superficial ways: for example, Cecilia Connage, sister of Amory's girlfriend, remarks that a general loosening of morals among the young – more smoking, more drinking, more frequent kissing – is "one of the effects of the war."[35]

Fitzgerald himself was just too young to see active military service, but Nick Carraway, narrator of *The Great Gatsby*, says that he enjoyed the war and came back restless, feeling that his native Midwest now appeared to be "the ragged edge of the universe" rather than, as formerly, its "warm center." Carraway has been unsettled by the war, saying that he "wanted the world to be in uniform and at a sort of moral attention forever," and Gatsby himself is also said to be a war veteran, with the years spent traveling with the army initially bringing him into contact with Daisy Buchanan, but also causing him to miss his initial opportunity with her.[36] In this sense, Stein's famous remark to Hemingway about how his was a "lost generation," which the latter recalled in *A Moveable Feast* (1964), has a particular resonance for Fitzgerald's work as well.[37] Ann Douglas has suggested there is a theological implication behind Stein's notion of a "lost" generation, and aspects of this postlapsarian sensibility are more obviously applicable to the work of Fitzgerald and Hemingway than to the writing of Stein herself.[38] In *Tender is the Night* (1934), Dick Diver's professional occupation as a psychiatrist offers an opportunity for the traumatic effects of the Great War to be discussed by his colleague, Dr Gregorovius, who says that even though Diver lacks direct experience of war, that does not mean he may not have been "changed like the rest." Later in the book, Diver has "a long dream of war," and when he wakes up he speaks in a "half-ironic" way of "Non-combatant's shell-shock." Most of this novel is set on the French Riviera, but there is also a scene where Diver visits the battlefields of the Somme with his friends, Abe North and Rosemary Hoyt, and exclaims: "All my beautiful lovely safe world blew itself up here with a great gust of high explosive love."[39] *Tender is the*

Night thus allegorically associates Dick Diver's own mental disintegration with what Fitzgerald took to be the increasingly shell-shocked condition of the twentieth-century world, a theme explored in his 1936 essay "The Crack-Up."

Whereas Fitzgerald and Hemingway both represent the Great War as an epitome of modernist fate, there were other writers, particularly during the early war years, who fiercely opposed American involvement in this conflict on political grounds. H.L. Mencken, of German ancestry himself, was one of the most prominent of these, while various other Greenwich Village radicals, including Max Eastman and Randolph Bourne, campaigned vigorously before 1917 against the prospect of world war. Theodore Dreiser, another writer of German extraction, was similarly aware of himself as being in a marginal position, and his fictional works consciously incorporate various aspects of ethnic difference that serve to position his narratives in an oblique relation to the nationalistic imperatives of American life. Such imperatives were, of course, particularly pressing around the time of the Great War, and it is important in this context that Dreiser's first language was not English but German; his father was a German immigrant who still spoke in his native tongue at home and who insisted on sending his son to a parochial school, where the nuns gave priority to instruction in German rather than English. The Dreiser novel which addresses this ethnic heritage most explicitly is *Jennie Gerhardt* (1911), where the heroine's father is said to wear a "knotted and weather-beaten German" countenance, and where, as the narrator makes clear, much of the novel's dialogue is reported in translation:

> He sat down calmly, reading a German paper and keeping an eye upon his wife, until, at last, the gate clicked, and the front door opened, Then he got up.
> "Where have you been?" he exclaimed in German.[40]

Andrew Delbanco has suggested that Dreiser's German inheritance may be "one reason his sentences often reflect some discomfort with customary English word order," and it is true that Dreiser's style seems always to preserve a distance from Anglo-Saxon syntactical norms, hinting at forms of linguistic and cultural defamiliarization.[41] There is a tendency towards compound words, as in hyphenated constructions like "race-thought," and towards circuitous grammar rife with subordinate clauses: "This added blow from inconsiderate fortune was quite enough to throw Jennie back into that state of hyper-melancholia from which she had been drawn with difficulty during the few years of comfort and affection which she had enjoyed with Lester in Hyde Park."[42] All of this gives the reader the curious impression that the whole of

Jennie Gerhardt, and not just Gerhardt's own speeches, might almost have been translated from the German.

Thomas P. Riggio described Dresier as a "hidden ethnic," someone whose German provenance is not always self-evident in his writing, and it is true that we do not automatically identify Caroline Meeber, the heroine of *Sister Carrie* (1900), as being from a German-American family, in the more obvious way that we see the characters of Ole Rolvaag, for example, as emerging from a Norwegian-American background.[43] Nevertheless, as Stuart P. Sherman observed in a 1915 essay, Dreiser's outlook does not seem to fit comfortably within an American tradition of moral realism, and for Mencken and other commentators associated with the Greenwich Village journal *Seven Arts*, Dreiser's detachment from the received patriotic wisdom of this era, along with his acknowledged anglophobia, became positive sources of approbation.[44] Bourne in 1917 called Dreiser "a true hyphenate, a product of that conglomerate Americanism that springs from other roots than the English tradition," adding that though his work was "wholly un-English" it was also "not at all German," but rather "an authentic attempt to make something out of the chaotic materials that lie around us in American life."[45] Bourne's perception here of Dreiser's "hyphenate" status points to a thread of doubleness that is indeed a constant factor throughout his narratives; while evading any separatist account of ethnicity, Dreiser's texts refract American national values aslant, as it were, mimicking the mythologies of United States nationalism while reframing them within a different linguistic and cultural context, so that the familiar American rags-to-riches paradigm is reproduced within a quizzically transnational framework.

After the Great War had ended in 1918, however, such oppositional voices became harder to find. The 1920s was generally a more conservative decade than its predecessor, one in which the systematic promotion of US national values became increasingly prominent. Such quiescence was not simply a consequence of the war itself; as Neil Smith has remarked, it was the Russian Revolution and perceived socialist threats deriving from labor unrest at home that helped to bring about at this time a "deglobalization of sorts," with the US Senate in 1919 rejecting membership of the League of Nations and Congress rescinding most of the progressive measures that had been passed during the war.[46] One consequence of this increasingly reactionary atmosphere was that questions of "taste and cultural value," as Susan Hegeman has observed, came to be articulated during the 1920s as never before or since in "geographical terms."[47] There was increased antagonism between country and city, with traditional rural communities expressing horror over social changes wrought through processes of modernization, while in turn Mencken and others in New York circles openly disdained the South and Midwest as primitive and backward. Sinclair Lewis's *Main Street* (1920), with its conflict between the values of Gopher Prairie, Minnesota, and modernization – Blodgett College, which the novel's inquisitive heroine Carol Kennicott attends, is said to be "still combating the recent heresies of Voltaire, Darwin, and Robert Ingersoll" – foreshadowed a series of novels in the 1920s where isolated and backward-looking communities were played off against the allure of progressive, free-thinking big cities.[48] This trend, in turn, fed into the demonization of the Midwest by the likes of Mencken, and it also contributed to the sense of restlessness that was endemic to fiction of the 1920s, where, as in Sherwood Anderson's *Winesburg, Ohio* (1919), the hero eventually feels compelled to abandon his provincial past in search of the riches of modern life.

Repression, then, was one of the general themes of fiction of the 1920s, not just the institutional repression of small-town life but also the psychic repression arising out of sensibilities shaped by the First World War. Sigmund Freud, who gave a series of lectures in Massachusetts in 1909, was very well known in America by the 1920s, and although of course his theories of psychoanalysis were often reworked into popular self-help narratives, the United States generally welcomed his work more readily than did traditional Europe, where the very notion of an unconscious was often considered suspect. Freud suggested in 1915 that wartime can last beyond the end of hostilities, and, as Marianna Torgovnick has written, this sense of the "cultural memory" of war is one of the starting points for *The Great Gatsby*, where Nick Carraway recalls at the beginning how he "participated in that delayed Teutonic migration known as the Great War" (p. 6).[49] A more systematic use of Freudian motifs manifests itself in Ludwig Lewisohn's novel *The Island Within* (1928), whose very narrative trajectory, chronicling a Jewish genealogy from nineteenth-century Prussia to twentieth-century America, might be seen in itself as an extended form of therapy, an attempt to delve back into the past so as to establish cultural identity more securely in the present. "Until the other day we Americans lived as though we had no past," says the narrator on the book's first page, but *The Island Within* then moves on deliberately to trace the contours of the past in order to excavate and explain the idea of ethnic difference. The notion of psychoanalysis is foregrounded in the narrative through Arthur Levy's professional practice as a therapist, and the whole structure of this novel is that of a man talking to himself, or perhaps a patient on a couch working through issues associated with the "inferiority complex" frequently cited here. After graduating from Columbia in 1914, Levy feels perturbed by the outbreak of European war, which he feels "to be something irrational – a hiatus in the march of civilization," but as the book goes on this sense of "irrational" agents in human affairs appears to be increasingly validated, with the hero drawn back towards his own Jewish heritage that he feels has left "an indelible stamp" on him.[50] Arthur's marriage to his non-Jewish wife, Elizabeth, consequently falls apart, with the compulsive though not entirely rational business of "reidentifying oneself with one's own people or group or clan" coming to supersede what are perceived to be the illusory freedoms of secular thought: "You didn't know you were going to resurrect the Jew in you," concludes Elizabeth plaintively at the end of the novel. For Levy, then, the traumatic disruptions of the Great War, which is said to have "loosened the taut strain of Puritan morals," shift his attention away from his narrow medical studies and expose him to the more uncomfortable aspects of "a barbarous world," where rationalizations of all kinds appear shallow when set against the atavistic nature of human instincts.[51]

These kinds of "herd prejudices," as *The Island Within* describes them, were not just found within the latent structures of psychoanalysis but also circulated more widely on the American political scene at this time.[52] The entry of America into the First World War in 1917 sparked a wave of intense nationalism, fuelled not only by the normal jingoistic rhetoric of wartime but also by a determined effort on the part of political leaders to consolidate the official position of English by suppressing the teaching of other immigrant languages. It was this kind of nationalism that helped to push the subject of American literature into a more prominent place on high school curricula, and the 1920s was also the decade when American literature began fully to establish itself as an academic subject at university level. In his introduction to *The Reinterpretation of American Literature*, Norman Foerster declared that there was a new need in the wake of the First World War to know what America "really is." Whereas the field of American history had become professionalized, said Foerster, questions of American literature had so far been left to "facile journalists and ignorant dilettanti."[53] But the events of war had served to focus attention on the United States as an independent powerful nation rather than merely a series of local cultures: "Throwing our nineteenth century into clearer perspective, the Great War removed from large numbers of Americans the sectional spectacles that had distorted their vision."[54] It would hardly be going too far to say that it was this "Great War" that effectively invented the idea of "American literature," not only in an institutional sense, as Foerster suggested here, but also conceptually. As Walter Benn Michaels has argued, the intense concern among writers of the 1920s with "nativism" as an ineradicable marker of cultural identity – the obsession of Hemingway, William Carlos Williams, and other American modernists with "America" itself as a sign of racial authenticity – produced an intellectual framework within which American literature, simply because of its Americanness, could be categorized as inherently different from other national idioms.[55]

While the American novel of the early twentieth century has become widely associated with the "Jazz Age" through the texts of Fitzgerald, Hemingway, and others, it is important to recognize how the dislocating experiences of the Great War were also an important contributory factor to this formative moment of cultural nationalism. The early novels of William Faulkner testify in interesting ways to the manner in which the shadow of the First World War hovers over literature of the 1920s. Faulkner himself had minimal exposure to military activity; keen to be a pilot, he joined the Royal Air Force in Canada and was posted to Toronto to be trained, but found his ambitions thwarted when the war finished before his training was complete. Although discharged as a cadet, Faulkner nevertheless purchased an officer's uniform, which he wore on the train home to Mississippi, where he subsequently regaled his old friends with tall tales of the wounds he had suffered in air conflict. More important than this, however, is the way in which Faulkner's first novel, *Soldiers' Pay* (1926), recasts his native South in the light of the Great War. Set mostly in Georgia rather than in Faulkner's mythological Mississippi, and noticeably oriented more towards the modern world in its evocation of recent historical events, *Soldiers' Pay* chronicles the return home of Donald Mahon, a pilot who has been shot down in Flanders and who now wears a permanent scar on his face. The rupture and transformation of war are epitomized in the figure of Mahon, of whom a local doctor says: the "man that was wounded is dead and this is another person, a grown child." This notion of a "grown child" anticipates Faulkner's later novel *The Sound and the Fury* (1929), where Benjy is an adult of 33 who is said to have a mental age of three, and it suggests ways in which Faulkner was attracted to the war partly as a way of approaching one of the key thematic concerns throughout his work: the disruption and reorganization of chronological sequence. In *Soldiers' Pay*, people once considered too young to marry now find that "war makes you older," the reverse of the grown child syndrome, while the scope of the conflict also effectively remaps the spatial co-ordinates that link the rural country to national events. "To feel provincial," says the narrator, involves "finding that a certain conventional state of behavior has become inexplicably obsolete overnight."[56]

Soldiers' Pay thus repositions the American South in the aftermath of the Great War, reconfiguring nature itself through metaphors of battle – "The stars swam on like the masthead lights of squadrons" – and contemplating "the hang-over of warfare in a society tired of warfare." More realist in its style than most of Faulkner's later fiction, *Soldiers' Pay* could be seen as his Jazz Age novel, since it describes the appearance of flappers and comments on how new social mores have brought about "physical freedom" for women, with a girl's "young, uncorseted body" seeming to be "flat as a boy's, and, like a boy's, pleasuring in freedom and motion." Many of the novels written in the shadow of the Great War react self-consciously against traditional gender codes associated with military life, with fictional characters such as Jake Barnes in *The Sun Also Rises* and Dick Diver in *Tender is the Night* represented as having lost their masculinity in various ways, and in this sense *Soldiers' Pay* touches on a theme fairly common to war novels of this era. The plot of Faulkner's novel revolves around whether Cecily Saunders will fulfill her promise to marry Mahon despite his war injury, or whether instead she will take off with her able-bodied suitor, George Carr. There is a veiled discussion here of Mahon's possible impotence – whether, as Mrs Powers puts it, he is "all right ... for marriage," since she says "a man ain't no right to palm himself off on a woman if he ain't" – and the idea of sexual relations here is presented in the kind of brutal, unsentimental way that later attracted censure to Faulkner for *Sanctuary* (1929). What is more striking, though, is the strong emphasis in Faulkner's narrative on sexuality in general, along with a tone that often verges toward the cynical; such features were characteristic of iconoclastic writing in the 1920s, but they caused such outrage in Faulkner's home state that the book was initially banned at the University of Mississippi.

The particularly provocative dimension of *Soldiers' Pay* lies in the way sexuality is associated implicitly not with spirit but with a world of matter, as if to align the narrative with the controversies of the Scopes trial which had taken place in Tennessee the previous year (in 1925), a trial that set Christian fundamentalists against those who advocated the teaching of evolution in high schools. College teacher Januarius Jones, for example, scrutinizes Cecily here as if she were an embodiment of Darwinian principles – "Her long legs, not for locomotion, but for the studied completion of a rhythm carried to its *nth*: compulsion of progress, movement; her body created for all men to dream after" – with the implication that his scholarly interests in Latin play second fiddle here to his frustrated sexual urges. In addition, the frequent references in *Soldiers' Pay* to icons of the Decadent movement (A.C. Swinburne, Aubrey Beardsley, and so on) enhance the reader's impression of a world where conventional moral values have fallen into disrepair and where a wider sense of degeneration – what Margaret Powers, thinking of Jones, describes as "an impression of aped intelligence imposed on an innate viciousness" – has become the order of the day.[57]

It was Sherwood Anderson who helped to get *Soldiers' Pay* published, and Faulkner dedicated to Anderson one of his subsequent novels, *Sartoris* (1929), which bridges the Jazz Age qualities of *Soldiers' Pay* with an immersion in the cyclic history of Mississippi that was to become Faulkner's authorial trademark. *Sartoris* is the first Faulkner work to be set in Jefferson, and it features a wartime aviator, Bayard Sartoris, returning home to the changing South. The old housekeeper Miss Jenny is generally unsympathetic to the idea of men going off to "play soldier," and in particular to Bayard's decision to come back to America in the middle of the war to get married. She compares Bayard unfavorably to his twin brother John, who "at least had consideration enough, after he'd gone and gotten himself into something where he had no business, not to come back and worry everybody to distraction."[58] But John is killed in the war, whereas Bayard eventually returns to Mississippi with a taste for speed, machinery, and accidents; he buys an automobile, kills his grandfather in a car crash, then flees to South America, where he meets an airman in a bar and, unable to resist the allure of flying again, subsequently dies in an aviation experiment at the age of 27. Faulkner thus portrays Bayard as caught up within a cycle of obsessive behavior, compelled to repeat the violence of war to a point of self-destruction. These psychopathological repetitions also merge here into Faulkner's more general view of the South, where the fate of young Bayard mirrors the self-immolation of his namesake in the American Civil War 50 years earlier.

In this sense, the trauma of the Great War for the Sartoris clan introduces a larger Faulkner theme, "the perverse necessity of his family doom," the ways in which ancestral bonds circumscribe individual destiny, a theme we see developed in relation to the Compson family in Faulkner's most famous novels. The prospect of social change is generally viewed askance by the characters in *Sartoris*. The black soldier Caspey claims he "don't take nothin' fum no white folks no mo'," saying that "War done changed all dat. If us cullud folks is good enough ter save France fum de Germans, der us is good enough ter have de same rights de Germans is." But Simon, a fellow African American, is less open to new ideas, insisting that he still prefers horses to automobiles, and appealing to the "arrogant shade" of "Marse John" Sartoris to rebuke Caspey's uppity notions. Later in the book we are told that "Caspey had more or less returned to normalcy," but the question of what is "normalcy," and the way in which the representation of Caspey's speech as a form of dialect serves effectively to marginalize him within this world, epitomize both the power and the problems of Faulkner's writing.

The troublesome nature of Faulkner's work lies in the way it conflates racial stereotypes and hierarchies with a state of nature, as if such differentiations arose out of the cycles of the earth; its strength, however, lies in its radically inchoate character, the way it textually evokes opposing forces without seeking to impose any kind of premature closure upon them. *Sartoris* brings European war and American pastoral, modernity and Mississippi, into violent juxtaposition, but rather than seeking any kind of sentimental resolution, it allows these divergent pressures to work themselves out in circuitous ways. Although the lawyer Horace Benbow returns from the European front to idealize his Jefferson home in "a golden Arcadian drowse," saying that "the reason for wars" is "[t]he meaning of peace," Faulkner's complex, multivalent novel does not altogether endorse such a regressive view of domestic bliss.[59] Indeed, it is the burden of Faulkner's modernist rhetoric to bring alternative discourses and interpretations of the world into conflict, so that characters with different views on law and race are implicitly at war with each other. Unlike in the more emollient world of postmodernist narrative, where different world views are often allowed to operate harmoniously alongside each other, Faulkner's personae exist within the more fraught circumstances of modernism, where they find themselves tormented by an impulse to achieve states of purity and truth. In this sense, the figure of the Great War comes for Faulkner to have a wider metaphorical resonance, since violence, conflict, and rupture are the dynamics upon which his fictional world turns.

In the twenty-first-century world of high-tech warfare, when international conflict has become a highly specialized operation, it is sometimes difficult to reconstitute the very different twentieth-century mindset, when world war involved the threat of universal conscription. War in the early years of the twentieth century was a labor-intensive occupation where lives were easily expendable and where the prospect of lay people being drawn into the conflict was much more evident. Although the United States itself was never a theater of conflict and did not have to endure mass bombing, the traumas suffered by servicemen on behalf of the country as a whole helped to shape the direction of the American novel throughout the 1920s. Faulkner published *Sartoris* in January 1929, just a few months before *The Sound and the Fury* appeared in October of that year, but even in Faulkner's later novels the echoes of war still reverberate, and the way in which he often imaginatively conflates the First World War with the US Civil War suggests how this wartime aesthetic had a durable effect on his fiction. Indeed, whereas from the synoptic retrospective gaze of the second half of the twentieth century the First World War was often regarded as merely a prelude to the Second World War, for Faulkner, as for other writers of this period, it was comparisons with the US Civil War that were more pressing. Henry James similarly begins his essay "Within the Rim" by evoking the shade of this earlier conflict: "The first sense of it all to me after the first shock and horror was that of a sudden leap back into life of the violence with which the American Civil War broke upon us, at the North, fifty-four years ago, when I had a consciousness of youth which perhaps equaled in vivacity my present consciousness of age." While James recognizes the similarity of these historical situations in terms of their conditions of violence, he is also astute enough to acknowledge the "illusion" of the "analogy," and part of the disorienting aspect of the Great War for American writers was precisely that this new kind of international conflict pulled them out of their familiar and accustomed national orbits.[60] For Faulkner, as for many other Americans of this era, the issue of active military engagement was ultimately less significant than the ways in which the country appeared to be drawn into more extensive social and political circuits, with the circumference of world war positioning US culture differently in relation to the march of global events.

4.2 The Esthetics of Contradiction

Within the world of poetry, the choice whether or not to write from within the American behemoth seemed in the period immediately after the Great War to take on significant political as well as cultural overtones. William Carlos Williams, who worked as a medical doctor in New Jersey, wrote scathingly at the beginning of his long poem *Paterson*, published in five volumes from 1946 to 1958, about how other American poets had "run out – / after the rabbits," and he entertained a distinct personal loathing throughout his life for T.S. Eliot, the native of St Louis, Missouri, who had gone as a student to Paris and Oxford and then stayed to make his literary career in London.[61] Ezra Pound, born in Idaho but driven out of his teaching appointment at a small college in Indiana after the authorities there accused him of impropriety with a visiting chorus girl, was another who fled to Europe, associating the Midwestern states in particular with a blockheaded stupidity that impeded the free circulation of art and ideas. This was an era of spatial hierarchies, where cultural capitals such as London and Paris (and, to some extent, New York) were regarded as the apex of all creative activity and places such as Idaho or Indiana merely the boondocks, and the trajectory of Pound's career reflected his intense desire to be at the center of things. Such ambition manifests itself in the way his poetry self-consciously modernizes esthetic forms through its deployment of Imagism and other avant-garde techniques. It is typical, for example, that his most famous Imagist poem, "In a Station of the Metro" (1912), which compresses perception into two lines, was based on an Underground station in Paris rather than in any American city:

> The apparition of these faces in the crowd;
> Petals on a wet, black bough.[62]

But Pound's restless ambition was evident also through his attempt in the *Cantos* to marry art and economics in the interests of mapping out an alternative version of world history. Never content to speak from merely a provincial viewpoint, Pound's *Cantos* engage with (among other things) classical Greek and Roman myth, the culture of the Orient and the American Revolutionary era driven by political leaders such as John Adams and Thomas Jefferson. Pound attempts poetically to batter the cultural history of the past into some kind of teleological order by linking the turbulence of the present to similar anxieties in previous eras, and all of his work aspires to expand the circumference of the world around him by juxtaposing proximate circumstances with events more distant in space and time. In his 1917 essay "Provincialism the Enemy," Pound celebrates Henry James, along with other writers such as Turgenev and Flaubert, for the way their "internationalism" and their crusade against "the hundred subtle forms of personal oppressions and coercions" effectively support "the whole fight of modern enlightenment" against more stifling forces of provincialism.[63]

There were, of course, other poets in this era who focused more specifically on quintessentially American landscapes. Many of them were associated with Chicago, which became established as the symbolic apex of a modernism rooted specifically in the American heartland, rather than one over which a transatlantic specter always tended to loom, as was the case in New York in part because of its geographical location on the Eastern seaboard. The poems of Vachel Lindsay, who was born in Illinois and studied at the Art Institute of Chicago, pioneered a style of poetry rooted in folk themes that was designed to be sung or chanted, with the composer Charles Ives actually setting to music Lindsay's first famous poem, "General William Booth Enters into Heaven" (1912). Booth was a British Methodist preacher who founded the Salvation Army and became its first "General," and Sandburg produced a similarly spiritualist ambience in his poem "Abraham Lincoln Walks at Midnight" (1914), which portrays Lincoln resurrected from his eternal sleep and walking the streets of Springfield, Illinois, where he ruminates on the depredations of the modern world that had led to the outbreak of the First World War.

Other poets who were associated with the so-called "Chicago Literary Renaissance" were Carl Sandburg and Edgar Lee Masters, both of whom were promoted (along with Lindsay) by Harriet Monroe in her influential journal *Poetry: A Magazine of Verse*, which became strongly identified with this Chicago school after its first appearance in 1912. Masters's *Spoon River Anthology* (1915) is made up of a series of interlinked poems that describe the inhabitants of a fictional Midwestern community called "Spoon River," with each poem comprising an epitaph for a dead citizen and the work as a whole evoking a compelling if macabre style of gothic humor. (Ezra Pound, in his review of *Spoon River Anthology*, declared: "At last! America has discovered a poet!")[64] Masters's book sold some 80 000 copies in four years, a remarkable figure for a volume of poetry, and it clearly touched a nerve in the American community. Sandburg's verse did not sell so well, but one of his most famous poems, "Chicago" (1914), was described by the author as "a chant of defiance by Chicago ... its defiance of New York, Boston, Philadelphia, London, Paris, Berlin and Rome," with the author adding: "The poem sort of says 'Maybe we ain't got culture, but we're eatin' regular.'"[65] The adversarial style of Sandburg's poem is evident in its declarative idiom:

> Hog Butcher for the World,
>   Tool Maker, Stacker of Wheat,
>   Player with Railroads and the Nation's Freight Handler;
>   Stormy, husky, brawling,
>   City of the Big Shoulders:
>
> They tell me you are wicked and I believe them, for I have seen your
>   painted women under the gas lamps luring the farm boys.
> And they tell me you are crooked and I answer: Yes, it is true I have
>   seen the gunman kill and go free to kill again.
> And they tell me you are brutal and my reply is: On the faces of
>   women and children I have seen the marks of wanton hunger.
> And having answered so I turn once more to those who sneer at this
>   my city, and I give them back the sneer and say to them:
> Come and show me another city with lifted head singing so proud to
>   be alive and coarse and strong and cunning.

The long lines here indicate a Whitmanian largesse, a willingness to break through conventional boundaries in the interests of representing a new kind of democratic freedom in poetry. The last line of the poem describes Chicago as "proud to be Hog Butcher, Tool Maker, Stacker of Wheat, Player with Railroads and Freight Handler to the Nation," and Sandburg's imagination is exercised by the position of Chicago at the center of the United States, something he represents proudly as a national (rather than global) position.[66] As with Masters, there is also a defensive aspect to the way in which Sandburg extols his native Midwest, a desire specifically to bring previously neglected landscapes to the attention of a wider literary world.

The 1920s was the era in which there was a concerted attempt for the first time to identify American literature as a separate subject in the public domain as well as the academic sphere. Initially, pressure for this was brought to bear among the bohemian circles in Greenwich Village and within the radical circles of journalism based in New York. It was this milieu that produced Mencken's work *The American Language*, first published in 1919, one that sought to valorize idiomatic American expressions as a particular (and not necessarily inferior) version of English. It also produced the critical writings of Bourne, Van Wyck Brooks and Edmund Wilson, all of whom scorned academic pedantry and sought to justify contemporary American writing as a dynamic response to the challenges of the modern world. Wilson spent his college years at Princeton between 1912 and 1916, served (like Dos Passos and Hemingway) in the Ambulance Corps in France during World War I, and then wrote for various magazines in New York throughout the 1920s. He worked for *Vanity Fair*, whose circulation reached 80 000 in 1920, for the *Dial*, which first published in 1922 T.S. Eliot's *The Waste Land* along with an essay by Wilson explicating the poem, and also for the *New Republic*, where his review of Joyce's *Ulysses* in the July 1922 issue elicited from the grateful author a letter thanking Wilson for his "very appreciative and painstaking criticism."[67]

It is easy to see how sharp would have been the distinction in Wilson's mind between this vibrant cultural milieu and the supine world of Princeton, which was, according to Morris Dickstein, "in many ways far from a serious university" during the first two decades of the twentieth century, an institution where "the gentleman's C was a way of life and there was a long tradition behind it."[68] Although Wilson remained indebted to his undergraduate teacher Christian Gauss, to whom his critical work *Axel's Castle* (1931) is dedicated, there is no doubt that Wilson considered New York the only possible location for his literary career after his return from wartime France. When Wilson graduated from Princeton there were only two university professors of English in the entire United States who specialized in American literature – Fred Lewis Pattee at Penn State and William B. Cairns at Wisconsin – and this neglect was compounded by the condescension of the Ivy League establishment towards contemporary literature in all its forms.[69] American literature in particular stood in the early twentieth century in the same relation to canonical English literature as English itself had stood during the nineteenth century to the study of Greek and Roman classics; among traditionalists, the new subject was always considered too soft, too susceptible to merely impressionistic reactions, to be worthy of serious intellectual pursuit. In 1928, Wilson complained with typical obstreperousness of how "[s]ince the death of Stuart P. Sherman, who was second-rate at best, there has not been a single American critic who regularly occupied himself in any authoritative way with contemporary literature."[70]

This long-standing academic hostility towards the vulgarities of contemporary culture was given particular resonance in the 1920s by the increasing prominence of the New Humanists, with whom Wilson and his New York contemporaries were in rebarbative dialogue. Centered around Harvard professor Irving Babbitt and Princeton guru Paul Elmer

More, the New Humanists laid emphasis upon their own interpretation of classical civilization and what Babbitt described as "proportionateness through a cultivation of the law of measure."[71] In the critical anthology *Humanism and America* (1930), editor Norman Foerster defined humanism as involving "a resolute distinction between man and nature and between man and the divine," and he declared humanists to be more "academic" in their orientation than "workaday journalist critics" since they were committed to exploring "a wisdom deeper than that of the market-place."[72] Foerster, as we have seen, was also one of the pioneers in the academic professionalization of American literature, with his anthology of critical essays *The Reinterpretation of American Literature* having appeared in 1928. There was in fact an overlap between the contributors to these two volumes, with Harry Hayden Clark of the University of Wisconsin declaring in 1928 that there was "a crying need for at least one learned journal devoted exclusively to publishing material on American literature." The academic journal *American Literature* was duly founded in 1929, and in the *Humanism and America* volume of 1930, Clark outlined the mythic conception of an American arcadia that would be consonant with how "great art has always been organic with and supported by the life and vision of a whole people." Such utopian designs led Clark in the latter essays to evoke a specter that was to haunt Americanist criticism over the next half century: "When such scholar-critics have developed such a social imagination, such a popular unanimity of hope," he wrote, "we shall be ready to receive the artist of genius who is to write for us the great American novel."[73] This "Great American Novel" became something of a cliché during the modernist period, suggesting not only the nationalist incentive that drove American writers during this era but also a spirit of defensiveness, as though these writers had some catching up to do.

Wilson's essays on literature and culture in the 1920s are taking issue both with the tenets of New Humanism and with the reification of American literature, great American novel and all, as "a popular unanimity of hope." For Wilson, such hortatory exercises in popular pedagogy were associated in various ways with what he took to be the desiccated world of higher education, and part of his self-definition as a writer during the 1920s involved an escape from such strictures. Wilson himself had been a contemporary (and competitor) of Scott Fitzgerald at Princeton, and his portrait was included, along with those of Fitzgerald, Dos Passos, John Peale Bishop, and Stephen Vincent Benét, in a 1922 *Vanity Fair* tribute to "The New Generation in Literature." At the same time, for all his iconoclasm and commitment to contemporary culture, Wilson also had one foot in the traditionalists' camp. His eulogistic tribute after Gauss's death in 1951 suggests a love-hate relationship with his alma mater, with Wilson celebrating his "great teacher" as "part of that good eighteenth-century Princeton." Gauss's easy familiarity with a vast range of subjects, said Wilson, indicated "fidelity to a kind of truth that is rendered by the discipline of aesthetic form, as distinct from that of the professional moralist."[74] In this way Wilson sharply differentiated Gauss from his fellow Princetonian, Paul Elmer More, in whom, said Wilson in a 1937 obituary, the "moralist" triumphed over the "poet"; Gauss, declared Wilson, was "much subtler a mind than More, with so much wider a range of imaginative sympathy, and correspondingly so much less fixed in his opinions."[75]

Such a sense of stylistic hybridity, oscillating between journalistic and academic vantage points, is developed in Wilson's early work to embrace a systematic esthetic of contradiction, where it is the interaction between street burlesque and classical form that defines the tenor of his art. Wilson wrote several appreciative essays on New York burlesque theater in the 1920s – his acquaintances E.E. Cummings and Hart Crane were also devotees of burlesque performance – and in his essay collection *The Shores of Light: A Literary Chronicle of the Twenties and Thirties*, Wilson's piece on the Minsky Brothers' Follies is directly preceded by his illuminating 1927 essay "A Preface to Persius: Maudlin Meditations in a Speakeasy." Here Wilson portrays himself alone in a New York diner reading an eighteenth-century edition of Persius, the Roman author who lived in the crime-ridden era of Nero and who consequently expressed himself "confusedly, inelegantly and obscenely." By drawing attention to the inconsistencies between Persius's inchoate style and the tamer idiom of eighteenth-century editor William Drummond, who blandly criticizes Persius for his lack of "elegance" and "urbanity," Wilson highlights discrepancies between the actual stuff of classical history and the way it has been domesticated by American neoclassical traditions.[76] Through foregrounding the similar confusions and follies of his own day – the provision of illegal wine and the boisterous presence of Cummings in the speakeasy, along with arguments over the impending execution of Italian-American anarchists Sacco and Vanzetti – Wilson seeks to present the chaotic scene of New York in the 1920s as a critique both of New Humanist complacency and also its unwarranted appropriation of classical history for narrow ideological purposes. Wilson thus represents burlesque as something like an ontological condition, where abstract ideals are brought low by the compulsive nature of material desire, but he simultaneously uses this classical model of Persius to reposition the New York speakeasy within an archetypal framework, thereby seeking intellectually to authenticate a common language, as Joyce did in *Ulysses*, through linking it analogically with mythological prototypes.

In intellectual terms, part of the challenge associated with academic institutionalizations of American literature involved the emergence of this field in parallel to American history, as the adumbration of a narrative about the development of a nation. Foerster's own contribution to his critical anthology *The Reinterpretation of American Literature* places special emphasis on what he takes to be the key national themes – the Puritan tradition, the frontier spirit, romanticism, and realism – as well as paying particular homage to Frederick Jackson Turner, arguing that Turner had professionally "revolutionized the study of American history" in a way American literature had yet to match. Turner's 1893 essay "The Significance of the Frontier" argued that the exceptional qualities of US cultural experience were shaped in profound ways by a frontier spirit, and Foerster consequently emphasized the transformational qualities of "physical America," as he called it. "In race and tradition we are fundamentally European," Foerster concluded, "but our geography is our own, and the consequences of our geography can scarcely be exaggerated."[77]

This focus on American culture as embodying a frontier spirit was very influential in how American literature generally came to be understood and institutionalized, particularly in the post-1945 period. The poet Charles Olson, for example, declared in 1949 that the "SPACE" was "the central fact to men born in America," a conception that informs not only his own poetry but also that of his acolytes, such as the Western poets Ed Dorn and Robert Creeley.[78] The obvious problem with such a formulation, however, is that it tends to restrict American literature to epiphenomena of national archetypes, as if textual complexities could be thematically compressed to expressions of an American myth. This narrows the critical parameters of the field unconscionably, as if a poet could be recognized only as "American" if he grappled with questions of space. But it is significant that Olson's maxim on American space was not gender neutral – "*men* born in America" – and his mythic assumption does not carry such obvious relevance either to women or to immigrant minorities who were generally clustered in urban centers.

Such slanted perspectives have often had a deleterious effect also on the critical reception of canonical American writers, as we see for instance in the often cumbersome ways in which the work of Hart Crane has been circumscribed by the academy. Born in the Midwest (in Ohio) in 1899, Crane's poetry in many ways conforms to traditional American models, examining the nature of beauty and the allure of a mythic *topos*, something explored most fully in his long poem *The Bridge* (1930), which projects Brooklyn Bridge as a symbol for America. Yet Crane, like Edmund Wilson, enjoyed the metropolitan scene of New York in the 1920s, integrating burlesque explicitly into *The Bridge* through a section of the poem named after the National Winter Garden burlesque theater in Manhattan. He also engaged intellectually with surrealist circles and with the work of Joyce, visiting Paris himself in 1929, and Crane's enthusiastic involvement with gay subcultures on both sides of the Atlantic helped to ensure that his epic poem was a multifaceted achievement, one self-consciously incorporating elements of comedy and popular culture alongside its high romantic strain. Yet none of this was of much interest to American critics in the middle years of the twentieth century – R.W.B. Lewis, L.S. Dembo, and others – who routinely castigated Crane for what they took to be the failure of his idealist vision.[79] Basing their critical approaches both on Christian symbolism – Catholic convert Allen Tate, who critiqued *The Bridge* in similar terms, was an important early influence on the poem's reception – and on an assumption of nationalist teleology turning upon the premise that Crane was attempting to inscribe national epic in the tradition of Whitman, these critics radically shortchanged *The Bridge* by approaching the poem through an excessively narrow interpretive model. American literature within the academy, in other words, had after World War II taken on certain rigid institutional parameters, linked to the "myth and symbol" critical format through which key American texts were expected to conform to nationalist archetypes, and works that flouted this pattern were downgraded accordingly.

These academic blindspots created a skewed pattern in the ways American literature was understood in the middle years of the twentieth century. Kenner's *A Homemade World* read American modernist writers – Faulkner, Fitzgerald, Hemingway, Williams, Stevens – alongside the world of Pound, Joyce, and Eliot, arguing that the work of these American writers was shaped by the "American conditions" and "peculiar homemade strengths" that informed their writing.[80] Similarly, Harold Bloom's *Wallace Stevens: The Poems of Our Climate* (1980) took a proprietorial attitude towards Stevens, aligning the idea of "our" climate with Stevens's modernist renegotiation of a transcendentalist poetic lineage deriving from Emerson and Whitman.[81] Both Kenner and Bloom were excellent critics, of course, but their polemical emphasis on a "homemade" aspect to American modernism tended to downplay how the intellectual influences on these writers derived from contexts that could not be confined to any national circumference. Bloom, for example, overlooks ways in which Stevens's early poetry was partially shaped by French surrealism and other avant-garde artistic movements that flourished outside the United States, even though Charles Altieri plausibly argues that Stevens was stylistically "closer to Mondrian and Picasso than to Whitman or Wordsworth."[82]

Although Cubism and other forms of modernist painting were introduced to the United States by the 1913 Armory Show, such iconoclastic modes of representation were never easily accepted by those who preferred the commercially driven realism that dominated the American art marketplace at that time. While the Armory Show also included the first public exhibition of works by significant American modernist painters such as John Marin and Joseph Stella, the popular reaction to this New York exhibition tended to dismiss abstraction itself as pretentious and nonsensical. Similarly, Kenner's designation of an American domestic milieu effectively prioritizes a nationalist agenda, even though, in the case of Fitzgerald and Hemingway, many of the key works of these authors were written outside the United States. Even William Carlos Williams, who campaigned relentlessly for an authentic American voice in art and culture, was indebted intellectually to international styles of painting such as the Cubism and Post-Impressionism then coming out of Paris, as chronicled in his *Autobiography* (1948), and Williams's own poetry is concerned in complex ways to integrate local and familiar scenarios within a framework of cosmopolitan, transnational esthetics. The motto with which Williams became famously associated – "no ideas but in things," as he expresses it in *Paterson* – did not mean that ideas could necessarily be reduced to inanimate objects but, rather, that all abstractions should bear a symbiotic relation to material phenomena.[83]

As Malcolm Bradbury acknowledged in his respectful rejoinder to Kenner's thesis: "To most Americans, Modernism was foreign; but since it was modern they wanted it, but made in a homemade way."[84] This suggests the manifold contradictions associated with American modernism, the ways in which it sought to speak to national and international agendas both at once. Lawrence Rainey has written insightfully about the "resolute contradictoriness" of modernism – the way that it both internalized and sought through a privileging of esthetic autonomy to keep its distance from the world of commerce and mass culture.[85] Vincent Sherry has advanced a similar argument in relation to the temporality of modernism, pointing out how Pound's slogan "make it new" was not concocted until 1934, while also commenting on how modernism's flamboyantly avant-garde stance incorporated much imagery from the artistic worlds of nineteenth-century decadence, so that modernism might be understood paradoxically as backward-looking as much as forward-looking.[86]

The same kind of conundrum manifests itself in relation to the worlding of modernism. For example, Gertrude Stein, who was born in Pennsylvania in 1874 and educated at Harvard and Johns Hopkins University, always insisted in her work that she was immutably American, a nationalistic theme promoted in her novel *The Making of Americans* (1925) where the emphasis falls on forms of classification by racial or other forms of typology, and an idea reinforced in her non-fictional *Wars I Have Seen* (1945), where she associates citizenship exclusively with a "right of birth" and therefore dismisses the idea of "naturalization" as "foolishness."[87] In this sense, Stein's commitment to esthetic and sexual radicalism ran alongside a much more conventional investment in the idea of national identity as an irreducible phenomenon. Her quip that America was her country and Paris was her home town thus spoke to a transnational paradox that ran all the way through this modernist era.

Given such paradoxes, transnationalism should be understood as a constitutive feature of American modernism, albeit one that often manifested itself in oblique or circuitous ways. Anita Patterson, for example, has written of how the poems of Langston Hughes appear at first glance to fit well with what recent commentators on modernism such as T.J. Clark, Wanda Corn and Walter Benn Michaels have "with misleading generalization, described as the purism and cultural nationalism of the modernist movement."[88] Yet, as Patterson went on to observe, Hughes not only read European writers such as Joyce, Joseph Conrad, and D.H. Lawrence, but was also actively involved in an extensive transnational literary network, one that included figures such as Marianne Moore, W.H. Auden, André Malraux, Pablo Neruda, and others. Hughes also met Tristan Tzara in Paris during the summer of 1937, and he drew on the kind of montage technique practiced by the Surrealists and Dadaists in order to fabricate his own poetic version of temporal and spatial compression, as in "The Negro Speaks of Rivers" (1921):

> I've known rivers:
> I've known rivers ancient as the world and older than the flow of
>   human blood in human veins.
>
> My soul has grown deep like the rivers.
>
> I bathed in the Euphrates when dawns were young.
> I built my hut near the Congo and it lulled me to sleep.
> I looked upon the Nile and raised the pyramids above it.
> I heard the singing of the Mississippi when Abe Lincoln
>   went down to New Orleans, and I've seen its muddy
>   bosom turn all golden in the sunset.
> I've known rivers:
> Ancient, dusky rivers.
> My soul has grown deep like the rivers.[89]

It is possible to discern here the influence on Hughes of American poets such as Carl Sandburg, with their emphasis on an authentic speaking voice and a chant-like style of delivery. Ann Douglas is also right to say that New York itself was a "magnet" in the 1920s for "the African-American movement of liberation," whose dynamic center in the Harlem Renaissance, of which Hughes was a part, was galvanized by the fact that all cultural media in this early modernist era were initially based in Manhattan.[90] But in the emphasis on "deep" time and space, and in the way Hughes juxtaposes his own spiritual experience with the alternative spatial dimensions of Asia and Africa, it is also not difficult to see how he deliberately links the culture of his homeland "(the singing of the Mississippi)" to a wider global circumference. Although he is a poet of Harlem, Hughes also merges local scenes into global events. The conception of "geomodernisms" outlined by Laura Doyle and Laura Winkiel suggests how the histories of modernism "are multiple and interconnected in surprising, unforeseen ways," and the manner in which Hughes brings Africa and America into poetic juxtaposition in "The Negro Speaks of Rivers" testifies to the way in which, for him, "African American" is a double and hybrid rather than merely a singular adjective.[91]

4.3 American Studies and World Literature: *The Great Gatsby* and *The Grapes of Wrath*

American studies as it developed in the years after World War II, like other manifestations of area studies at this time, tended to emphasize the notion of the United States having, in Susan Hegeman's words, "a coherent, consensual, transhistorical national character," with particular texts exemplifying such "character."[92] Such willingness to allegorize particular texts as synecdochic of an American spirit carried its own risk of exceptionalism; Michaels argued in *Our America* that the modern concept of culture was not a critique of racism but was itself a form of racism, since it was predicated upon an idea of national identity that had become reified. Examples of this oversimplified alignment of text and context can be seen in the educational readiness to read Fitzgerald's *The Great Gatsby* as a typically American text of the 1920s or John Steinbeck's *The Grapes of Wrath* as a typical text of the 1930s.

The idea of types itself has a complicated intellectual history in America, from the use of typology to establish correspondences between divine revelation and secular time in Puritan typology of the seventeenth century through to the emphasis on representative identity in Chinese American novelists Gish Jen's *Typical American* (1991). But for *Gatsby* and *The Grapes of Wrath*, this assumption of representative identity tended too often to remain insufficiently theorized, with no indication of how such correlations between text and context were adduced. It is, nevertheless, easy enough in both cases to understand how such symbiotic equations came about, and indeed Fitzgerald's own essay "Echoes of the Jazz Age" (1931) retrospectively aligns the rich, carefree years of the 1920s with a largesse that he said had subsequently passed. But *The Great Gatsby* is in its own way as intensely regional a novel as is Steinbeck's, which is set famously on the Western highways between the dustbowl of Oklahoma and the promised land of California. Fitzgerald's narrator Nick Carraway enjoys parties both in Manhattan and at Gatsby's mansion on Long Island, with his awed reaction to this kind of bohemian hedonism being contrasted in his mind with his childhood train journeys "coming back West from prep school and later from college at Christmas time." Thinking of "the murky yellow cars of the Chicago, Milwaukee and St Paul railroad," Carraway realizes "that this has been a story of the West after all," since its main characters "were all Westerners, and perhaps we possessed some deficiency in common which made us subtly unadaptable to Eastern life" (pp. 136–137). Regionalist variation in American literature might be understood as a parallel to transnational frameworks, since it fractures the putative organic homology of a national body and recognizes the cultural terrain instead as a tissue of multiple interlocking strands, and in both *The Great Gatsby* and *The Grapes of Wrath* there is a distinct tension between national and regional tropes.

Both of these novels aspire self-consciously to represent themselves as epitomizing an American condition, particularly in *Gatsby*'s final chapter where Carraway associates the hero's vision of his future with that of the Pilgrim Fathers, evoking "the old island here that flowered once for Dutch sailors' eyes – a fresh, green breast of the new world" (p. 140). Yet the multiple ironies in both books link this kind of transcendent vision to a much more extensive and dispersed consciousness. Fitzgerald himself was born to Midwestern parents of Irish descent who were both practicing Catholics, and there is an important sense in which a Catholic esthetic sensibility, displaced into cultural and secular forms, helps crucially to shape the direction of Fitzgerald's most famous novel. Indeed, in the very first draft of his narrative, Fitzgerald envisaged a prologue that sought to explain the main character's early life through recounting a confession he made when young to a priest, and, although this idea was ultimately dropped, the remaining fragment, featuring a character called Rudolph Miller, was published separately as a short story in 1924 under the title "Absolution."

Given all the interest in recent times in the diverse, multicultural ethnic strands of American literature, it might be considered somewhat surprising that Fitzgerald is not regarded more as a forerunner of Gish Jen or Jhumpa Lahiri in the way he interrogates boundaries between alien or immigrant cultures and the American mainstream, but such critical blindness to *The Great Gatsby*'s Irish Catholic dimensions testifies to the way in which the book has, over the past 50 years, become thoroughly institutionalized. The book was distributed by the Armed Services to American military personnel during World War II to remind them of the values they were fighting for, and the text has, since the 1950s, become established as a standard part of the American high school curriculum.

Of course, such processes of normalization do indeed speak aptly to one particular aspect of *Gatsby*, the side that emphasizes conventional paths to success in American society. This is the dimension that draws overtly on Benjamin Franklin's *The Way to Wealth*, the model upon which the youthful Gatsby's rigorous daily routine, as inscribed on the fly-leaf of his dog-eared copy of *Hopalong Cassidy*, is based. However, such educational norms have also over time had the negative effect of glossing over the more disjunctive, violent undercurrents that are also integral to Fitzgerald's masterpiece. The author signals clearly the racism of Tom Buchanan, Daisy's husband, through the fact that Buchanan is said to be reading "*The Rise of the Colored Empires* by this man Goddard," where the idea is, as Tom explains it, that "if we do not look out the white race will be utterly submerged" (p. 14). James L. West III, who edited the text of *Gatsby* for Cambridge University Press, reported that film director Baz Luhrmann before his 2013 film version of *Gatsby* emailed him with questions about the likely ethnic provenance of Buchanan's house servants and whether or not African Americans would have been included in the invitations to Gatsby's parties on Long Island, and such inquisitiveness suggests an attention to racial mixes that is, to say the least, not common among Hollywood directors making adaptations of famous novels.

In a 1924 letter to the author, Fitzgerald's editor, Maxwell Perkins, having read the novel in manuscript, said it had "a sense of eternity" about it, and Fitzgerald was clearly seeking here to write not just a social commentary on 1920s America but a much broader critique of the philosophy and ideology informing American romance.[93] The overriding theme of the book is not greed or money but, rather, the nature of perception: not only how Gatsby projects and distorts Daisy, but also how Carraway interprets Gatsby. (The novel would of course have been entirely different if it had been a first-person narrative recounted by Gatsby himself.) After Gatsby's death, Carraway records that the East has been "distorted beyond my eyes' power of correction" (p. 137), and such a focus fits with the recurring motif of Dr T.J. Eckleburg, an advertising hoarding for an optician's practice that looms over the Valley of Ashes, the highway community midway between Long Island and Manhattan where Tom Buchanan's mistress, Myrtle Wilson, lives with her garage mechanic husband. In this industrial wasteland, smoke is said to rise only "with a transcendent effort" (p. 21), and Fitzgerald here consciously projects an ironic slant on the kind of Puritan-inflected idealism that has been so influential upon canonical American culture. As Sacvan Bercovitch argued in *The Puritan Origins of the American Self*, such an impetus has run from the days of the Pilgrim Fathers, who attempted hermeneutically to apotheosize brute matter into a realm of the spirit, through to the visionary poetics of nineteenth-century transcendentalists such as Emerson and Whitman, for whom the romantic sublime involved reducing the external world, as Emerson said in *Nature*, to "only a realized will, – the double of the man."[94]

Fitzgerald's novel does not work exactly as a parody of transcendentalism but it preserves a double-edged attitude toward this kind of discursive matrix, exemplifying a capacity to be, as Carraway says in the narrative, "within and without, simultaneously enchanted and repelled" by life's "inexhaustible variety" (p. 30). The book rotates on a structural double-bind, whereby Gatsby himself is at the same time both a corrupt bootlegger – a "common swindler," as Tom Buchanan calls him (p. 104) – and also a grand visionary. On one level, of course, it might appear absurd to juxtapose the "green light at the end of Daisy's dock" (p. 141) with the Puritans' apprehension of the "fresh, green breast of the new world" (p. 140), but Fitzgerald's style involves elements of distortion and forced juxtaposition, the kind of idiom that was characteristic of surrealist art of the 1920s. Early in the book, Carraway relates the perception of Long Island as "a source of perpetual wonder to the gulls that fly overhead" to "the Columbus story" (p. 8), whereby the mariner confounded his audience, who maintained an egg could not be stood on its end, by cracking the shell and doing it through another route, thereby demonstrating the power of lateral thought to rotate any given situation on its axis.

The Great Gatsby is testimony to the potential power of the human mind to frame the world differently, but it always holds such aspirations in check, by playing off the Promethean imagination against a sense of the world's ontological limitations. Such principled contradictions are the source of the book's philosophical irony, where the abstractions of mind are contrasted with the corporeal nature of matter, and this suggests ways in which metaphysical debates are always implicit within the narrative. In the last pages of the novel, Carraway imagines West Egg "as a night scene by El Greco" (p. 137), thereby relating how the lights at Gatsby's parties "grow brighter as the earth lurches away from the sun" (p. 34) to the somber spirit of the Spanish painter, in whose work partially luminous religious shades are constantly hovering. Medievalism is another specter in *Gatsby*: Daisy Faye's maiden name echoes that of Morgan Le Fay in Arthurian legend, while Gatsby's house is said to make a "feudal silhouette against the sky" (p. 71), all of which implies systematic nostalgia for a lost era.

This is not to suggest, of course, that *The Great Gatsby* is a religious book in any literal or theological sense. Unlike his parents, Fitzgerald himself was not in adult life a practicing Catholic, although he did attend church while at Princeton and it was not until 1918, at the age of 21, that he confided to his journal that this would be his "last year as a Catholic."[95] The more general intellectual argument here, however, is that, coming as he did from an Irish-Catholic cultural context, Fitzgerald was always interested in exploring how the material phenomena of commercial culture might be embodied within the American Dream, rather than being seen merely as a vulgar debasement of it. Just as the evening sun is said to provide a "benediction over the vanishing city" (p. 119), thereby metaphorically incorporating New York within a sacramental gesture, so the guest lists in Chapter 4 express something like a liturgical or ritualistic sense of community, and in their distinctive valorization of the social body they are worlds away from the self-authenticating individualism of an Emerson or a Thoreau, grounded as were the works of those great writers on an ethic of spiritual retreat and pastoral purity. Instead, Fitzgerald greatly admired his fellow lapsed Catholic James Joyce, whom he met during his time in France in the early 1920s, and indeed he was heavily influenced when writing *Gatsby* by Joyce's *Ulysses*, published in 1922. Just as Joyce in that work seeks to adduce parallels between daily life in twentieth-century Dublin and the legends of classical Greece, so Fitzgerald's first version of *Gatsby*, entitled "Trimalchio in West Egg," sought to make analogies between contemporary Long Island and the world of ancient Rome. Trimalchio was renowned in Nero's Rome as a former slave who, after working his way into the inner echelons of society, became famous for holding orgies. Trimalchio's career is recounted in Petronius's *Satyricon*, a book that became famous in the early 1920s because of attempts to censor a modern edition, and through this channel it attracted the attention of both Joyce and Fitzgerald. Acting on the advice of Max Perkins, Fitzgerald eventually chose to eliminate most of these classical Roman parallels so as to make his novel more realistic and thus easier to read, although one allusion to this ur-text still remains in Chapter 7 of *Gatsby*, when Carraway in elegiac tone recalls of the chief protagonist how, "as obscurely as it had begun, his career as Trimalchio was over" (p. 88).

In this sense, *Gatsby* can be understood as a text redolent of international modernism's classical and universal trajectories. Although embedded in the culture of 1920s America, the book seeks simultaneously to relate its narrative to more expansive temporal horizons. In Chapter 5 of the novel, Carraway says of Gatsby's mansion: "There was nothing to look at from under the tree except Gatsby's enormous house, so I stared at it, like Kant at his church steeple, for half an hour" (p. 69). Again, this underlines questions of perception, with Fitzgerald's narrator contemplating Gatsby in the same way as Immanuel Kant, the German philosopher who was a prime influence on the transcendentalist movement, contemplated the church in his native Königsberg. Kant argued that it is human perception that structures natural laws, that space and time should be understood merely as extensions of human consciousness, and that, as he put it, "objects must conform to our cognition."[96] This made Kant the particular *bête noire* of Catholic theologians and philosophers in the nineteenth century, because of the way he chose to disregard Aquinas's emphasis on the substantiality of natural objects and instead related knowledge back to the faculty of the human mind. In Fitzgerald's novel, though, there is a sustained consideration of both the power and limitations of a human being's capacity to remodel the world in his own image, with Gatsby's effort to arrest time – "'Can't repeat the past?' he cried incredulously. 'Why of course you can!'" (p. 86) – running alongside various episodes where characters play with self-consciously fake forms of transformation and transubstantiation. There is an example of this in the first chapter, when Daisy, welcoming her second cousin to the dinner table, says he reminds her of "a rose, an absolute rose," to which Carraway responds skeptically: "This was untrue. I am not even faintly like a rose" (p. 15). Along similarly parallel lines, the structure of Fitzgerald's book is elaborately patterned, with various scenes echoing each other in a dance of reduplication: for example, Tom's adultery with Myrtle Wilson mirrors Daisy's affair with Gatsby, while the formal dinner at the Buchanans' residence on Long Island is subsequently reflected in the drunken party held at Myrtle's apartment in New York.

All of this has the cumulative effect of introducing into Gatsby a double-edged note, a half-suppressed tone of parody, as if the narrative can never quite decide whether or not to believe in the fanciful analogies and mirror images that are being adduced here. In this sense, *The Great Gatsby* is positioned ambiguously as both invested in the American Dream and also, at the same time, alienated from it. Fitzgerald said in his 1936 essay "The Crack-Up" that "the test of a first-rate intelligence is the ability to hold two opposed ideas in the mind at the same time and still retain the ability to function," and his own novel perfectly fulfills that objective of being, like Carraway, both "within and without" the world it describes.[97] Rather than simply epitomizing the Jazz Age, Fitzgerald's novel ruminates on it from an estranged position, both geographically and philosophically, as he uses his Midwestern Catholic sensibility to frame New York high society within a more global perspective.

Steinbeck's *The Grapes of Wrath*, by contrast, is notable for its almost total elimination from its purview of the US East Coast. Freeman Champney suggested of Steinbeck that "[m]ore perhaps than any other important contemporary American writer, except William Faulkner, his writing has grown out of a special region."[98] Yet Steinbeck clearly did not intend simply to limit himself to regional fiction set in California since all his novels contain Biblical resonances, while the 16 "interchapters" of *The Grapes of Wrath*, comprising one-sixth of the narrative, create a kind of chorus effect that throws the novel's individual protagonists into relief. The book's title is taken from "The Battle Hymn of the Republic" – "Mine eyes have seen the glory of the coming of the Lord / He is trampling out the vintage where the grapes of wrath are stored" – and the story of flight outlined in the Book of Exodus shadows the dustbowl migration from Oklahoma to California that is delineated here.

Writing some years later in *Travels with Charley: In Search of America* (1962), Steinbeck suggested that "Americans are a restless people, a mobile people, never satisfied with where they are." He also declared that "for all of our sectionalism, for all of our interwoven breeds drawn from every part of the ethnic world, we are a nation, a new breed. Americans are much more American than they are Northerners, Southerners, Westerners, or Easterners ... The American identity is an exact and provable thing."[99] Yet this conflation of an American national mythology with archetypes of mobility does not accord exactly with the textual dynamics of his fictional narratives, which often create their affective power from a sense of the random and aleatory. It may well be true to say that Steinbeck "belongs to the line of American transcendentalism," as Bradbury put it, "the Emersonian idealism of those who saw a unified soul in man and nature, and who sought that soul's deliverance in a new America seen as a paradisial Eden."[100] But one dominant impression for the reader of *The Grapes of Wrath* is the novel's compelling evocation of the more impersonal, anonymous details of Western life: the truck stops, the highway cafés, the used car lots, the ubiquitous pre-moving yard sales. Although the author says of the Joads that "their eyes focused panoramically, seeing no detail, but the whole dawn, the whole land, the whole texture of the country at once," his own narrative trajectory does not support unproblematically such a synoptic vision.[101] Indeed, the novel flirts with an idea of this utopian promise as a form of false consciousness, a dream of redemption in the West destined to be frustrated by the material conditions associated with the organization of the Californian agricultural industry in the 1930s. This political theme is addressed overtly in Steinbeck's earlier novel *In Dubious Battle* (1936), which focuses on a strike of apple pickers in the early 1930s, at the onset of the Great Depression. *The Grapes of Wrath* similarly had its origins in representations of current events, specifically in this case through photojournalism, after George West had asked Steinbeck to take a trip for the *San Francisco News* to observe migrant farm workers. Steinbeck undertook a similar commission for *Life* magazine in 1938, although this time he accepted only expenses for himself, saying "I'm sorry but I simply can't make money on these people ... The suffering is too great for me to cash in on it."[102]

The high profile of *The Grapes of Wrath* in the popular media helped ensure it was a bestseller after its publication in 1939 and thus that it had an immediate political effect. Oklahoma congressman Lyle Boren denounced the book as "a black, internal creation of a twisted, distorted mind," thereby testifying ironically to its visibility and success, and this hold on the mind of the general public was strengthened after the release of a film version directed by John Ford in 1940, just one year after the novel's initial publication. The director Joseph Losey later remarked that Ford's *Grapes of Wrath* was the only Hollywood film to have a real left-wing impact.[103]

Steinbeck's popularity, however, was never an uncontested phenomenon. Michael Denning has pointed out that the novel's "racial populism" avoids any representation of the Mexican immigrants who actually formed a significant portion of the Californian agricultural laboring force at this time.[104] Indeed, Steinbeck's narrator specifically disowns any non-white progeny among the displaced Okies, declaring: "We ain't foreign. Seven generations back Americans, and beyond that Irish, Scotch, English, German. One of our folks in the Revolution, an' they was lots of our folks in the Civil War – both sides. Americans."[105] This exemplifies Steinbeck's attempt to seek wide popularity for his novel by mythologizing his story of a westward journey, thereby integrating it not only with a national prototype but also a Biblical allegory, as if the promise of redemption were itself an exclusively American prerogative. Yet the author's deliberate attempt to blend different strands within his narrative was reflected by the way avant-garde French composer Edgard Varèse was the first to recognize how Steinbeck exploited techniques of musical composition in his writing.[106] Varèse similarly used random street noises in his experimental works of the 1920s: *Ionisation, Amériques*, and so on. Steinbeck also met John Cage in 1938, and in 1941 Cage discussed with Varèse the possibility of the French composer working with Steinbeck, viewing it as an interesting possibility, even though Cage did ultimately express doubts over whether Steinbeck "has a real appreciation of music of contemporary spirit."[107]

Whatever the extent of Steinbeck's musical knowledge, his association with Cage, an apostle of radical West Coast esthetics, belies the snobbish notion that Steinbeck was merely a populist backwoodsman. After he had won the Nobel Prize in 1962, the *New York Times* wrote that it was a pity the prize had not been given to a writer whose work had "made a more profound impression on the literature of our age," and Steinbeck was widely derided throughout his career by New York intellectuals such as Edmund Wilson, Mary McCarthy, and Alfred Kazin.[108] Interestingly, however, both Wilson and Kazin critiqued Steinbeck for the way his characters appeared to lack humanist distinctiveness. Wilson argued in the *New Yorker* in 1936 that "Mr Steinbeck almost always in his fiction is dealing either with the lower animals or with human beings so rudimentary that they are almost on the animal level," while Kazin complained that "Steinbeck's people are always on the verge of becoming human, but never do."[109] Yet the swerve away from humanist consciousness in Steinbeck's work and the attempt to adduce analogies between human and animal consciousness – evident also in other popular novels of his, such as *Of Mice and Men* (1937) – might be seen from another perspective as an indication of a progressive posthumanist consciousness. Steinbeck was great friends with Californian marine biologist Ed Ricketts, who worked in a laboratory at Monterey and published with Jack Calvin the academic monograph *Between Pacific Tides* (1939), a study of the intertidal ecology of the Pacific Coast, with Ricketts's emphasis on the interrelatedness of ecological phenomena being something that strongly influenced Steinbeck's imagination.

It was through Ricketts that Steinbeck met John Cage, and though Ricketts was killed in a car crash in 1948, it is not difficult to see how his emphasis on the autonomy of the environment has anticipated later forms of progressive thinking that have subsequently emerged from California in particular, as for example in the work of Donna Haraway. Haraway's posthuman focus on how the human frame relates to ecological or biological phenomena resonates with Steinbeck's fictional explorations, and from this perspective Edmund Wilson's grumpy complaint that his narratives downplay the significance of human consciousness might be seen merely as symptomatic of the prejudices of a particular time and place. Wilson was working during an era when New York assumed itself to be the cultural capital of the world and when the idea of existential consciousness, typically refracted in the US during the years after World War II through political and cultural forms of liberalism, was at the forefront of intellectual attention. By contrast, Steinbeck's radical reimagining of American culture – he admired *Moby-Dick*, for example, not for its political engagement but for its "non-teleological" emphasis – anticipates more recent postnationalist critiques of Melville, as for example in the work of Lawrence Buell, which has highlighted Melville's attention to oceanic phenomena rather than to the more transitory apparatus of Manifest Destiny.[110]

In the cases of both *The Great Gatsby* and *The Grapes of Wrath*, texts that have been taken to be emblematic of the condition of America in the 1920s and 1930s can be seen to relate just as pertinently to other contexts. *Gatsby*'s transnationalism, like the posthumanism and ecological consciousness that pervades *The Grapes of Wrath*, enables us to understand these works not just as national allegories but as epitomes of the situation of American literature within a wider world. All critical frameworks are arbitrary in their own way, of course, but the tendency to appropriate canonical texts for exclusively national purposes has led on occasion to a damaging parochialism in American literary studies, and if the worlding of American literature does not necessarily lead in itself to a fuller understanding of any given fictional narrative, it might at least challenge the more domesticated readings that seek to interpret the literature of the United States purely on a proximate and proprietorial basis.

References

1 Gerald Kennedy, J. (1993). *Imagining Paris: Exile, Writing, and American Identity*, 28. New Haven: Yale UP.
2 Miller, H. (2005). *Tropic of Cancer* (1934; rpt.), 157. London: HarperCollins.
3 Smith, N. (2003). *American Empire: Roosevelt's Geographer and the Prelude to Globalization*, 454. Berkeley: U of California P.
4 James, H. (1999). Within the Rim (1917). In: *Henry James on Culture: Essays on Politics and the American Political Scene* (ed. P.A. Walker), 179–180. Lincoln: U of Nebraska P.
5 Fussell, P. (2000). *The Great War and Modern Memory*, 2e, 80, 21. New York: Oxford UP.
6 James, "Within the Rim," 183, 181.
7 Cowley, M. (1934). *Exile's Return: A Narrative of Ideas*, 47. New York: Norton.
8 Dos Passos, J. (1966). *Nineteen*, in *U.S.A.* (1938; rpt.), 495. New York: Penguin.
9 Cowley, M. (1973). *A Second Flowering: Works and Days of the Lost Generation*, 9. New York: Viking Press.
10 Cummings, E.E. (1999). *The Enormous Room* (1922; rpt.), 86–87, 18, 164–165. New York: Penguin.
11 Stein, G. (1962). The Autobiography of Alice B. Toklas (1933). In: *Selected Writings of Gertrude Stein* (ed. C. Van Vechten), 205. New York: Random House.
12 Steiner, G. (1972). *Extraterritorial: Papers on Literature and the Language Revolution*. London: Faber.

13 Edwards, B.H. (2003). *The Practice of Diaspora: Literature, Translation, and the Rise of Black Internationalism*. Cambridge: Harvard UP.

14 Passos, J.D. (2003). *One Man's Initiation: 1917*. In: *Novels 1920–1925*, 2, 3, 4, 57. New York: Library of America.

15 Dos Passos, *One Man's Initiation*, 44, 74–75.

16 Dos Passos, *Three Soldiers*. In: *Novels 1920–1925*, 119, 184, 179.

17 Dos Passos, *Three Soldiers*, 383, 221, 467.

18 Dos Passos, *Three Soldiers*, 387, 267, 335, 368.

19 Denning, M. (1996). *The Cultural Front: The Laboring of American Culture in the Twentieth Century*, 177. London: Verso.

20 Bradbury, M. (1987). The nonhomemade world: European and American Modernism. *American Quarterly* 39(1): 28.

21 Lentricchia, F. (1994). *Modernist Quartet*, 107. Cambridge: Cambridge UP.

22 Armstrong, T. (1998). *Modernism, Technology, and the Body: A Cultural Study*. Cambridge: Cambridge UP.

23 Anderson, S. (2015). *Poor White* (1920; rpt.), 97. Jefferson Press.

24 Saint-Amour, P.K. (2003). Modernist Reconnaissance. *Modernism/ Modernity* 10(2): 349, 368.

25 Lynn, K.S. (1987). *Hemingway*, 179. Cambridge: Harvard UP.

26 Stein, *Autobiography*, 73.

27 Lawrence, D.H. (1982). Calendar of Modern Letters, April 1927. In: *Hemingway: The Critical Heritage* (ed. J. Meyers), 73. London: Routledge and Kegan Paul.

28 McCormick, J. (1971). *American Literature, 1919-1932: A Comparative History*, 58. London: Routledge and Kegan Paul.

29 Hemingway, E. (1935). *A Farewell to Arms* (1929; rpt.), 144. London: Penguin.

30 Baker, C. (1969). *Ernest Hemingway: A Life Story*, 153. London: Collins.

31 Hemingway, E. (1977). In Our Time (1924). In: *The Essential Hemingway*, 302–303. London: Panther-Granada.

32 Levin, H. (1951). Observations on the Style of Ernest Hemingway. *Kenyon Review* 13(4): 606.

33 Wharton, E. (1998). *A Backward Glance: An Autobiography* (1934; rpt.), 6. New York: Touchstone-Simon and Schuster.

34 Stein, *Autobiography*, 206.

35 Scott Fitzgerald, F. (1963). *This Side of Paradise* (1920; rpt.), 192–193, 57, 155. London: Penguin.

36 Scott Fitzgerald, F. (1991). In: *The Great Gatsby* (ed. M.J. Bruccoli), 6, 5. New York: Cambridge UP). Subsequent page references to this edition are cited in parentheses in the text.

37 Hemingway, E. (1977). *A Moveable Feast* (1964; rpt.), 29. London: Panther-Granada.

38 Douglas, A. (1995). *Terrible Honesty: Mongrel Manhattan in the 1920s*, 42. New York: Farrar, Straus and Giroux.
39 Scott Fitzgerald, F. (1982). *Tender Is the Night* (1934; rpt.), 128, 192, 67. London: Penguin.
40 Dreiser, T. (1991). *Jennie Gerhardt* (ed. Mitchell, L.C.), 37, 55. Oxford: Oxford UP.
41 Delbanco, A. (1989). Lyrical Dreiser. *New York Review of Books* 23: 32.
42 Dreiser, *Jennie Gerhardt*, 352, 338.
43 Riggio, T.P. (1984). Theodore Dreiser: hidden ethnic. *MELUS* 11(1): 53–63.
44 Sherman, S.P. (1955). The barbaric naturalism of Mr. Dreiser. In: *The Stature of Theodore Dreiser: A Critical Survey of the Man and His Work* (ed. A. Kazin and C. Shapiro), 71–80. Bloomington: Indiana UP.
45 Bourne, R. (1917). The art of Theodore Dreiser. *The Dial* 14: 509.
46 Smith, American Empire, 454.
47 Hegeman, S. (1999). *Patterns for America: Modernism and the Concept of Culture*, 23. Princeton: Princeton UP.
48 Lewis, S. (1992). *Main Street* (1920; rpt.), 5. New York: Library of America.
49 Torgovnick, M. (2005). *The War Complex: World War II in Our Time*, 1. Chicago: U of Chicago P.
50 Lewisohn, L. (1928). *The Island Within*, 1, 216, 125, 262. New York: Harper.
51 Lewisohn, *Island Within*, 241, 263, 158, 235.
52 Lewisohn, *Island Within*, 117.
53 Foerster, N. Introduction. In: *Reinterpretation of American Literature* (ed. N. Foerster), vii, viii.
54 Foerster, N. Factors in American literary history. In: *Reinterpretation of American Literature* (ed. N. Foerster), 24.
55 Michaels, W.B. (1995). *Our America: Nativism, Modernism, and Pluralism*. Durham: Duke UP.
56 William Faulkner, *Soldiers' Pay* (1925; rpt. London: Random House-Vintage, 2000), 97, 230, 164.
57 Faulkner, *Soldiers' Pay*, 201, 164–165, 214, 186, 205.
58 Faulkner, W. (1929). *Sartoris*, 57, 54. New York: Harcourt, Brace and Co..
59 Faulkner, *Sartoris*, 312, 62, 113–114, 199, 169.
60 James, "Within the Rim," 177.
61 Williams, W.C. (1963). *Paterson*, 3. New York: New Directions.
62 Pound, E. (1975). *Selected Poems*, 53. London: Faber.
63 Pound, E. (1973). Provincialism the enemy. In: *Selected Prose of Ezra Pound 1909-1965* (ed. W. Cookson), 159. London: Faber.
64 Pound, E. (1915). Webster Ford. *The Egoist* 2(1): 11.

65 Corwin, N. (1961). *The World of Carl Sandburg*, 32. New York: Harcourt, Brace and World.
66 Sandburg, C. (1914). Chicago. *Poetry: A Magazine of Verse* 3(6): 191–192.
67 Meyers, J. (1995). *Edmund Wilson, A Biography*, 78. Boston: Houghton Mifflin.
68 Dickstein, M. (2005). *A Mirror in the Roadway: Literature and the Real World*, 77–78. Princeton: Princeton UP.
69 Douglas, *Terrible Honesty*, 160. On this topic, see also Vanderbilt, K. (1986). *American Literature and the Academy: The Roots, Growth, and Maturity of a Profession*. Philadelphia: U of Pennsylvania P, and Renker, E. (2007). *The Origins of American Literature Studies*. Cambridge: Cambridge UP.
70 Wilson, E. (1952). The critic who does not exist. In: *The Shores of Light: A Literary Chronicle of the Twenties and Thirties*, 370–371. London: W. H. Allen.
71 Babbitt, I. (1967). Humanism: an essay at definition. In: *Humanism and America: Essays on the Outlook of Modern Civilisation* (1930; rpt.) (ed. N. Foerster), 30. Port Washington: Kennikat Press.
72 Foerster, N. Preface. In: *Humanism and America* (ed. N. Foerster), vi, xi.
73 Clark, H.H. American literary history and American literature. In: *Reinterpretation of American Literature* (ed. N. Foerster), 190.
74 Wilson, E. Prologue, 1952: Christian Gauss as a teacher of literature. In: *The Shores of Light*, 8, 5, 11.
75 Wilson, E. Mr. More and the Mithraic bull. In: *The Triple Thinkers*, 10–11, 6.
76 Wilson, E. A Preface to Persius: Maudlin meditations in a speakeasy. In: *The Shores of Light*, 270, 267.
77 Foerster, "Factors in Literary History," 27–28.
78 Olson, C. (1997). Call me Ishmael (1949). In: *Collected Prose: Charles Olson* (ed. D. Allen and B. Friedlander), 17. Berkeley: U of California P.
79 Lewis, R.W.B. (1967). *The Poetry of Hart Crane: A Critical Study*. Princeton: Princeton UP; Dembo, L.S. (1960). *Hart Crane's Sanskrit Charge: A Study of The Bridge*. Ithaca: Cornell UP.
80 Kenner, H. (1974). *A Homemade World: The American Modernist Writers*. New York: Knopf.
81 Bloom, H. (1977). *Wallace Stevens: The Poems of Our Climate*. Ithaca: Cornell UP.
82 Altieri, C. (1989). *Painterly Abstraction in Modernist American Poetry: The Contemporaneity of Modernism*, 413. Cambridge: Cambridge UP.
83 Williams, *Paterson*, 6.
84 Bradbury, "The Nonhomemade World," 27.

85 Rainey, L. (1998). *Institutions of Modernism: Literary Elites and Public Culture*, 172. New Haven: Yale UP.
86 Sherry, V. (2015). *Modernism and the Reinvention of Decadence*, 14. Cambridge: Cambridge UP.
87 Stein, G. (1984). *Wars I Have Seen* (1945; rpt.), 131. London: Brilliance Books.
88 Patterson, A. (2008). *Race, American Literature and Transnational Modernisms*, 94. Cambridge: Cambridge UP.
89 Rampersad, A. (ed.) (1994). *The Collected Poems of Langston Hughes*, 23. New York: Knopf.
90 Douglas, *Terrible Honesty*, 5.
91 Doyle, L. (2005). Introduction: the global horizons of modernism. In: *Geomodernisms: Race, Modernism, Modernity* (ed. L. Doyle and L. Winkiel), 14. Bloomington: Indiana UP.
92 Hegeman, *Patterns for America*, 169.
93 Kuchl, J. and Bryer, J.R. (ed.) (1971). *Dear Scott/Dear Max: The Fitzgerald-Perkins Correspondence*, 84. New York: Scribner's.
94 Emerson, "Nature," 25.
95 Bruccoli, M.J. (1981). *Some Sort of Epic Grandeur: The Life of F. Scott Fitzgerald*, 89. New York: Harcourt Brace Jovanovich.
96 Kant, I. (1855). *Critique of Pure Reason* (trans. J.M.D. Meiklejohn), xxviii. London: Bohn.
97 Scott Fitzgerald, F. (1965). The crack-up. In: *The Crack-Up with Other Pieces and Stories*, 39. London: Penguin.
98 Champney, F. (1972). John Steinbeck, Californian (1947). In: *John Steinbeck: Twentieth Century Views* (ed. R.M. Davis), 21. Englewood Cliffs: Prentice-Hall.
99 Steinbeck, J. (1980). *Travels with Charley: In Search of America* (1962; rpt.), 80, 159. London: Penguin.
100 Bradbury, M. (1983). *The Modern American Novel*, 110. Oxford: Oxford UP.
101 Steinbeck, J. (2000). *The Grapes of Wrath* (1939; rpt.), 118. London: Penguin.
102 Stoddard, M. (1983). *California Writers: Jack London, John Steinbeck, The Tough Guys*, 82. London: Macmillan.
103 Swenson, J.R. (2015). *Picturing Migrants:* The Grapes of Wrath *and New Deal Documentary Photography*, 56. Norman: U of Oklahoma P.
104 Denning, *The Cultural Front*, 267.
105 Steinbeck, *The Grapes of Wrath*, 244.
106 Benson, J.J. (1984). *The True Adventures of John Steinbeck, Writer*, 393. London: Heinemann.
107 Kuhn, L. (ed.) (2016). *The Selected Letters of John Cage*, 51. Middletown: Wesleyan UP.

108 Benson, *True Adventures*, 914.

109 Loftis, A. (1990). A historical introduction to *Of Mice and Men*. In: *The Short Novels of John Steinbeck, with a Checklist to Steinbeck Criticism* (ed. J.J. Benson), 46. Durham: Duke UP; Kazin, A. (1942). *On Native Grounds: An Interpretation of Modern American Prose Literature*, 394. New York: Harcourt, Brace and World.

110 Englert, P.A.J. (1997). Education of environmental scientists: should we listen to Steinbeck and Ricketts's comments?. In: *Steinbeck and the Environment: Interdisciplinary Approaches* (ed. S.F. Beegel, S. Shillinglaw, and W.N. Tiffney), 186–187. Tuscaloosa: U of Alabama P; Buell, L. (2001). *Writing for an Endangered World: Literature, Culture, and Environment in the U.S. and Beyond*, 196–223. Cambridge: Harvard UP.

5

Postmodernism, Globalization, and US Literary Culture

5.1   The Politics of Postmodernism

Debates around the definition of postmodernism turn in most cases upon whether the idea should be understood primarily in formalist or historical terms. Those who argue for a formalist category, such as Ihab Hassan, tended to compare and contrast modernism to postmodernism, suggesting that the emphasis in the former on such qualities as "form (conjunctive, closed)" or "hierarchy" could be contrasted with "antiform (disjunctive, open)" and "anarchy" in the latter.[1] But, as Marjorie Perloff has cogently argued, such distinctions would seem to risk oversimplification, since any competent reader would recognize elements of "disjunctive" aesthetics in, say, Ezra Pound's *Cantos*, which are commonly regarded as a key work of high modernism.[2] It is true that postmodernism may be generally more hospitable towards indeterminacy – as in the poetry of John Ashbery, for example – but there have also been many writers associated with postmodernism who have had conservative or even religious sympathies: David Foster Wallace, for example, comes to mind. There has also been a substantial body of work on relations between postmodernism and theology, from Mark C. Taylor and others.[3]

Overall, then, it would seem to make most sense to regard postmodernism as a loose historical period, one conventionally associated with post-1960 literature and culture. The sociologist C. Wright Mills heralded in 1959 what he called a "post-modern period," and although such a designation would of course only constitute a rough guide, it does fit with the general scheme of periodization outlined by John Carlos Rowe, who described three overlapping phases of postmodernism.[4] The first of these for Rowe centered on literary experimentation, from about 1965 to 1975; the second emphasized themes of poststructuralism and deconstruction, from 1975 to 1985; and the third, since the mid-1980s, has been increasingly dominated by changes in the information economy

American World Literature: An Introduction, First Edition. Paul Giles.
© 2019 John Wiley & Sons Ltd. Published 2019 by John Wiley & Sons Ltd.

and service industries, which have brought about fundamentally different conditions of production and reception within the digital economy.[5] Since the turn of the twenty-first century, there has also been a greatly increased focus on environmental issues, with global warming and other threats to the planet increasingly dominating the artistic and cultural landscape.

Some critics have attempted to confine postmodernism to one or other of these strains, but just as modernism is now generally considered to be a capacious container, embracing the realism of Steinbeck and Dos Passos as well as the traditional high modernism of Pound and Stevens, so it would be most useful to think of how postmodernism operates across a broad conceptual spectrum. The situation is further complicated by some critical assumptions that postmodernism itself should be considered a specifically American phenomenon, with Andreas Huyssen arguing that it began in the United States in the 1960s, when novelists such as John Barth and Donald Barthelme began drawing on popular culture to interrogate conservative Western hierarchies.[6] Although Huyssen's hypothesis is doubtful, considering how quickly the idea of postmodernism spread around the world, it is certainly the case that the comic brio evident in such iconoclastic American works as Barth's *Lost in the Funhouse: Fiction for Print, Tape, Live Voice* (1968) or Barthelme's *Snow White* (1967) exemplified a multimedia element, as both authors played with representational models of literary form to humorous effect. In *Snow White*, for example, the author interrupts his narrative to pose questions directly to his readers:

1) Do you like the story so far? Yes ( ) No ( )
2) Does Snow White resemble the Snow White you remember? Yes ( ) No ( )

By rendering conventional literary assumptions explicit, Barthelme effectively mocks them, disrupting the familiar "suspension of disbelief" through which readers customarily enter imaginatively into fictional worlds. Barthelme's narrator goes on:

9) Has the work, for you, a metaphysical dimension? Yes ( ) No ( )
10) What is it (twenty-five words or less)?[7]

Just as radical film-makers of this era such as Jean-Luc Godard made the apparatus of the camera visible, so Barthelme foregrounds and implicitly parodies the apparatus on which a fictional universe depends.

One of the reasons American fiction of the 1960s seemed particularly brash and innovative was because it was willing to incorporate artistic experiments across other media within more prosaic literary formats.

While English fiction of the 1960s tended to stick to tried and tested styles of realism, the American postmodern fabulists of the 1960s – Robert Coover and John Hawkes, as well as Barth and Barthelme – seemed to emerge in a direct line from the Beat writers of the 1950s (Jack Kerouac, Norman Mailer) in the way they were willing to push the genre of the American novel into frontier territory. This romance of the new also fitted with a traditional view of American literature as being inclined always to stake out uncharted territory, in accordance with the understanding of it as an exceptionalist enterprise whose leading edge of postmodernity was helping to shape a brave new artistic world.

More recent critical work has emphasized the importance of links between American postmodernist fiction and Latin American magical realism, with Coover in particular (whose wife is Spanish, and who is himself fluent in the Spanish language) acknowledging a debt to the work of Julio Cortázar, Carlos Fuentes, and Gabriel García Marquez, but when they first appeared on the scene these American postmodernists seemed to speak not only for the brash novelty of American literature but for the national agendas exemplified by its radically experimental qualities.[8] Just as the Apollo missions to the moon in the 1960s bore witness to American technological prowess, so its exuberant experimental fiction of this era exemplified a pioneering spirit in the literary realm.

In subsequent decades, American postmodernism involved as much a decreative as a creative strand. The kind of deconstruction of master narratives undertaken by Barth and Barthelme took on more distinctly political forms from the 1970s onwards, with Adrienne Rich's poetry and critical prose in the last three decades of the twentieth century applying to Western culture more generally the iconoclastic dynamic that Barth and Barthelme had applied more narrowly to literary forms. Laura Kipnis in 1989 described "feminism" as "the political conscience of postmodernism," specifically defining feminism as "a decolonizing movement," one linked to the "*world* system of patriarchy" that it sought to deconstruct.[9] Rich's early poetry, published in the 1950s, had been more formalist in orientation, offering models of containment and quiescence that were reminiscent of the poetic style of her contemporaries such as Richard Wilbur. "Autumn Equinox," from Rich's collection *The Diamond Cutters* (1955), represents a domestic scene within a landscape of poise and tranquility, even though the poem expresses discontent at the way worldly goods are husbanded within the academic study of the woman narrator's aging husband:

> Along the walls
> Of Lyman's study there were steel engravings
> Framed in black oak: the crazy tower of Pisa,
> The Pyramids, rooted in desert sand,

> Cologne Cathedral with its dangerous spires
> Piercing the atmosphere. I hated them
> For priggishly enclosing in a room
> The marvels of the world, as if declaring
> Such was the right and fitting rôle of marvels.[10]

In her 1974 foreword to a selection of her poems, however, Rich recalled how in the mid-1950s she "had come to the end of the kind of poetry I was writing in *The Diamond Cutters* and felt embarked on a process that was tentative and exploratory, both as to form and materials."[11] Her subsequent poetry was far less constrained by systems of enclosure and tradition, and it juggles various forms of contradiction, often self-consciously playing off a subjective narrative voice against forces by which the poetic self finds itself fractured and decentered. Rich drew explicitly upon images of cinematic reflexivity in her poems "Images for Godard" (1970) and "Pierrot le Fou" (1969), the latter taken from the title of a 1965 Godard film. Although Rich developed at this time a powerful political voice, one that articulated a repressed feminist history in American culture, she also framed this lost world within an esthetic of contradiction through which the autonomy of a poetic voice was always subject to ironic displacement. While Rich was in many ways indebted to familiar conceptions of American romanticism – Whitman's landscapes, she remarked in 2003, are "vistas of possibility" – her poems also explore internal dialogues evoking the kind of philosophical turbulence and structural dissonance typical of postmodern writing, as we see in the "Contradictions: Tracking Poems" section of *Your Native Land, Your Life* (1986), where she says: "Don't let the solstice fool you: /our lives will always be/a stew of contradictions."[12]

There has been a long critical tradition of reading American poetry accordingly to narrowly defined nationalistic templates, with the great postmodernist poet John Ashbery, for example, celebrated by Harold Bloom for his renegotiation of the legacy of Whitman and Stevens, even though Ashbery was deeply influenced by French surrealism, having spent many years working as an art critic for the *New York Times* in Paris, where he wrote his first book on the French poet Raymond Roussel. Rich, similarly, has been categorized too frequently in nationalist terms, as the heir of American women poets whom she celebrates in her own work – Anne Bradstreet, Emily Dickinson, and others – even though her own artistic horizons were much broader, embracing European modernism and political tensions in the Middle East, with the author addressing throughout her poetry her own Jewish heritage. Both Ashbery and Rich thus blend an internationalist style with an American idiom, refracting domestic popular culture (in Ashbery's case) or a vernacular idiom (in

Rich's) through an artistic circumference that seeks to identify points of overlap or friction between American local space and the wider world. In this sense, the title of Rich's 1991 poem "An Atlas of the Difficult World" might be seen to typify her work more generally, where the difficulty of mapping co-ordinates between local and global is made explicit.

Politically, the 1980s and early 1990s was a conservative era in the United States, one governed by two Republican presidents in Ronald Reagan and George H.W. Bush. Reagan himself had of course been a Hollywood film actor prior to becoming Governor of California, and his administration was marked above all by great skill in public relations and communication, with Reagan able to manipulate his presidential image to project an effervescent vision of "Morning in America." This reduction of substance to slogan was itself characteristic of a postmodern idiom, one impugned by Daniel J. Boorstin in his 1961 book *The Image*, where he lambasted the way media companies could create "pseudo-events" for the purposes of generating advertising and publicity. (One of Boorstin's examples was of a hotel celebrating in grand style its own 30th anniversary.)[13] This suggests ways in which postmodernism at this time cut a broad swathe across the entire cultural spectrum. Reagan, Barthelme, and Rich could hardly have been more various in their political assumptions, but they all thrived professionally in an environment where older institutional models were being refurbished. Reagan's manipulation of his presidential image was in some ways antithetical to Rich's manipulation of the literary canon, but they were both working out of an assumption that older established forms were cultural rather than natural formations, ones that were malleable and therefore susceptible to change.

The art of Andy Warhol between the 1960s and his death in 1987 epitomized the kind of ambiguity that was often associated with postmodernism, since his style both exemplified the commodity capitalism that his iconic portraits represented and, more arguably, sought simultaneously to parody it. By creating replicas of Jacqueline Onassis or Marilyn Monroe that sold for millions of dollars, Warhol was not only manipulating this capitalist dynamic but also foregrounding the ways in which it operated. Critics disagreed about whether Warhol was seeking simply to exploit the market or to deconstruct its operations in a more Brechtian fashion, but in any case his work suggested ways in which the condition of postmodernity at this time appeared to acquire something like a universal status. British cultural critic Stuart Hall in 1986 declared that the term *postmodernism* primarily signified "how the world dreams itself to be American," and the dreams of an unfettered global marketplace dominated by Western capitalism, a fantasy that became more prevalent after the fall of the Berlin Wall in 1989, led to an assumption in some quarters during the last decade of the twentieth century that the values of US postmodernism were simply going to conquer the world.[14]

The most famous (or infamous) exponent of this emollient thesis was political scientist Francis Fukuyama, whose *The End of History and the Last Man* (1992) was based on the premise that the "spread of a universal consumer culture" to the wider world – along with its natural allies, a free market and "prosperous and stable liberal democracies" – offered the promise that historical and political conflict would simply disappear. Fukuyama suggested "a remarkable consensus concerning the legitimacy of liberal democracy as a system of government" and "a universal evolution in the direction of capitalism," while proclaiming, like a proselytizer for the New Jerusalem, that "good news has come."[15] In the wake of 9/11 and the ravages of the War on Terror, such blithe optimism might seem simply laughable, but Fukuyama was writing at a utopian moment when, in the wake of the disappearance of its long-standing Soviet foe, American culture aspired towards a universal purchase. The Japanese-American scholar Masao Miyoshi similarly envisaged in 1993 a "borderless world," and although this vision of a world without frontiers might now seem as illusory as the gaudy capitalist spectacles of the Jazz Age, it is important for cultural historians to recognize how powerful was this vision of a millennial America in the last decade of the twentieth century. Miyoshi's essay invoked the nation state as "a nostalgic and sentimental myth" and envisaged a world dominated by transnational corporations.[16] But it is clear that within this paradigm such corporations were centered firmly in the United States, which was effectively exporting itself in this sense as a global empire, one driven by the transfer of information across national borders.

5.2   Styles of Globalization

Globalization since 1980 has been impelled by various factors, the most conspicuous of which is a revolution in communications technology that has made the transmission of ideas and commodities across national frontiers much easier, and which in turn has left the economies of nation states more exposed to rapid transfers of global capital by multinational companies and others. It was in the 1980s, according to Roger Burbach, that "finance capital began to exert a more decisive influence over state policies," with cuts in public funding running alongside a shift from labor-intensive to capital-intensive industry, as a process of economic globalization was driven by the "transnationalization" of production and of capital ownership.[17] All this happened quite suddenly: as Thomas L. Friedman remarked, when Clinton was elected president in 1992 virtually no-one outside exclusive government circles had access to email, and it did not become widespread in universities until a year or two later but by the end of the 1990s email forms of communication, to which national frontiers were no impediment, had become equally ubiquitous as, and distinctly cheaper than, conversations on the telephone.[18]

In the last two decades of the twentieth century there was thus a convergence of different types of social formation, with the widespread availability of information technology (in international forms such as satellite television and mobile phones as well as the internet) running alongside, and indeed arguably helping to bring about, the collapse of the Berlin Wall in 1989. This meant that the "three worlds" theory, the established basis for familiar assumptions about the geopolitical and geocultural order since World War II, gave way to a new perception that the world was, in fact, interconnected in a single system or network. As Michael Denning observes, the term "globalization," with its implication of amorphous boundaries, effectively superseded "international," the "keyword of an earlier moment," which tended by contrast to indicate a process of interaction across still stable national domains.[19] The classic statement of globalization by Arjun Appadurai in 1996 posited five dimensions of global cultural flow – ethnoscapes, mediascapes, technoscapes, financescapes, and ideoscapes – all of which testified to ways in which various forms of social, economic, and ideological capital were circulating transnationally, as both people and commodities began to cross national borders with an ease and regularity unknown in previous eras. Noting the absence of "isomorphism" in new conceptions of locality, Appadurai proposed instead "the configuration of cultural forms in today's world as fundamentally fractal."[20]

In American literature of this time, the hard edges of globalization were represented most obviously by writers such as William Gibson, a native of South Carolina whose science fiction narratives projected versions of technological displacement from his base in Vancouver BC, and Don DeLillo, whose later novels such as *Cosmopolis* (2003) and *Falling Man* (2007) focused on the more dehumanized qualities of money markets and global terrorism. The multibillionaire hero of *Cosmopolis* regards "data itself" as "soulful and glowing, a dynamic aspect of the life process," as expressed in "the eloquence of alphabets and numeric systems, now fully realized in electronic form, in the zero-oneness of the world, the digital imperative that defined every breath of the planet's living billions."[21]

The globalization of American literature during this period was also underwritten by the increasing prominence of English as an international language – not, usually, as a replacement for local languages, but as something to run alongside them, a lingua franca. As David Crystal has explained, the "world status" of the English language was primarily the result of two factors: "the expansion of British colonial power, which peaked towards the end of the nineteenth century, and the emergence of the United States as the leading economic power of the twentieth century."[22] This increasing viability of English as a world language thus helped to create a new, international version of it as an agent of communication, most obvious perhaps in the truncated codes used by air traffic control systems and the like, and this again helped to disseminate the idea of American culture as a global rather than a narrowly nationalist phenomenon. Much of Gibson's *Neuromancer* (1984) is set in Japan, with Gibson (who did not himself visit Japan until 1988) claiming that he prepared for the novel by observing "Japanese tourists" in Vancouver and by taking the street scenes for his fictional Chiba City "from a Japan Air Lines calendar."[23] Even if this is not altogether accurate, it exemplifies ways in which local and global jostle together linguistically and culturally in his work. Rather than romanticizing the idea of exile, as did Ernest Hemingway and the members of his "Lost Generation," Gibson's narratives prefer creatively to dissolve categorical divisions between home and abroad.

Addressing this conception of globalization as universalism, political theorist Anthony King argued in 1991 how the basic paradox of globalization was the way its exposure of seemingly new horizons led to a sense of societal and ethnic difference grounded upon identity politics, a reaction that effectively served to obscure the common social and economic sources that in fact produced such diversity: "the degree to which cultures are self-consciously 'different,'" wrote King, "is an indication of how much they are the same."[24] Slavoj Žižek, in a 1997 essay, similarly linked the new-found popularity of multiculturalism in institutional terms to the rise of multinational capitalism, arguing that both involved trading in commodified versions of diversity, where sentimentalized versions of cultural pluralism and difference could exist alongside a political investment in the new liberal world order. Žižek went on to describe "multiculturalism" as "a disavowed, inverted, self-referential form of racism," a "racism with a difference," and it is certainly true that American literature of the 1990s now often appears somewhat quaint in its instinctive assumption of the United States as the privileged center to which the rest of the world appears peripheral or subordinate.[25]

In much popular ethnic writing in the United States during the postmodern era, there has often been an effort to domesticate globalization, to represent it not as something disturbing or disruptive but as a prospect fundamentally consonant with larger American narratives. For example, the 1996 novel by Chinese American author Gish Jen, *Mona in the Promised Land*, draws upon the iconography of a "promised land" to evoke a world where the fluidity of social and ethnic transformation (in this case, a metamorphosis of Chinese into Jewish) can be valorized: "Tell them this is America," says the heroine's best friend, "anything is possible."[26] Such a notion of infinite possibility is associated here with old American pioneers such as Lewis and Clark, and ultimately with Ovid's testimony to the powers of change, flux and motion, as cited in the novel's epigraph. It is also noticeable how much of Jen's narrative takes place in educational settings, both Mona's high school and her elder sister's Harvard, thus creating for this rite-of-passage novel something like a pedagogic imaginary, where coming of age involves being initiated into the moral circumference of American civic life. Even Ovid is being read in Mona's high-school English class, and indeed at one point the novel draws this analogy between education and civic life directly, saying how Mona "understands that this is how life operates in America, that it's just like the classroom. You have to raise your own hand – no one is going to raise it for you – and then you have to get ready to stand up and give the right answer so that you may gulp down your whole half-cup of approval."[27] It is true that there are in Jen's novel elements of pastiche and irony hedging in all these invocations of a promised land, an iconography which is both evoked and revoked simultaneously. What this book does suggest, however, are the powerful institutional and pedagogic reasons for wanting to cling on to an idea of national promise, even at a time when the theoretical premises of US exceptionalism have been all but exhausted.

As time passes, the idea of American literature of the 1990s constituting a period with definable characteristics has come into clearer focus. Philip E. Wegner has identified the "long nineties" as running from the fall of the Berlin Wall in November 1989 to the sudden impact of 9/11 on September 11, 2001, a span over the course of which American attention gradually shifted from the external threat of communism to that of radical Islam.[28] But the 1990s represented a hiatus during which the United States entertained the idea that it had triumphed in the Cold War and that its conception of free market values enjoyed universal approval. As we have seen in discussing Thomas Paine and others, the idea of globalization was not of course something that originated in the twentieth century, with many scholars having drawn attention to earlier iterations of interactive world systems. It was, however, a concept that came to enjoy particular prominence in the new financial and technological conditions that appertained after 1980. This conception of America interfacing with extraterritorial space also came to have a particular political charge in the 1990s, with Bill Clinton choosing to make the "global" a key point of reference in his 1992 election campaign, linking both the threats and the opportunities for the United States to a global landscape that was postindustrial as well as post-Communist.[29]

One aspect of this globalization process involved a shift in social and economic power from national jurisdictions to transnational corporations, with (for instance) the GNP of Shell at this time being three times larger than that of Guatemala. This new scope for economic control across an international axis reinforced the power of the United States as what Michael Hardt and Antonio Negri called a "decentered and deterritorializing" empire, one grounded not upon the occupation of land but incorporating "the entire global realm" within its orbit of transnational capital and influence.[30] George H.W. Bush announced in 1991 a "New World Order" in response to the demise of the Soviet Union, and, as Jay Prosser has suggested, it is possible that some of the peremptory overseas interventions by US forces in the 1990s (Iraq, Somalia, Haiti, Bosnia) served ultimately to heighten a "backlash" against US hegemony that manifested itself in subsequent attacks upon the blithe equation of American free market fundamentalism with a universal order. It is, however, equally important to recognize how globalization formed part of the popular imaginary in the United States during the 1990s, with big global corporations such as Microsoft and Starbucks seeming to be, in Prosser's words, "everywhere and indispensable."[31]

Various technological changes associated with globalization also threatened the institutional position of literature itself, with Jeremy Green commenting on how "the *literary field* in advanced capitalism" inevitably involved a negotiation with computers, the commodifications of mass culture, and the all-pervasive spirit of television star Oprah Winfrey's Book Club.[32] In this sense, the increasingly permeable boundaries of national formations coincided with a tectonic shift from print to electronic media, so that the morphing of national into global narratives could be seen to overlap with an equivalent form of globalization within the realms of media production and distribution. *The Sopranos*, a work made for television by the Home Box Office cable channel that is now regularly cited as one of the most enduring works of fiction from this era, is firmly located in plot terms within the purlieus of the New Jersey Mafia, but it rapidly achieved global status through overseas television and DVD channels after its first series aired in 1999.

At the end of the 1980s, there were various well-publicized "Culture Wars," with Stanford University's decision in 1989 to replace its first-year course "Western Culture" with the unit "Culture, Institutions, and Values" attracting national attention. Stanford was criticized by Reagan's Secretary of Education, William Bennett, for neglecting works anchored in the traditions of Western civilization, and this controversy carried particular resonance for American literature, whose academic canon was then undergoing radical scrutiny from scholars seeking to re-establish hitherto marginalized works by women and people of color. American novels published around this time – Bharati Mukherjee's *Jasmine* (1989), Jessica Hagedorn's *Dogeaters* (1990), Julia Alvarez's *How the García Girls Lost Their Accents* (1991), as well as Sandra Cisneros's collection of short stories *Woman Hollering Creek* (1991) – were implicitly intervening in these culture wars, since their female protagonists were claiming equal rights within the fabric of American society. All these fictional works retell stories of immigration and accommodation within the broad matrix of US culture, with their clear implication being that American literature should be seen as a multicultural phenomenon made up of multinational strands. Mukherjee's *Jasmine* tracks the progress of its heroine from the Hindu constraints of a small Indian village, where daughters were considered curses, to Elsa County, Iowa, with the central protagonist priding herself on her capacity for change. Jasmine's openness to personal "transformation" is linked explicitly to the American frontier myth: "Adventure, risk, transformation: the frontier is pushing indoors through uncaulked windows."[33] However, this susceptibility to metamorphosis is also interestingly aligned with Hindu traditions of reincarnation, and part of the book's traction derives from the various ways in which Jasmine feels herself "suspended between worlds" as she "shuttled between identities." It is clear that the superimposition of an American future upon Jasmine's Indian past creates stress in the heroine's "fragmentary" life – she talks of how "extraordinary events can jar the needle arm, jump tracks" – but it is also evident how she regards this psychological violence as a price she is willing to pay for the benefits of personal renewal: "There are no harmless, compassionate ways to remake oneself. We murder who we were so we can rebirth ourselves in the images of dreams."[34]

Mukherjee's novel has been frequently criticized for the way in which it appears to eulogize American values of mobility, and it is true that there is a seemingly heartless dimension to Jasmine's sense of her own providential place in "God's plans," something manifested in her willingness to drop her American husband Bud after he has been shot and maimed.[35] Caught as she is "between the promise of America and old-world dutifulness," the heroine turns "Jasmine the reliable caregiver" into "Jane the prowling adventurer," with the book's epigraph from James Gleick's *Chaos* – "It is a geometry of the pitted, pocked, and broken up, the twisted, tangled, and intertwined" – speaking to the fractious and "intertwined" nature of Mukherjee's immigrant landscape.[36]

Generically, one characteristic that Mukherjee's novel shares with others at the turn of the 1990s is its mediation of a distant, overseas past through the voice of a female narrator who looks back at her native heritage from a position safely ensconced within the American heartland. Jessica Hagedorn's *Dogeaters* is set in the Philippines of the 1950s, and it evokes the hybrid nature of this island society, where influences from American popular culture have become all-pervasive. Hagedorn's narrator Rio luxuriates in recalling how the 1951 film *A Place in the Sun*, starring Elizabeth Taylor, was "condemned by the Archdiocese of Manila as vile and obscene."[37] She also remarks that her "philosophy of life" involves "keeping things slightly off-balance," with the transnational affiliations of her father – he has "dual citizenship, dual passports, as many allegiances to as many countries as possible at any one given time" – speaking to her own narrative's multidirectional aspects. The way Hagedorn interweaves the voice of her narrator with extracts from the fictional newspaper *The Metro Manila Daily* and from Jean Mallat's historical work *The Philippines* (1846) lends this whole text a deliberately decentered idiom, as though its multiple fragments were formally reflecting the "fragmented nation" of the Philippines, "our tropical archipelago of 7100 known islands."[38] But Rio grows up to live in the United States, in the midst of all the American popular culture she experienced as a child only by proxy, and the final scenes of the novel focus on the processes of memory and the difficulties of aligning retrospective recollections with contemporary experience: "All Souls' Day, 1959. Or 1960 – why is it so difficult to recall? Why didn't I write it all down, keep diaries and journals …" For all of the liveliness of Filipino society as recollected here, it also represents "a corrupt regime – a *dictatorship*," against which the United States is positioned as a point of security.[39]

Similarly, the final chapter in Alvarez's *How the García Girls Lost Their Accents* focuses upon the narrator Yolanda's escape from "the dictator Trujillo" in the Dominican Republic and the flight of her family to the safe haven of the Bronx.[40] Alvarez's work is told chronologically in reverse order, starting in 1989 and then tracking back to the Dominican Republic in the 1950s, and this again serves to foreground the discourse of memory, how past experiences continue to shape present perspectives. Indeed, the whole of this fictional narrative is structured like a discourse of therapy, with Yolanda's mother continually saying she wants to forget the past even though she "remembers everything," her father "haunted" by the memory of Trujillo for the rest of his life, and her sister Carla growing up to be a "child psychologist." Alvarez's emphasis is upon excavating the past, and on how the modernity of the United States relates to a formative cultural heritage that is kept here at a distance, both spatially and temporally. Yolanda, after immigrating to the United States, feels she "would never find someone who would understand my peculiar mix of Catholicism and agnosticism, Hispanic and American styles," but her fictional memoir inscribes precisely such a style of principled hybridity, where Dominican assumptions can be assimilated within the ever-expanding circle of US multiculturalism.[41]

In 1991, the same year that Alvarez's novel appeared, Betty Jean Craige published in the prominent academic journal *PMLA* an essay entitled "Literature in a Global Society," which described a "clash between traditionalism, manifesting itself in nationalism, and cultural holism, manifesting itself in globalism." Craige's agenda involved "appreciating the world's variety of human expression" through "promoting cultural exchange on a global scale," with her "hope" being "that eventually a widespread appreciation of diversity, which multicultural education fosters, and a desire for co-operation will supplant the intercultural competition that now predominates."[42] While this emphasis on an emollient "holism" now looks quite dated, its key terms, *multicultural* and *diversity*, speak aptly to the political engagements and alliances that were current in this era.

Sandra Cisneros's *Woman Hollering Creek* is another text that looks backwards, correlating its memories of the narrators' Hispanic pasts with a focus on life on both sides of the Mexican border. In Cisneros's case, this bilateralism also expresses itself in bilingualism, with the story "Little Miracle, Kept Promises" including letters written in Spanish as well as English. As in Alvarez, the idea of past time here takes on a recursive quality, with the narrator of *"Bien* Pretty" saying: "We have to let go of our present way of life and search for our past, remember our destinies, so to speak."[43] For Cisneros, this temporal shift takes on a reflexive quality, with these rhetorical paradoxes ("remember our destinies") mirroring divisions in the narrator's subjectivity. Such textual instabilities, characteristic of postmodernism, epitomize ways in which the characters' minds are shaped by linguistic difference: in *"Bien* Pretty," the narrator suggests how the "true test of a native Spanish speaker" is when he yells "¡Ay!" rather than "Ouch" when accidentally hammering his thumb.[44] By thus relating multiculturalism to a play of the sign, Cisneros accommodates postmodernism's contingent dynamic, suggesting how ethnicity is a linguistic and cultural construction rather than an essentialist form of identity.

In the 1994 book *Nations Unbound,* a team of social scientists described a situation where old distinctions between temporary migrants and permanent immigrants were falling into disrepair, with many US residents developing "networks, activities, patterns of living, and ideologies that span their home and the host society."[45] Multicultural American literature of the postmodern era often reflected this pattern in the way it represented what Michael S. Laguerre called a "politics of simultaneity" rather than a "politics of succession," whereby the old country came to seem connected to the American mainland through cheap flights and new communications technologies.[46] Peggy Levitt in 2001 described what she called a "new cartography" of transnational villages, where migrants opt to participate in different societies simultaneously.[47] There is, in other words, a characteristic tension in ethnic fiction of this era between narratives that regard the United States in time-honored fashion as a providential resting place for beleaguered immigrants, and a bifocal structure whereby the narrative voice switches backwards and forwards between alternative domains, thereby opening up American scenes to concurrent transnational horizons. Jhumpa Lahiri's fiction, which James Annesley accuses of incorporating "a homogenizing dynamic" underwriting "implicit celebrations of Americanness," might be seen from another perspective to embody precisely these cross-cultural tensions, since the Indian-born narrator of "The Third and Final Continent" (1999), now securely resident in the suburbs of Boston, nevertheless uses his retrospective voice not only to recall his own past in Calcutta, but also to defamiliarize the routine world of American domestic landscapes.[48] Lahiri's understated, limpid style is beguiling in part because of the way it combines an air of transparency with a capacity to make strange, and the implicit comparison adduced by this story's narrator between his own arrival in the United States and the "moon shot" in 1969 when American astronauts first "landed on the shores of the Sea of Tranquillity" has the effect of rendering proximate scenes distant, as though, by a kind of *mise-en-abîme* effect, this comfortable American home might open up at any point to radically different vistas.[49]

DeLillo's major work *Underworld* (1997) represents a very different form of globalization, although the use of *world* in the second part of this novel's title points clearly enough to its global reach. DeLillo's theme here is connection in all of its facets, how events that might seem distant in time and space are in fact inextricably conjoined. The connections forged through collective memory – the book starts with a 1951 baseball game between the Giants and the Dodgers – thus become analogous to an American culture whose environmental affairs are bound symbiotically to its systems of waste management: "waste is the secret history, the underhistory, the way archaeologists dig out the history of early cultures, every sort of bone heap and broken tool, literally from under the ground."[50] This archeological imagination, intent as it is upon excavating sedimented layers of past time, also leads *Underworld* to make connections between post-Enlightenment America and medieval societies. The book's prologue is entitled "The Triumph of Death," with the title of its third part being taken from Julian of Norwich's fifth-century treatise *The Cloud of Unknowing*, and all of these analogies are designed to correlate twentieth-century American culture with its medieval antecedents. DeLillo's ancestral Catholicism is clearly one source for this universalism – Sister Edgar is described as "a figure from a universal church with sacraments and secret bank accounts and a fabulous art collection" – and DeLillo's Italian Catholic roots become more evident in this novel than in any of his others.[51] The point here, though, is not to inscribe a particular version of ethnic identity, but rather to project an alternative version of US culture, one predicated not upon the romantic exceptionalism of the frontier tradition but upon the communal sharing of everyday household gods: "home alone, surrounded by all the things and textures that make you familiar, once again, to yourself." In this sense, the idea of the global becomes for DeLillo an ontology, with "the force of converging markets" and the worlding capacity of the internet – "The real miracle is the web, the net, where everybody is everywhere at once" – serving to illuminate the style of cosmic communitarianism that has, according to DeLillo, always been implicit within the American body politic.[52]

In a 1991 interview with Anthony DeCurtis, DeLillo spoke of his "sense that we live in a kind of circular or near-circular system and that there are an increasing number of rings which keep intersecting at some point, whether you're using a plastic card to draw money out of your account at an automatic teller machine or thinking about the movement of planetary bodies."[53] The great skill of *Underworld*, however, is to reposition this "circular system" of contemporary life within an alternative spatiotemporal genealogy, so that the banking and internet systems come to evoke an environment where the relation between America and the wider world appears qualitatively different. Hence the medieval topography that informs *Underworld* – the modern urban mall which is described as resembling a "medieval town, with the castle smack at the center" – makes the United States in the last decade of the twentieth century appear co-extensive with European landscapes of 1000 years earlier.[54] Tony Tanner, in an essay on *Underworld*, described DeLillo as "some kind of latter-day American urban Transcendentalist," but this is true only to the extent that DeLillo is specifically quarreling with the premises of transcendentalism.[55] Rather than taking the natural world to be an extension of the subjective self, DeLillo's work dissolves the self-aggrandizing subject into a global nexus whose expansive orbits exceed any imaginative subjugation of it. Writing specifically of DeLillo's *White Noise* (1985), Thomas Peyser admitted there "is nothing new about globalization," but he suggested what was "startlingly and even shockingly new" in the 1990s was "the sway that the idea of globality holds over the imagination."[56] In DeLillo's case, it is this framework of globalization, with its austere parallel to Catholic universalism, that gives the author intellectual distance from American mythologies of possessive individualism.

It was a fundamental disagreement over the nature of such individualism that fired the dispute in 1997 between John Updike and David Foster

Wallace, after the latter had written a scathing review of Updike's *Toward the End of Time*, accusing the senior novelist of neglecting his large-scale canvas of how a "Sino-American war" in 2020 had killed millions and ended US central government in favor of much more self-indulgent ruminations about the narrator's home and "how his ocean view looks in different seasons."[57] There was a generational aspect to such differences, with Wallace regarding the globalized condition of his American world as a *fait accompli* in a way that Updike found more difficult to admit except on sufferance, but this also overlapped with important artistic divergences. Wallace's 1993 essay "E Unibus Pluram: Television and U.S. Fiction" came to stand as a manifesto for his generation of fiction writers, with Wallace arguing here that American writers under 40 – born, in other words, after 1953 – had been conditioned to a world within which the ubiquity of television was a plain fact, with such stratification by "generation" carrying more purchase than older nostrums whereby writers would be categorized according to "regions" or "ethnicity."[58]

Dave Eggers's *A Heartbreaking Work of Staggering Genius*, published in 2000, fully exemplifies this television sensibility in the way it incorporates an esthetic of interchangeability, presenting the narrator as "the common multiplier for 47 million" and using the image of a "lattice" to evoke "the connective tissue" that binds his contemporaries together.[59] There are innumerable references in *A Heartbreaking World* to specific television programs, with the casts of these televisual worlds coming to operate for Eggers's personae as a surrogate family after the loss of their own parents. Also revealing in generational terms is the idea expressed in the novel's first pages that "death is literally around each and every corner," the fear that "each and every time an elevator door opens, there will be standing, in a trenchcoat, a man, with a gun."[60] In her introduction to a 2003 anthology of American fiction by writers "quite different in spirit from the generation that preceded them," Zadie Smith remarked that one characteristic of this "chorus of melancholy" was its acknowledgment of how "Fear of disease, accident and attack is everywhere."[61] In Eggers's case, this sense of an amorphous looming threat, something that predates 9/11, is connected to the radical instability of family situations, along with the frenetic pace of technological and economic change. Whereas the literary generation that came to maturity after World War II often wrote about family relationships as a claustrophobic impediment to liberal individualism, younger writers active in the 1990s tended to be nostalgic for the kind of family security and cultural continuity that now seemed to them only a distant dream. Caren Irr has written of "the specific insecurities, and vertiginous sense of placelessness" associated with "economic neoliberalism," citing as an example how Jonathan Franzen's *The Corrections* (2001) tracks back from its projection of Eastern Europe and the volatility of the global stock market to reimagine the Midwestern family home as "a site of reconciliation."[62]

The novelist of the 1990s who expressed this generational sensibility most acutely was Douglas Coupland, a native of Vancouver, Canada, whose observation that "Vancouverites" have more in common with "West Coast Americans" than with East Coast Canadians spoke aptly to the transnational framework of his times.[63] Coupland's iconic work *Generation X* was published in 1991, and the book foregrounds the question of planetary rotation in its very first sentence, recalling as it does the narrator flying as a 15 year old across the continent "to witness a total eclipse of the sun."[64] All Coupland's fictional works are attuned to the cycles of time, with *Microserfs* (1995), which starts very precisely in 1993, chronicling ways in which social relationships are shaped by the development of technological drivers. The Microsoft campus outside Seattle, the fulcrum of this narrative, is said to make people rethink the relationship between their brains and bodies, and in this rapidly developing environment the borders between life and work have become blurred, memory has replaced history, with the narrator Daniel commenting on how "we can edit ourselves as we go along, like an on-screen document."[65] In the 1990s such generational self-consciousness became particularly acute, since structural changes in the global economy – the shift from labor-intensive to capital-intensive industry, with a concomitant loss of long-term professional security – created a situation of disproportionate unemployment among the young, so that, as Saskia Sassen observed, many young adults in the last years of the twentieth century developed "only weak ties to the labor market."[66] Just as Scott Fitzgerald's "lost generation" was shaped by the experience of World War I, so Coupland's generation was shaped by fallout from pressures of globalization associated with the revolution in information technology.

One of the most compelling fictional accounts of this uncomfortable transition from a national to a global imaginary is Bob Shacochis's *Swimming in the Volcano*, published in 1993, but set 16 years earlier, in 1977. Shacochis's novel focuses on American diplomats, executives, and Peace Corps volunteers who get caught up in various disorienting experiences on the fictional Caribbean island of St Catherine. Sally, who fled Kansas out of dismay at the prospect of a "quiet life" with her dull boyfriend Jerry, finds herself out of her psychological depth in this farrago of drugs, corruption, and violence, and she asks rhetorically: "What was everybody doing here?"[67] Mitchell, burdened with the presence of his former girlfriend Johnnie, contemplates the "naiveté" of Americans who, having been tempted to take "an unmediated leap out onto the globe," believe that the world's landscapes should be "as simple to change as a television channel." Mitchell finds his compatriots who have never been "out of the States before" have a tendency "to judge a place by what was missing, the cancellation of entitlements."[68]

There are various intertextual references here, to the Gothic forms of William Burroughs ("this naked lunch of an island"), to Joseph Conrad's *Heart of Darkness* ("He felt like cartoon footage, the Saturday-night evolution of Kurtz"), and to Evelyn Waugh's fictional encounters with Africa and South America in novels such as *Black Mischief* and *A Handful of Dust*, with Adrian, taking time out from her work in a New York art gallery, describing her American friends as living out a scenario of "Evelyn Waugh gone to pot."[69] All of this attests to a sense of "debasement" in this Caribbean environment, something that threatens "the march of European sensibilities" and of US assumptions of world order modeled on "the efficacy of the Monroe Doctrine," the principle of US foreign policy originally articulated in 1823 by President James Monroe, which insisted the continent of the Americas fell within a US sphere of influence and that any intervention there by external powers was potentially a hostile act against the United States itself. At the same time, these American innocents abroad are drawn psychologically to such atavistic landscapes, where the memory of slavery still lingers: "What was it there in the puritan heart that so idolized corruption; or was it capitalism, the New England slave traders, exchanging syrup for souls, for more syrup and more souls, in an unabashed triangle of profit between continents?"[70] The book's titular metaphor of a dormant volcano is paralleled by the smoldering passions for sex and violence that lie buried within these characters, with the imagery here making connections between global geography and internal landscapes. For example, Johnnie, who "attracted a devil" in Mitchell, is described in geopolitical terms – "the two hemispheres of her hair," "the gaunt hemispheres of her buttocks" – while the narrator describes how Sally "sometimes felt equatorial, a narrow imaginary line of contact between the frictional polarity of hemispheres."[71]

All of this serves forcibly to impress a global consciousness upon these American characters, and the novel turns upon ways in which domestic assumptions, both psychological and political, find themselves upended by this "parallel universe," an "island of contradictions," where "the world spun in both directions."[72] Shacochis's careful situating of his narrative in the recent past allows him not only to chronicle the emergence of an embryonic form of globalization during the years of the Carter administration, but also to suggest the limits of any US attempt to colonize the globe. Mitchell thinks at one point that he "didn't know what the world would look like ten years into the future, or who would win the Cold War, but [he] suspected that for orphans like St Catherine it couldn't possibly matter."[73] Don H. Doyle has argued that a guiding principle of US culture in general is not its exceptionalism but its universalism, the notion that everyone should want what America values, with the Declaration of Independence typically attesting to the nation's claim on universal standards rather than codes of custom most appropriate to itself.[74] But if the immigrant fictions of Mukherjee and Hagedorn tend to postulate an Americanization of the entire globe, *Swimming in the Volcano* tends rather in the opposite direction, towards (in Irr's phrase) situating "the United States on a variegated international map rather than universalizing its time-space."[75] By forcing US culture into alien encounters, Shacochis's novel effectively reconstitutes the rhetoric of globalization from what the author here calls an "arse-backwards topsy-turvy" perspective.[76]

Another work of fiction that combines a digital with a transnational sensibility is Geoff Ryman's *253*, a novel that first appeared on the internet in 1996 and then in book form (with a subtitle "the print remix") two years later. Ryman's narrative, brilliantly original in form and execution, chronicles a London Underground train carrying 252 passengers and its driver on a seven-minute journey between two tube stations on 11 January 1995, from 8.35 to 8.42 a.m. The book operates as a paean to contingency, with the way these passengers are brought together reflecting a sense, as *253* says on its second page, of how "the universe is not held together by cause and effect alone, but by mysterious patterns," patterns that mirror the catalogues and networks of the World Wide Web.[77] Although we become partially privy to the characters' inner lives here, with the sketch of each individual being confined to 253 words, the author also tells us how they are bound by an "inexorable logic of age, gender, genes, character, their time in history, luck" and in this sense, the minimalist verbal box within which each person is presented comes to epitomize the genetic "logic" that circumscribes their terrestrial incarnation.[78] All of the metafictional apparatus that frames Ryman's novel – its passenger maps, its incorporation of pseudo-advertisements and a final "Reader Satisfaction Survey" – involves the kind of comic reflexivity that is reminiscent of classic postmodernist texts such as Barthelme's *Snow White*, and there is no doubt that Ryman takes pleasure in spoofing the received assumptions that underlie London life.[79]

The author, who was born in Canada but moved to the United States at the age of 11 and studied at UCLA before relocating to England in 1973, brings to his fiction a transnational imagination that enables him to approach the scenarios of British culture from many different directions. The book is rooted quite specifically in the events of the mid-1990s – it mentions, for instance, "Tony Blair having a go at the lefties over Clause Four," something that led to the Labour Party constitution being amended in April 1995, thereby ending the Party's long-standing commitment to nationalization – and it turns an ironic eye on the oppressive nature of

British bureaucracy: "Gwen firmly believes that the entire NHS should have an ISO standard quality accreditation."[80] But rather than leaving this merely at the level of acerbic observation, Ryman uses his paratextual paraphernalia to situate English culture within a broader spatiotemporal matrix, incorporating for example a long discursive footnote on William Blake, the Londoner of 1795, and commenting pointedly on the ubiquity of surveillance systems: "The English live in *1984* and don't know it," even though "it's illegal to spy on people in America."[81] Such an implicitly comparative framework serves to relativize the visible world, to make all these scenes appear contingent in time and space. The author uses his god-like position to chart future events – we are proleptically informed, for example, of how Passenger 40 "will have an embarrassing meeting in 20 minutes' time with Passenger 38" – but this self-conscious play with omniscience seems again to reflect the all-encompassing tentacles of computer technology rather than aspiring towards any kind of artistic omnipotence.[82] Ryman himself worked for a time in 1994 at the UK government's Central Office of Information, and his novel reflects, albeit in a sardonic way, how labyrinthine systems of administrative control operate.

Frederick Buell complained in 2001 of how environmental concerns, which he believes should have been a key part of globalization debates in the 1990s, in fact failed to make much general impact during that decade. Observing how "global environmental discourse" was "quickly dropped from Clinton's popular globalization package in the 1990s," Buell attributed this to the "neo-liberal affirmation" of a "global economy," one valorized ideologically by a "new cosmopolitanism" that embraced "multiculturalism" as its slogan.[83] It was also the case that a collective fixation on the capacities of new digital systems, together with an assumption that winning the Cold War would ensure for the United States an unchallenged global hegemony, created an illusory sense of security that came crashing down, quite literally, on 9/11. From our later vantage point, however, it is now obvious enough that the United States in the last decade of the twentieth century was blind not only to how Islamic fundamentalism was generating an oppositional impetus but also to the multiple complexities associated with "environmental crisis." Rather like the 1920s before the Wall Street Crash, American literature of the 1990s operated within a climate of utopian promise generated in part by technological novelty, one that tended silently to suppress more disruptive factors that were to become increasingly visible in later years.

Joseph O'Neill's *Netherland* (2008) is a novel that exemplifies this state of disruption. It is set in the post-traumatic landscape of New York after 9/11, where the hero, a native of Holland who has married an English woman and now works on the American stock market, has all kinds of bureaucratic tussles with the federal department of Homeland Security, an agency set up after 9/11 to protect the nation's borders. Nevertheless, what really takes the interest of Hans van den Broek here is the evolution of cricket in America, inspired by a chance meeting with a native of Trinidad, Chuck Ramkisson, who has drawn up all kinds of business plans to build a sports stadium and market cricket in the United States. As the novel goes on, it becomes clear that this is not purely a pipe-dream; according to the latest census, so we are told, there are nearly a million English-speaking West Indians in the New York metropolitan area, and at one point Hans joins Chuck and his friends in a sports bar to watch a cricket match between Pakistan and New Zealand being "broadcast live from Lahore." Chuck also persuades Hans that cricket actually has a long buried history in America, that "Benjamin Franklin himself was a cricket man," and that the "first international team sports fixtures anywhere were cricket matches between the USA and Canada in the 1840s and 1850s."[84] These are historical facts, and they lend the novel's transnational dimension an air of authenticity. At the same time, cricket clearly represents an alien culture in terms of mainstream modern America. Chuck says at one point: "You want a taste of how it feels to be a black man in this country? Put on the white clothes of the cricketer. Put on white to feel black." And later on, after Chuck's shady connections with the gangster world have caused him to be murdered, his former business associate Farek Patel says: "There's a limit to what Americans understand. The limit is cricket." The idea here, as Chuck himself puts it, is that for all of their global ambitions, "Americans cannot really see the world. They think they can, but they can't."[85] There is, in other words, a tension in this novel between a theoretical receptiveness in the United States to the impulse of globalization and the kind of entrenched, defensive mentality that actually characterized the country in its fearful post-9/11 state.

The way Hans attempts to reconcile these two contradictory forces is by remapping the history and terrain of the United States to encompass its Dutch origins. This provides the source of the novel's title, *Netherland*, which speaks not only to the country of the Netherlands but also to the idea of a land beneath the country's topography, a "nether-land" in that double sense. Describing himself at one point as a Rip van Winkle figure, Hans also imagines the American countryside outside New York morphing into the landscape of Netherlanders and Indians that comprised Dutch national territory in the seventeenth and eighteenth centuries. All this is highly reminiscent of Scott Fitzgerald's *The Great Gatsby*, at the end of which the narrator Nick Carraway links Gatsby's home landscape of Long Island with "the old island here that flowered once for Dutch sailors' eyes" (p. 140). What O'Neill's novel does, in effect, is intertextually to rewrite *The Great Gatsby* for the twenty-first century, redescribing the history of America as properly a multiethnic phenomenon, and correlating the promise that Carraway finds in Gatsby with the willingness to make "a go of things" that Hans admires in Chuck. For all its multiethnic inventiveness, then, *Netherland* ultimately acquiesces in a traditional myth of American exceptionalism, of America as a "providential country," where the new conditions of multiculturalism have been harnessed in the name of a refurbished and updated national narrative.[86]

The alternative version of the New York past inscribed in O'Neill's *Netherland* epitomizes the kind of revisionist impetus that has become characteristic of the globalization thesis in general. Influenced in part by poststructuralist conceptions of the malleable nature of historical narratives, exponents of globalization in various different fields have sought to redescribe American cultural history as a transnational phenomenon comprising multiple border zones and intersections, rather than one determined merely by unilinear teleologies of immigration and assimilation. In January 2001, *PMLA* published a special issue on "Globalizing Literary Studies," whose general hypothesis was that nation-based approaches to literary study had simply become superannuated; such ideological "coherence," suggested Paul Jay, "was rooted in a cultural moment that has passed."[87] A discourse of globalization was consequently mobilized in critical terms to dismantle what were thought to be the increasingly archaic structures of national narratives. It is, however, abundantly clear from events of the first decade of the twenty-first century – not only 9/11 but also the global financial crisis of 2008 – that there are what Appadurai in 2006 called many "darker sides to globalization."[88] Appadurai contrasted the "high globalization" theory prevalent in the 1990s, when an ebullient rhetoric of open markets and free trade predominated, to "the phenomenon of grassroots globalization, globalization from below," that has become more visible since the turn of the millennium.[89] This new dynamic of activist resistance to transnationalism first came to general prominence in the riots at the World Trade Organization ministerial conference held in Seattle in 1999, when there was widespread protest against the negative effects of transnational corporations on domestic environments, but the subsequent widespread misery brought about through cumulative domino effects after the collapse of the US sub-prime mortgage market in 2008 was ample testimony to how closely the world's national economies are now interlinked. In addition, as Appadurai noted, terrorism might aptly be described as "a kind of metastasis of war, war without spatial or temporal bounds," a phenomenon that updates the idea of war for the global age. "Terror divorces war from the idea of the nation," wrote Appadurai, and he consequently called terror "the nightmarish side of globalization," one that "cannot be divorced from certain deeper crises and contradictions that surround the nation-state."[90]

In truth, however, such "contradictions" have always been endemic to globalization processes of many different kinds. Expansive global horizons have long borne as their shadow the prospect of a systematic destabilization of local identity, something that has often carried as its corollary a threat of violence, either literal or metaphoric. The disruptions wrought in the heart of the American republic by the twenty-first-century "War on Terror" or the First World War of 1917–1918 are not altogether different in kind from the threats to the US body politic about which Adams and Jefferson were concerned in the 1790s, in the wake of the French Revolution. Globalization in the United States has a long history, but it is a checkered history, and to trace the fluctuations in its fortunes over the course of two centuries is to bear witness also to how the concomitant narrative of cultural nationalism has similarly ebbed and flowed. Exceptionalism and globalization might thus be regarded as different sides of the same coin within the American domain, cultural inclinations that are symbiotically attached to each other but destined always to present alternative faces to the world.

While the larger fate of globalization in the twenty-first century remains uncertain, it seems unlikely that US literary studies will ever be able again simply to locate itself "in the American grain," in the way William Carlos Williams recommended at the historical moment of the subject's nationalist emergence in 1925. For better or worse, such nativist impulses and exceptionalist assumptions have in the twenty-first century been forced to enter into negotiation with more extensive transnational currents, and the historical map of American literature has necessarily been redrawn to reflect this wider global provenance.

5.3 Disorientation and Reorientation: Kincaid, Morrison, Kingston

Part of the rationale for the realignment of American literature within a world framework in the second half of the twentieth century involved, as Michael Bérubé put it, "the attempt of American literature to become a world literature of a stature appropriate to newfound American global power." This marked a significant change from the 1940s and 1950s, when, as Bérubé also observed, American literature constituted "an *oppositional* canon," one that, taking its cue from Melville's "NO! in thunder," highlighted ideas of darkness and the grotesque amidst a more conventional culture of light and affirmation.[91] American literature at that time might in fact be understood as having enjoyed a doubly oppositional status, since it was frequently positioned as the junior partner on college curricula, where the classics of English literature were traditionally given priority, with Melville or Twain often being regarded as appropriate subject matter for the junior year and Milton or Shakespeare for the senior year. By the beginning of the twenty-first century, however, these canonical English writers were usually not so central to the structure of undergraduate degrees in English, and the cultural prestige of contemporary American writers had risen correspondingly. In both Europe and the United States itself, students were more likely to enroll for classes that offered the prospect of reading *When the García Girls Lost Their Accent* rather than *Paradise Lost*, and in an era of mass higher education, when student demand and satisfaction were increasingly key criteria within institutional settings, the academic profile of American literature as a subject shifted accordingly.

Nevertheless, many of the most interesting American writers of fiction at the turn of the twenty-first century tended in one way or another to problematize relationships between the United States and the wider world. Rather than simply representing the United States itself as a multicultural haven, in the way we saw in Hagedorn's *Dogeaters*, the fiction of Jamaica Kincaid proposes a more complex relation between the Caribbean, the British colonial burdens under which her native Antigua labored, and the differential but ambiguous prospects of liberty offered by American culture. John Carlos Rowe has written of how "Americans' interpretations of themselves as a people are shaped by a powerful imperial desire and a profound anti-colonial temper," and he argued that "[t]he internal colonization of different peoples depended centrally on hierarchies of race, class, and gender to do the work of subjugation and domination."[92] The premise of Rowe's work is thus not that the theory of US liberty itself was partial or contingent, but that there was in practice a hypocritical gap between abstract formulation and empirical event, so that marginalized groups – Native Americans, African Americans and others – did not get included within this charmed circle. But in Kincaid's more radical work this conception of liberty itself is problematized, so that the transnational dimensions in her fiction speak to the fractious relationship between American literature and the ghosts of postcolonialism.

Kincaid was born in 1949 as Elaine Potter Richardson on the Caribbean island of Antigua, a British colony until it became self-governing in 1967. She lived in Antigua until 1965, when she went to Scarsdale, New York, to work as an au pair. She subsequently wrote "Talk of the Town" pieces for the *New Yorker*, changed her name in 1973 – choosing "Jamaica," so she said, as "symbolic" of the Caribbean – and is now settled in the United States, where she lives in Vermont and teaches writing at Harvard.[93]

Kincaid has always said that the decision to come to the United States is one she has "never regretted."[94] Even though she declared in 1991 that she would "never become an American citizen," considering herself "a citizen of Antigua" and so "Caribbean," she in fact subsequently took US citizenship in 1993, largely because of Bill Clinton, whom in 2006 she still thought to be "as great an American President as I can expect in my lifetime."[95] She also credits the transformative energy of the United States with giving her the temerity to "invent" herself anew, to rebel against the "patriarchal nineteenth-century English view" of the world with which she was inculcated during her upbringing in the colonial West Indies.[96] As Bérubé observed, Kincaid's "success in mainstream American venues" has led to her being "widely considered to be 'almost' an American writer," although Kincaid herself has long cherished what she calls her "life of contradiction": "Even as I live in America and can vote and do all the things an American can do, I don't feel I'm an American in a certain way."[97] Kincaid thus uses a strategic form of "exile" to triangulate British, Antiguan and US national identities, thereby provoking awkward, uncomfortable questions about how the specter of postcolonial domination relates to an American cultural context.[98]

This pattern of contradiction and mirroring is particularly evident in Kincaid's scathing account of Antiguan history, *A Small Place*. Here the wrongs of empire are plentifully enumerated, with the English denounced as a "bad-minded people" who used the Caribbean for the trading of slaves and other kinds of economic exploitation; the author points out how many streets in Antigua are named after "English maritime criminals": Nelson, Hood, Hawkins, Drake, and others. But this is not simply a cry of outrage, nor a song of freedom, for Kincaid chronicles here the psychological and political paradoxes at the heart of what she calls Antigua's "postcolonial" condition. She describes how the islanders, to celebrate their new-found independence from Britain, "go to church and thank God, a British God"; she also describes how, in this "small place" that is apparently contracted in time as well as space, there appear to be no conventional chronological divisions into past, present, and future: "they speak of emancipation itself as if it happened just the other day, not over one hundred and fifty years ago." This is an Alice in Wonderland world, where temporal boundaries seem to have collapsed, where slavery is still part of the collective imagination, where emancipation and subjugation are simultaneous rather than sequential phenomena. Consequently, the anger in *A Small Place* is directed not just against the English but also against the Antiguans, herself included, for their willingness passively to subscribe to colonial myths and also their gullibility in romanticizing the island's slave past as a picturesque "pageant full of large ships sailing on blue water." Written as a pastiche travel narrative by a supposedly ignorant tourist, *A Small Place* not only critiques the assumptions inherent in more conventional travel writing but also, crucially, explores the limits of cultural and political agency. The author equates the general narrowness of vision in Antigua with the island's political smallness: "the people in a small place cannot see themselves in a larger picture," she writes, so that it is "as if everything and everybody inside it were locked in and everything and everybody that is not inside it were locked out."[99] At the same time, it is precisely this sense of enclosure that becomes the catalyst for the narrative's frantic anger. Smallness here becomes, in other words, something like an ontological category, the restrictive force that enables the voice of protest against a dominant oppressor, even as its inferior position ironically disallows any prospect of ameliorating such a belittled state.

Kincaid herself joked to an interviewer that anger was the source of her literary creativity: "If I ever find myself not getting angry ... I'll go to a psychiatrist to regain my anger."[100] Postcolonialism for Kincaid thus signifies a realm of the split subject: not simply a mythical transition from one point to another, from slavery to freedom, but a legacy of rupture and violence turned back against the self. Her works tend accordingly to be more pessimistic in tone than many of those celebrated in the US literary canon, since her triangulated version of the colonial/postcolonial dynamic annuls in advance any prospect of transcendence. Whereas classic American literature has typically involved a progressive erasure of postcolonial consciousness, as though the trauma of violent conflict could simply be purified out of the system, Kincaid's self-lacerating narratives reject that spirit of pastoral regeneration and represent the anger associated with a fissured condition as a prerequisite for the reconstitution of a postcolonial subject. This is why Kincaid has deliberately positioned herself in an estranged relation to the institutional assumptions of US culture, taking issue with "that line in the Declaration of Independence, 'the pursuit of happiness,'" a phrase which she believes "has no meaning at all" since, in her eyes, "you cannot pursue happiness." Similarly, she attributes "the sorry state of American writing" to the fact that "Americans ... like to laugh and they like a happy ending," whereas her own preferred creative mode, she observes drolly, is "to be depressing."[101] By contemplating the abstract conception of "freedom" as a form of false consciousness, Kincaid uses transnational dimensions to project her subjects within a wider sphere. As an American author in a double sense – a hemispheric American, with continuing loyalties to the Caribbean, and also since 1993 a citizen of the United States – Kincaid raises intriguing and complex questions about how the field of "American literature" should be described, and what the implications might be of certain models of inclusion or exclusion.

Toni Morrison is another American novelist whose fiction has been canonized in influential ways, particularly after she was awarded the Novel Prize for Literature in 1993. A native of Ohio, where she was born in 1931 under the name Chloe Anthony Wofford, Morrison projects in her fiction imaginative journeys where past and present merge and intermingle, so that the ghosts of old wrongs always haunt the contemporary scenes she describes. In this, she takes inspiration from William Faulkner, on whom she wrote her 1955 Master's thesis at Cornell, with the observation of Faulkner's lawyer Gavin Stevens in *Requiem for a Nun* that the "past is never dead. It's not even past" being echoed in the way Morrison's characters find themselves caught between alternative worlds.[102] The heroine of *Tar Baby* (1981), who is studying art history at the Sorbonne in Paris, attempts to resist racial stereotyping, saying that "sometimes I want to get out of my skin and be only the person inside – not American – not black, just me." Yet we are subsequently told that "Jadine's legs burned with the memory of tar," and it is this specter of memory, transposed from a personal to a collective dimension, that typically frustrates the desires of Morrison's dramatis personae for psychological emancipation.[103] *Song of Solomon* (1977) starts out with a description of Robert Smith's abortive aeronautical flight, and this anticipates the desire of Milkman to escape from his past: "He just wanted to beat a path away from his parents' past, which was also their present and was threatening to become his present as well."[104] But Milkman is trapped oedipally by his imposing father, Macon Dead Jr, as well as by his mother Ruth, who "milked" him until he was quite old, thereby giving him his nickname. The structure of this book follows the round of the Song of Solomon from which this novel takes its title, with a sense of the past intruding into the present. The confines of family comprise a significant part of this pattern, with incest being an important theme in both *Song of Solomon* and in Morrison's first novel, *The Bluest Eye* (1970).

Morrison herself has become expert at orchestrating the engines of publicity, having worked for many years as a senior editor for Random House publishers in New York, and her Norton lectures at Harvard published as *Playing in the Dark* (1992) elucidate ways in which familiar American tropes of flight and adventure were based on explicit or implicit repression of black voices. In this way, Morrison has performed the signal service for American literature of exposing ways in which many of its dominant assumptions in the second half of the twentieth century were based upon intellectual blindspots. Yet what is finally most interesting about Morrison's own fictions is the way in which their strands of emancipatory promise fail quite to cohere. As Heather Love has argued, Morrison's *Beloved* (1987), which is based on the historical anecdote of Margaret Garner in 1856 murdering her child rather than allowing her to be sold into slavery, is actually based around "documentary and description rather than empathy and witness," since Morrison stylistically balances the emotional impact of slavery against a more alienating structure where the past becomes impossible to reclaim with any transparency or sense of clarity.[105] In a conversation with Paul Gilroy, Morrison adamantly expressed opposition to what she understood to be the artificial literary form of magical realism, as developed most famously by Latin American novelists such as Marquez, and she emphasized instead her indebtedness to the authenticity of African American culture, which she linked to the affective qualities of black music.[106] Yet it is obvious enough that *Beloved* does invoke the mythopoeic power of language, not only in its Biblical references – to the four horsemen of the apocalypse, for example – but also in its deployment of various modes of anthropomorphism: "Winter stars, close enough to lick, had come out before sunset." This reflects the fault line running through *Beloved* more generally, between a desire mimetically to reflect the brutal historical reality of slavery – the book's epigraph, "Sixty Million and more," controversially implies how this "peculiar institution" led to more human slaughter than the Holocaust – and, conversely, a recognition of the partiality of all such historical reconstructions.[107] Linda Hutcheon has described what she called "historiographic metafiction" as one of the characteristics of postmodernism, a mode that shows "fiction to be historically conditioned and history to be discursively structured," and this is a textual labyrinth out of which Morrison's work cannot escape.[108]

Yet it is precisely this internal conflict between textuality and transparency that generates the unsettling power of Morrison's fiction. Love suggested that these fault lines helped to make visible in *Beloved* "the antihumanism of a text that has generally been understood as an exemplary instance of humanist ethics," where the losses of history are emphasized as much as its reparation, and it is arguable that the transnational dimensions of Morrison's fiction tend to problematize its status as an authentic expression of African American folk culture.[109] Tessa Roynon has shown how frequently Morrison draws upon classical tropes in her fiction – the author studied ancient Greek and Latin culture during her undergraduate college years at Howard University – and this again implies an uneasy juxtaposition between proximate and distant in Morrison's imaginative universe.[110] But it is precisely this sense of juxtaposition and incongruity – signaled in *Beloved* by another epigraph, this one taken from the Biblical Book of Romans: "I will call them my people, which were not my people" – that produces the mordant compulsions of Morrison's art. Like that of Kincaid, Morrison's fiction thrives on anger and insufficiency, turning not only on a discrepancy between word and object but, in a wider sense, on the agonies of a violent culture that is not to be easily assuaged by any redemptive rhetoric. Sethe, the main character in *Beloved*, is said to be "angry, but not certain at what," while this recursive pathology also extends to the slaves themselves, who "killed a boss so often and so completely they had to bring him back to life to pulp him one more time."[111]

This disquieting layering of psychological and historical levels is seen again in Morrison's novel *Home* (2012), where Korean war veteran Frank Money tracks back into his childhood home in the state of Georgia to rescue his sister from abuse and oppression. Again, Frank's twisted consciousness – "the free-floating rage, the self-loathing disguised as somebody else's fault" – is mapped on to a geographical model of transference and transposition, where the landscapes of Korea and Georgia come in his eyes to resemble each other. This raises the uncomfortable question of what "home" might mean to him, and Morrison's novel positions itself between alternative times and places, none of which can offer the protagonist any prospect of domestic security. Lotus, Georgia, seems to Frank "the worst place in the world, worse than any battlefield," with "no future, just long stretches of killing time" and as "the haunting images" of war dance before his eyes, Frank finds his memories of military conflict merging into a vision of the equally dehumanizing environment of the Deep South.[112] By aligning Georgia with Korea, Morrison extends her American literary imagination into the wider world, showing how familiar racial conflicts in the US South gain traction from being juxtaposed with the defamiliarizing dimensions of the war in Asia as Frank experiences it.

Korea in Morrison's *Home* operates as a site of disorientation, just as the Vietnam war does in Michael Herr's *Dispatches* (1977) or Francis Ford Coppola's film *Apocalypse Now* (1979). By contrast, Asia functions in the writing of Maxine Hong Kingston as a home base rather than an alien location, with San Francisco represented in her novel *Tripmaster Monkey* (1989) not as "the last city of bohemian migration," as it was for Beat writers such as Jack Kerouac, but rather, in Jason Arthur's words, "the first city of Asian America."[113] Kingston herself was born in Stockton, California, to a family of Chinese immigrants, and her writing systematically remaps the United States in terms of its connections with China and the rest of Asia. Her first published work, *The Woman Warrior* (1977), which is a blend of memoir and fantasy, takes the hyphenated status of "Chinese-Americans" to be synecdochic of the form of this book more generally, which zig-zags between past and present, commenting on how the Chinese world manifests itself differently in America and vice versa. Again, as in Morrison, the spectral presence of ghosts is an important thematic element for Kingston. In "At the Western Palace," one of the sections in *The Woman Warrior*, she describes the reappearance of his

Chinese wife to an American immigrant who has become a skilled surgeon and taken up with a young English woman, commenting on how the first wife "must look like a ghost from China."[114] The surreal flights of Kingston's writing, marrying fact and fable, have overtones of magical realists such as Salman Rushdie, and the style of Kingston, like that of Rushdie, flourishes through stylistic formations of structural paradox, where different cultural forces intersect and intertwine with each other. Recalling how "Time was different in China. One year lasted as long as my total time here," the narrator nevertheless uses these Chinese ghosts to problematize the naturalized condition of what she calls "my waking life American-normal." She also celebrates the way she becomes "a female avenger" within this new American environment, counterpointing this against the "Chinese word for the female *I*, which is slave."[115]

Kingston's second book *China Men* (1981), which was again a cross between alternative history and autobiography, similarly foregrounds the idea of inversion as a dynamic principle: "what topsy-turvy land formations and weather determine the crops on the other side of the world."[116] This work rewrites American history by chronicling how Chinese men worked on the railroads in nineteenth-century America, and it uses their involvement in the transcontinental crossing that joined New York to San Francisco as a metonym for conjunctions between East and West across a broader canvas: "After the Civil War, China Men banded the nation North and South, East and West, with crisscrossing steel. They were the binding and building ancestors of this place." The political commentary in *China Men* is quite direct and pointed, remarking how these nineteenth-century "Chinese were not white; this had been established legally in 1854 when Chan Young unsuccessfully applied for citizenship in Federal District Court in San Francisco and was turned down on grounds of race."[117] Yet just as *The Woman Warrior* observes how "fights are confronting as to who has won," so *China Men* generates a miscegenated style where transposition and confusion turn out to be more creative and illuminating than millennial notions of victory and defeat.[118] Kingston uses here the geopolitical position of Hawaii as a crossroads between America and Asia to elucidate the multidirectional emphasis of her prose: "I had gone east, that is west, as far as Hawai'i."[119] By turning "east" and "west" into reversible co-ordinates, Kingston highlights the reversible idiom that runs through her style of writing more generally.

Tripmaster Monkey is Kingston's great novel, the heavy-duty work of a Berkeley intellectual who seeks to reorient the American cultural tradition to make it face towards Asia rather than Europe. The novel's central character, Wittman Ah Sing, is a parodic derivation from Walt Whitman, with the novel's first two chapter titles – "Trippers and Askers" and "Linguists and Contenders" – being quotations from "Song of Myself," and Wittman himself later citing his namesake's "Facing West from California's Shores."[120] As Arthur observed, there is also a strong "stylistic correspondence" here between Kingston and Kerouac, with the Chinese American author seeking particularly to rewrite Kerouac's *The Town and the City* in her instantiation of San Francisco as a city lying to the east of Asia as much as to the west of New York.[121] Some readers have expressed impatience with *Tripmaster Monkey* for being too beholden to traditional standards of canonicity in the way it depends upon literary models only to invert them; the book presents itself self-consciously as an "echo-chamber tunnel," refracting established cultural icons through an idiom of postmodern reflexivity, which is related to Wittman's birth "backstage in vaudeville."[122] Yet Kingston herself in 1989 prophesied that "the dream of the great American novel" would be superseded by "the global novel" set "in the United States, destination of journeys from everywhere," and *Tripmaster Monkey*, published in the year that the Berlin Wall fell and the Cold War finally came to an end, executes this ambition with aplomb. Kingston added that "if you [are] going to write a great American novel, then it is also the global novel," and this explicit attempt to align American literature with a global dimension was characteristic of how this field evolved in the era of postmodernism.[123]

It would be easy enough, of course, to underline the partiality of Kingston's "global" perspective and the inevitability of how American world literature is always bound paradoxically to a particular place and perspective. Kingston's equation of "the great American novel" with "the global novel" is itself a symptom of a specific historical time, although, as we have seen, attitudes towards globalization have fluctuated markedly within American culture across the years. The idea of American world literature is of course itself a fiction, one inflected by global power relations as well as by the contrapuntal pull towards American exceptionalism that impelled its pastoral apotheosis as "a world elsewhere" in the middle years of the twentieth century. It is worth recalling Fredric Jameson's exhortation in 1986 that "one of our basic political tasks lies precisely in the ceaseless effort to remind the American public of the radical difference of other national situations."[124] Given such an emphasis on environments outside the American charmed circle, Jeffrey T. Nealon's summation of how within the world of what he called "post-postmodernism" – which he took to be an "intensification and mutation within postmodernism" – he found "Classic rock" to be "everywhere," with "the Eagles in the grocery store," should surely be seen as unduly restricted in its purview. Although Nealon presents this scenario as a universal paradigm, the Eagles are not generally heard in grocery stores in Africa, nor in Asia or Australasia. What would perhaps be a more reasonable inference is that "the new global casino capitalism," as Nealon called it, is intersecting in complex and often fractious ways with the contours of a wider world, with American literature written under the sign of transnationalism often positioning itself at these points of intersection, thereby illuminating ways in which US cultural assumptions coincide, or fail to coincide, with those of a more expansive planetary system.[125]

American world literature, as Moretti said of world literature in general, is accordingly "not an object" but a "*problem*," one that "asks for a new critical method."[126] To trace how the spheres of American literature and world literature have converged and diverged since white settlers first intruded on the North American continent in the seventeenth century is consequently to gain a clearer sense of how American literature has always accommodated a spherical trajectory, albeit in partial and asymmetrical ways, and should be seen as much more than merely a nationalist enterprise.

References

1 Hassan, I. (1982). *The Dismemberment of Orpheus: Toward a Postmodern Literature*, 2e, 267–268. Madison: U of Wisconsin P.
2 Perloff, M. (1992). Modernist studies. In: *Redrawing the Boundaries: The Transformation of English and American Literary Studies* (ed. S. Greenblatt and G. Gunn), 267–268. New York: Modern Language Association of America.
3 See, for example, Taylor, M.C. (1999). *About Religion: Economies of Faith in Virtual Culture*. Chicago: U of Chicago P.
4 Wright Mills, C. (1959). *The Sociological Imagination*, 166. New York: Grove Press.
5 Rowe, J.C. Postmodernist studies. In: *Redrawing the Boundaries* (ed. S. Greenblatt and G.B. Gunn), 180.
6 Huyssen, A. (1986). *After the Great Divide: Modernism, Mass Culture, Postmodernism*, 214. Bloomington: Indiana UP.
7 Barthelme, D. (1972). *Snow White* (1967; rpt.), 82. New York: Atheneum.
8 Gordon, L. (1983). *Robert Coover: The Universal Fictionmaking Process*, 13. Carbondale: Southern Illinois UP.
9 Kipnis, L. (1988). Feminism: the political conscience of postmodernism?. In: *Universal Abandon? The Politics of Postmodernism* (ed. A. Ross), 163, 165. Minneapolis: U of Minnesota P.
10 Rich, A. (1974). *Poems Selected and New, 1950–1974*, 25. New York: Norton.
11 Rich, *Poems Selected and New*, xv.
12 Rich, A. (2003). Six meditations in place of a lecture. In: *What Is Found There: Notebooks on Poetry and Politics*, 2e, 263. New York: Norton; Rich, A. (1986). *Your Native Land, Your Life: Poems*, 83. New York: Norton.

13 Boorstin, D.J. (1972). *The Image: A Guide to Pseudo-Events in America* (1962; rpt.), 10. New York: Atheneum.
14 Grossberg, L. (1986). On postmodernism and articulation: an interview with Stuart Hall. *Journal of Communication Inquiry* 10(2): 46.
15 Fukuyama, F. (1992). *The End of History and the Last Man*, xv, 12, xi, xiii. New York: Free Press.
16 Miyoshi, "A Borderless World?," 744.
17 Burbach, R. (2001). *Globalization and Postmodern Politics: From Zapatistas to High-Tech Robber Barons*, 7. London: Pluto.
18 Friedman, T.L. (2005). *The World is Flat: A Brief History of the Globalized World in the Twenty-First Century*, 10. London: Allen Lane-Penguin.
19 Denning, M. (2004). *Culture in the Age of Three Worlds*, 17. London: Verso.
20 Appadurai, A. (1996). *Modernity at Large: Cultural Dimensions of Globalization*, 46. Minneapolis: U of Minnesota P.
21 DeLillo, D. (2003). *Cosmopolis*, 24. New York: Scribner.
22 Crystal, D. (2003). *English as a Global Language*, 2e, 59. Cambridge: Cambridge UP.
23 McCaffery, L. (ed.) (1991). *Storming the Reality Studio: A Casebook of Cyberpunk and Postmodern Science Fiction*, 285. Durham: Duke UP.
24 King, A.D. (1991). The global, the urban, and the world. In: *Culture, Globalization and the World System: Contemporary Conditions for the Representation of Identity* (ed. A.D. King), 153. Basingstoke: Macmillan.
25 Žižek, S. (1997). Multiculturalism, or the cultural logic of multinational capitalism. *New Left Review* 225: 44.
26 Jen, G. (1996). *Mona in the Promised Land*, 84. New York: Knopf.
27 Jen, *Mona in the Promised Land*, 67.
28 Wegner, P.E. (2009). *Life Between Two Deaths, 1989–2001: U.S. Culture in the Long Nineties*, 2. Durham: Duke UP.
29 Buell, F. (2001). Globalization without environmental crisis: the divorce of two discourses in U.S. culture. *Symplokē* 9(1/2): 47.
30 Hardt, M. and Negri, A. (2000). *Empire*, xii. Cambridge: Harvard UP.
31 Prosser, J. (2008) Introduction. In: *American Fiction of the 1990s: Reflections of History and Culture* (ed. J. Prosser), 1–2. London: Routledge.
32 Green, J. (2005). *Late Postmodernism: American Fiction at the Millennium*, 3. New York: Palgrave Macmillan.
33 Mukherjee, B. (1991). *Jasmine*, 240. (1989; rpt.). London: Virago.
34 Mukherjee, *Jasmine*, 76, 125, 127, 29.
35 Mukherjee, *Jasmine*, 189. On the critical reception of Mukherjee, see Annesley, J. (2006). *Fictions of Globalization: Consumption, the Market and the Contemporary American Novel*, 141–142. London: Continuum.
36 Mukherjee, *Jasmine*, 240, 176.

37 Hagedorn, J. (1991). *Dogeaters*, 15. (1990; rpt.). New York: Penguin.
38 Hagedorn, *Dogeaters*, 37, 7, 100.
39 Hagedorn, *Dogeaters*, 238, 220.
40 Alvarez, J. (2004). *How the García Girls Lost Their Accents* (1991; rpt.), 146. London: Bloomsbury.
41 Alvarez, *How the García Girls*, 64, 146, 41, 99.
42 Craige, B.J. (1991). Literature in a global society. *PMLA* 106(3): 396, 397, 399.
43 Cisneros, S. (1991). *Bien* Pretty. In: *Woman Hollering Creek and Other Stories*, 149. New York: Random House.
44 Cisneros, "*Bien* Pretty," 153.
45 Basch, L., Schiller, N.G., Blanc, C.S. (1994). *Nations Unbound: Transnational Projects, Postcolonial Predicaments, and Deterritorialized Nation-States*, 4. Amsterdam: Gordon and Breach.
46 Laguerre, M.S. (1998). *Diasporic Citizenship: Haitian Americans in Transnational America*, 177. New York: St. Martin's Press.
47 Levitt, P. (2001). *The Transnational Villagers*, 11. Berkeley: U of California P.
48 Annesley, *Fictions of Globalization*, 128, 139.
49 Lahiri, J. (2000). The third and final continent. In: *Interpreter of Maladies: Stories* (1999; rpt.), 179. London: Flamingo.
50 DeLillo, D. (1998). *Underworld* (1997; rpt.), 791. London: Picador.
51 DeLillo, *Underworld*, 822.
52 DeLillo, *Underworld*, 482, 786, 808.
53 DeCurtis, A. (1991). 'An Outsider in This Society': an interview with Don DeLillo. In: *Introducing Don DeLillo* (ed. F. Lentricchia), 61. Durham: Duke UP.
54 DeLillo, *Underworld*, 109.
55 Tanner, T. (1998). Afterthoughts on Don DeLillo's *Underworld*. *Raritan* 17(4): 67.
56 Peyser, T. (1996). Globalization in America: the case of Don DeLillo's *White Noise*. *Clio* 25(3): 255.
57 Wallace, D.F. (2005). Certainly the end of something or other, one would sort of have to think (1997). In: *Consider the Lobster and Other Essays*, 55–56. London: Abacus.
58 Wallace, D.F. (1998). E Unibus Pluram: television and U.S. fiction (1993). In: *A Supposedly Fun Thing I'll Never Do Again*, 65. London: Abacus.
59 Eggers, D. (2000). *A Heartbreaking Work of Staggering Genius*, 236, 211. London: Picador.
60 Eggers, *A Heartbreaking Work*, xxviii–xxix.
61 Smith, Z. (2003). Introduction. In: *The Burned Children of America*, xv. London: Hamish Hamilton.
62 Irr, C. (2014). *Toward the Geopolitical Novel: U.S. Fiction in the Twenty-First Century*, 105, 118. New York: Columbia UP.

63 Coupland, D. (2000). *City of Glass: Douglas Coupland's Vancouver*, 106. Vancouver: Douglas and McIntyre.

64 Coupland, D. (1991). *Generation X: Tales of an Accelerated Culture*, 3. New York: St. Martin's Press.

65 Coupland, D. (1996). *Microserfs* (1995; rpt.), 253. London: Flamingo.

66 Sassen, S. (2006). *Territory, Authority, Rights: From Medieval to Global Assemblages*, 285. Princeton: Princeton UP.

67 Shacochis, B. (2004). *Swimming in the Volcano* (1993; rpt.), 249, 339. New York: Grove Press.

68 Shacochis, *Swimming*, 116, 27, 125.

69 Shacochis, *Swimming*, 340, 34, 302.

70 Shacochis, *Swimming*, 142, 136, 108, 389.

71 Shacochis, *Swimming*, 432, 48, 103, 343.

72 Shacochis, *Swimming*, 491, 511.

73 Shacochis, *Swimming*, 446.

74 Doyle, D.H. (2007). *American Nationalism and the Dark Side of Idealism*. Rothermere American Institute, University of Oxford, 26 April.

75 Irr, *Toward the Geopolitical Novel*, 185.

76 Shacochis, *Swimming*, 487.

77 Ryman, G. (1998). *253: The Print Remix*, 2. London: Flamingo.

78 Ryman, *253*, 339.

79 Ryman, *253*, 365–366.

80 Ryman, *253*, 76, 121.

81 Ryman, *253*, 185–189, 202.

82 Ryman, *253*, 62.

83 Buell, "Globalization without Environmental Crisis," 49–50.

84 O'Neill, J. (2008). *Netherland*, 51, 14, 98. London: Fourth Estate.

85 O'Neill, *Netherland*, 13, 243, 204.

86 O'Neill, *Netherland*, 158, 86.

87 Jay, P. (2001). Beyond discipline? Globalization and the future of English. *PMLA* 116(1): 43.

88 Appadurai, A. (2006). *Fear of Small Numbers: An Essay on the Geography of Anger*, 3. Durham: Duke UP.

89 Appadurai, *Fear of Small Numbers*, 2, x–xi.

90 Appadurai, *Fear of Small Numbers*, 92, 33.

91 Bérubé, M. (1994). *Public Access: Literary Theory and American Cultural Politics*, 214. London: Verso; Melville, H. (1993). Letter to Nathaniel Hawthorne, 16 April 1851. In: *Correspondence* (ed. L. Horth), 186. Evanston-Chicago: Northwestern UP-Newberry Library.

92 Rowe, J.C. (2000). *Literary Culture and U.S. Imperialism: From the Revolution to World War II*, 3, 7. New York: Oxford UP.

93 Cudjoe, S.R. (1989). Jamaica Kincaid and the modernist project: an interview. *Callaloo* 39(Spring): 400.

94 Dilger, G. (1992). 'I use a cut and slash policy of writing': Jamaica Kincaid talks to Gerhard Dilger. *Wasafiri* 16: 21.

95 Birsbalsingh, F. (1996). Jamaica Kincaid: from Antigua to America (1991). In: *Frontiers of Caribbean Literature in English* (ed. F. Birsbalsingh), 143. New York: St. Martin's Press. In a letter to the author, 18 June 2006, Kincaid also wrote that she specifically tried to take US citizenship "in time for the 1992 presidential election."

96 Birsbalsingh, "Jamaica Kincaid," 142.

97 Bérubé, M. (2002). Introduction: worldly English. *Modern Fiction Studies* 48(1): 13.

98 Birsbalsingh, "Jamaica Kincaid," 143.

99 Kincaid, J. (1988). *A Small Place*, 23–24, 43, 9, 54–55, 52, 79. London: Virago.

100 Brooks Bouson, J. 2005. *Jamaica Kincaid: Writing Memory, Writing Back to the Mother*, 91. Albany: State U of New York P.

101 Snell, M. (1997). Jamaica Kincaid Hates Happy Endings. *Mother Jones* (September–October). www.motherjones.com/news/qa/1997/09/snell. html (accessed 1 June 2006). For a fuller discussion of Kincaid's ambivalence towards American literature, see Giles, P. (2010). *Transnationalism in Practice: Essays on American Studies, Literature and Religion*, 202–232. Edinburgh: Edinburgh UP.

102 Faulkner, W. (2011). *Requiem for a Nun* (1951; rpt.), 73. New York: Random House-Vintage.

103 Morrison, T. (1983). *Tar Baby* (1981; rpt.), 45, 278. London: Granada.

104 Morrison, T. (1980). *Song of Solomon* (1977; rpt.), 181. London: Granada.

105 Love, H. (2010). Close but not deep: literary ethics and the descriptive turn. *New Literary History* 41(2): 375.

106 Gilroy, P. (1993). *Small Acts: Thoughts on the Politics of Black Cultures*, 181. London: Serpent's Tail.

107 Morrison, T. (1988). *Beloved* (1987; rpt.), 148, 174, vii. New York: New American Library.

108 Hutcheon, L. (1988). *A Poetics of Postmodernism: History, Theory, Fiction*, 120. New York: Routledge.

109 Love, "Close but not deep," 381.

110 Roynon, T. (2013). *Toni Morrison and the Classical Tradition: Transforming American Culture*, 12–13. Oxford: Oxford UP.

111 Morrison, *Beloved*, ix, 62, 109.

112 Morrison, T. (2012). *Home*, 15, 83, 97. London: Chatto and Windus.

113 Arthur, J. (2013). *Violet America: Regional Cosmopolitanism in U.S. Fiction since the Great Depression*, 66. Iowa City: U of Iowa P.

114 Kingston, M.H. (1977). *The Woman Warrior: Memoirs of a Girlhood Among Ghosts*, 5, 153. New York: Knopf.

115 Kingston, *The Woman Warrior*, 105–106, 87, 47.
116 Kinston, M.H. (1981). *China Men*, 43. London: Picador.
117 Kingston, *China Men*, 145, 151.
118 Kingston, *The Woman Warrior*, 51.
119 Kingston, *China Men*, 89.
120 Kingston, M.H. (1989). *Tripmaster Monkey: His Fake Book*, 162. New York: Knopf.
121 Arthur, *Violet America*, 71.
122 Kingston, *Tripmaster Monkey*, 5, 13.
123 Buell, L. (2016). *The Dream of the Great American Novel*, 344. Cambridge: Harvard UP.
124 Jameson, "Third-World Literature," 77.
125 Nealon, J.T. (2012). *Post-Postmodernism; or, The Cultural Logic of Just-in-Time Capitalism*, 44, 29. Stanford: Stanford UP, ix.
126 Moretti, F. "Conjectures on World Literature," 55.

Index

American World Literature: An Introduction, First Edition. Paul Giles.
© 2019 John Wiley & Sons Ltd. Published 2019 by John Wiley & Sons Ltd.

Dimock 18

Kaplan 18